Deepening Divides

Anthropology, Culture and Society

Series Editors:
Jamie Cross, University of Edinburgh,
Christina Garsten, Stockholm University
and
Joshua O. Reno, Binghamton University

Recent titles:

*The Limits to Citizen Power:
Participatory Democracy and the
Entanglements of the State*
VICTOR ALBERT

*The Heritage Machine:
Fetishism and Domination
in Maragateria, Spain*
PABLO ALONSO GONZÁLEZ

*Becoming Arab in London:
Performativity and the Undoing of Identity*
RAMY M. K. ALY

Anthropologies of Value
EDITED BY LUIS FERNANDO ANGOSTO-
FERRANDEZ AND GEIR HENNING
PRESTERUDSTUEN

*Vicious Games:
Capitalism and Gambling*
REBECCA CASSIDY

*Ethnicity and Nationalism:
Anthropological Perspectives
Third Edition*
THOMAS HYLLAND ERIKSEN

*Fredrik Barth:
An Intellectual Biography*
THOMAS HYLLAND ERIKSEN

*Small Places, Large Issues:
An Introduction to Social
and Cultural Anthropology
Fourth Edition*
THOMAS HYLLAND ERIKSEN

*What is Anthropology?
Second Edition*
THOMAS HYLLAND ERIKSEN

*At the Heart of the State:
The Moral World of Institutions*
DIDIER FASSIN, ET AL.

*Anthropology and Development:
Challenges for the Twenty-first Century*
KATY GARDNER AND DAVID LEWIS

*Children of the Welfare State:
Civilising Practices in Schools,
Childcare and Families*
LAURA GILLIAM AND EVA GULLØV

*Faith and Charity:
Religion and Humanitarian Assistance
in West Africa*
EDITED BY MARIE NATHALIE LEBLANC
AND LOUIS AUDET GOSSELIN

*Private Oceans:
The Enclosure and Marketisation
of the Seas*
FIONA MCCORMACK

*The Rise of Nerd Politics:
Digital Activism and Political Change*
JOHN POSTILL

*Base Encounters:
The US Armed Forces in South Korea*
ELISABETH SCHOBER

*Ground Down by Growth:
Tribe, Caste, Class and Inequality in
Twenty-First-Century India*
ALPA SHAH, JENS LERCHE, ET AL

*When Protest Becomes Crime:
Politics and Law in Liberal Democracies*
CAROLIJN TERWINDT

*Race and Ethnicity in Latin America
Second Edition*
PETER WADE

Deepening Divides

How Territorial Borders and
Social Boundaries Delineate Our World

Edited by Didier Fassin

First published 2020 by Pluto Press
345 Archway Road, London N6 5AA

www.plutobooks.com

Copyright © Didier Fassin 2020

The right of the individual contributors to be identified as the authors of this work has been asserted by them in accordance with the Copyright, Designs and Patents Act 1988.

British Library Cataloguing in Publication Data
A catalogue record for this book is available from the British Library

ISBN   978 0 7453 4042 5   Hardback
ISBN   978 0 7453 4043 2   Paperback
ISBN   978 1 7868 0562 1   PDF eBook
ISBN   978 1 7868 0564 5   Kindle eBook
ISBN   978 1 7868 0563 8   EPUB eBook

This book is printed on paper suitable for recycling and made from fully managed and sustained forest sources. Logging, pulping and manufacturing processes are expected to conform to the environmental standards of the country of origin.

Typeset by Stanford DTP Services, Northampton, England

Simultaneously printed in the United Kingdom and United States of America

Contents

1 Introduction: Connecting Borders and Boundaries 1
  Didier Fassin

PART I: POLITICAL AND MORAL ECONOMIES

2 What Money Can Buy: Citizenship by Investment on a Global Scale 21
  Kristin Surak

3 Monitoring International Labor Precarity: The State Management of Migrant Domestic Workers 39
  Rhacel Parreñas

4 When Migrants Claim Blood Kinship: Constructing Hierarchies of Human Worth 58
  Ayşe Parla

5 Family Resemblances: Binational Marriage, Muslim "Communalism," and the Patriarchal State 79
  Mayanthi Fernando

PART II: LEGAL DISBARRING

6 An Earlier Ban: Chinese Exclusion and Plenary Power 103
  Mae Ngai

7 Manners of Exclusion: From the Asiatic Barred Zone to the Muslim Ban 118
  Sherally Munshi

8 Brave New Worlds: The Racial Regimes of the Americas 144
  Michael Hanchard

9 The Outlawed: Landscapes of Human Rights 169
  Tugba Basaran

PART III: CREATING SPACES

10 Protection: Sanctuary and the Contested Ethics of Presence in the United States — 189
    Linda Bosniak

11 Ruination and Rebuilding: The Precarious Place of a Border Town in Gaza — 214
    Ilana Feldman

12 Symmetry and Affinity: Comparing Borders and Border-Making Processes in Africa — 233
    Paul Nugent

Notes on Contributors — 256
Index — 258

1

Introduction
Connecting Borders and Boundaries

Didier Fassin

We were expelled from Germany because we were Jews. But having hardly crossed the French borderline, we were changed into "boches."
—Hannah Arendt, "We Refugees"

On January 27, 2017, one of the first decisions made by Donald Trump as the newly inaugurated president of the United States was to issue Executive Order 13769 "to protect the American people from terrorist attacks by foreign nationals admitted to the United States."[1] This temporarily banned travel and immigration from seven countries: Syria, Iran, Iraq, Yemen, Libya, Somalia, and Sudan. Taking effect immediately, it generated chaos at airports due to refusals of entry, and it also created a surge of protests. Conspicuously, no citizen from these countries had been involved or was suspected of being involved in any fatal attack in the United States, while none of the countries whose citizens had actually carried out deadly attacks on US territory—Saudi Arabia, Egypt, United Arab Emirates, Pakistan, Russia, and Kyrgyzstan—was affected. Because the executive order targeted exclusively Muslim-majority countries without specific security justification, it was referred to as a "Muslim ban." The White House denied any discriminatory intention, but according to his personal lawyer the president had asked how to "legally" implement the ban he had explicitly designated as such. This affirmation and the various public statements made earlier by him during the presidential campaign were sufficient evidence for federal judges to consider the executive order unconstitutional, even after two modifications in its formulation, before the Supreme Court eventually upheld it. The selectivity of the executive order was nowhere more visible than in the case of refugees. Not only did the number of those admitted for protection dramatically decline, but the proportion of Muslims among them spectacularly decreased by six times compared to what it was before the executive order. However, the administration's discriminatory practices against immigrants were not only based on their religion. They also concerned their ethnicity, as was clear in the repeated singling out of Mexicans and more generally Latinos by the president, who iteratively described them as "drug dealers," "criminals," "terrorists," and "rapists," although he occasionally conceded that "some are good people." From this perspective, the Mexican border wall, the construction of which has been announced on numerous occasions, has been viewed as a "Latino wall" as much as the ban is a "Muslim ban." In both cases, the enforcement of border control is not the same for everyone. It more or less implicitly outlines boundaries based on faith or origin.

On October 31, 2017, the day before he announced the end of a state of emergency, Emmanuel Macron enacted a law "strengthening internal security and the fight against terrorism."[2] The state of emergency declared two years earlier, after the deadly attacks carried out in Paris, had been prolonged several times over the following twenty-four months. It gave the police additional powers in terms of identity checks, search warrants, and house arrests, at the same time as it allowed the state to prohibit demonstrations and close places of worship, while judicial control was henceforth limited in all these cases. Most of the measures, which had been used in practice much less to fight terrorism than to tackle ordinary delinquency and illegal immigration, were incorporated in the new law the day before the state of emergency was ended. The exception thus became the rule, to quote Walter Benjamin's famous phrase. The most remarkable, albeit little noticed, legal change was the extended opportunities of so-called border checks and searches. Indeed, after the 1993 creation of the Schengen Area, such police interventions had been authorized as far as 20 kilometers from the national border as well as at ports, airports, and international train stations. But the new legislation broadened the 20 kilometer perimeter of border checks and searches by applying it to 118 ports, airports, and stations. As a result, from then on it included all major urban areas of the country, corresponding to two-thirds of the population and the quasi-totality of people of immigrant origin, whether foreigners or French nationals. It was well known that checks and searches were mostly conducted on the basis of the physical appearance of individuals, focusing on Arab and black men, but in the absence of credible suspicion of involvement in a crime having been or on the verge of being committed, legal redress could be filed and several court decisions had condemned the state for racial discrimination. Under the new regulation, mere appearance became a legitimate reason for what was administratively designated as a border check and search since the redrawing of borders included in fact a large part of the territory. Consequently, this reshaping of national cartography indirectly sanctioned and even encouraged racial profiling. Moreover, with the increasing focus on Muslims in relation to both terrorist risk and veiling laws, this profiling also began to include religious criteria, which had not been the case until recently. In sum, the multiplication of internal zones of exception served as the justification for a surveillance system meant to be applied less to territorial borders than to racial and religious boundaries.

* * *

The evocation of these two recent situations—however different the historical and political contexts of the United States and France may be—shows both the volatility and intertwinement of borders and boundaries. While Donald Trump establishes new border controls allegedly to reduce the threat of terrorism or criminality linked to immigration, he endeavors to harden boundaries, which are religious in the case of the Muslim ban and ethnic in the case of the Mexican border wall, to satisfy the Islamophobic and xenophobic tendencies of the core of his constituency.[3] Whereas Emmanuel Macron displaces borders from the periphery of the national territory to the urban centers of the country, he simultaneously shifts the official goal of defending the security of the country from possible attacks toward the disguised objective of legalizing checks and searches on the basis of racial, ethnic, and religious boundaries.[4] In both cases, it is clear that borders cannot be thought of without the boundaries they establish or reinforce, and boundaries have to be analyzed in relation to the justifications they provide for the control or even the shifting of borders.

Yet, in theory, the difference between the two seems relatively straightforward. On the one hand, borders are generally considered to delimit territories (Rudolph 2005). They have to do with states and the space of exercise of their sovereignty. They entail law and its power to determine the perimeter of citizenship. They are political creations resulting from wars and peace treaties, colonialism, and the decolonization process. On the other hand, boundaries are habitually viewed as distinguishing between groups (Lamont & Molnár 2002). They have to do with representations and the establishing of categories. They encompass a multiplicity of potential criteria, such as race, ethnicity, language, religion, class, gender, and sexual orientation. They are social constructions proceeding from history and culture, identification and otherization. While both borders and boundaries involve relations of power and dynamics of the imagination, the former work on principles of inclusion and exclusion, and the latter on logics of solidarity and inequality.

But such straightforward characterizations tend to essentialize notions that are elusive and changing, as revealed in the two initial examples. When Étienne Balibar writes that "we cannot attribute to the border an essence which would be valid in all places and at all times, and which would be included in the same way in all individual and collective experience" (Balibar 2002: 75), his observation resonates with the argument developed by Fredrik Barth in his pioneering study of ethnicity where he argues that it is "the ethnic boundary that defines the group, not the cultural stuff that it encloses" (Barth 1998: 15). We should therefore avoid reifying borders or boundaries, but we should also be aware that the two are often linked. As the cases of the United States and France discussed above suggest, the clear-cut differentiation between the two entities is often blurred, and even what we think we know about each of them appears questionable and uncertain (Fassin 2012). Issues related to territorial, legal and political delimitations are interwoven with issues related to racial, ethnic, religious, gender, and sexual delineations. As Aristide Zolberg (2008) observes, viewing and even lauding the United States as a country of immigration comes down to forgetting that all along its history it has not been welcoming to all newcomers. The same is true for numerous countries in the world: immigrants are not all treated in the same way when they enter a foreign country (borders) and not all citizens are protected in the same way by their legal status (boundaries).

Past and present examples of the intertwinement of borders and boundaries abound, from the expulsion of the Jews in fifteenth-century Spain and the repression of Algerian colonial subjects in early twentieth-century France to the persecution of Tibetans in China, Rohingyas in Myanmar, and Kurds in Turkey in the present moment. The current situation of the Palestinians is a contemporary case in point, with the permanent reduction of the living space of those dwelling in the Occupied Territories, via the extension of settlements, destruction of fields, and construction of walls, and the growing deprivation of the civil rights of those residing in Israel, via religious and ethnic discrimination increasingly inscribed into the law. And the recent so-called refugee crisis in Europe also revealed how the control of borders at whatever cost in terms of human lives (more than 15,000 deaths were reported in the Mediterranean between 2014 and 2018) was linked to the making of racial and ethnic rather than merely national boundaries, which served to justify policies (there were more citizens of the United States obtaining a first residence permit than people from Africa and Asia trying to reach the continent by sea in 2017).[5] But the history of the overlapping of (national) borders and (ethno-racial) boundaries is fortunately not always as tragic, even if it remains quite problematic when one thinks of how it is also at play in the labor market, housing policies, legal matters, and even sports. The case of the Roma in Europe is of particular relevance since, despite the fact that, as citizens of Romania, Bulgaria, or Hungary, they belong to the European Union, they are nevertheless treated as aliens and even deported.[6] The most banal evidence of this overlapping is seen in the intergenerational transition from immigrants coming from the so-called Global South, who by definition have crossed a border, to their racialized or ethnicized children born in their host country, for whom the state and society at large often consolidate boundaries by not recognizing them fully as citizens or, when they do, as equals. Interestingly, in the parents' generation, there was little protest against the blatant discrimination of which they were victims since, as foreigners, they felt that they had no other choice than to resign themselves to their illegitimate status, while in the generation of the children, discrimination was not tolerated anymore since, for these often-French citizens also born in France, it was now unequal treatment that was viewed as illegitimate.

Connecting national territorial borders and ethno-racial boundaries is therefore crucial for scientific reasons (to understand the deepening divides of contemporary societies) as well as political ones (due to the sense of urgency resulting from the current situation). But in fact, this connection is more complex than suggested here. On the one hand, the most relevant borders are not necessarily those of the national territory. They can be supra-national, as was the case with the British Empire and is the case with the European Union today (Green 2013), especially in the context of the externalization of the control of immigration beyond the border, in Turkey, Libya, and Morocco. They can also be infra-national, as in Ireland during the so-called Troubles between nationalists and unionists, or Berlin, with the city physically divided in two during the Cold War by the Wall (Borneman 1992), the symbolic traces of which having remained long after its physical destruction. On the other hand, boundaries are not solely ethno-racial even if this is a major component at the border. They also involve religion, as illustrated by the previous examples of the United States and France, as well as class, gender, and sexuality. Social class appears to be an important element of differentiation between the wanted and the unwanted as well as in the public debate about selective immigration (Ypi 2018). Gender plays a less visible but no less important role in transnational networks and border control, including in sex work and domestic labor (Pessar & Mahler 2003). Disability has also been analyzed as a source of discrimination at the border in the name of what is criticized as "ableism" (El-Lahib & Wehbi 2012). But rather than examining these boundaries individually, it makes more sense to apprehend them from an intersectional perspective revealing the interactions between ethnic or racial characteristics, religion, class, gender, and disability.

A considerable literature has been dedicated to both borders and boundaries. This is not the place to review it in detail as there exist various comprehensive reviews (Schultz 2015; Winant 2000) and edited volumes (Goldberg & Solomos 2002; Wilson & Donnan 2012). Although the terms borders and boundaries are often used interchangeably, they have been the object of two distinct approaches and have generated two prolific fields of research. Borders, research into which overlaps with migration studies (Hollifield et al. 2014), have been analyzed in political geography in terms of the permanence of processes of inclusion and exclusion (Newman 2007), in international relations from the perspective of conflicts related to territorial disputes (Fravel 2008), in sociology through the question of detention and deportation of illegal migrants (Pratt 2005), and in anthropology via the production of borderlands as socially and culturally distinctive territories (Alvarez 1995). They have also been conceived of as a method to decipher contemporary crises, global transformations of economies, and local sites of violence (Mezzadra & Neilson 2013). Boundaries, which have been a major topic in the studies of race (Essed & Goldberg 2002), have been explored via the formation of hybrid identities resulting from the combination of ethnic, gendered, and sexual differences (Anzaldúa 1987), in terms of escape routes that allow people to cross them so as to redefine themselves and transcend ascribed identities (Telles & Sue 2009), and via the exclusionary strategies that they may reveal (Stolcke 1995) or, conversely, in terms of the politics of diversity and multiculturalism to which they have given birth (Brubaker 2015). They have also been examined by psychologists to apprehend group relations and conflicts (Prentice & Miller 1999). Thus, for the most part, borders and boundaries are inscribed in two separate sets of scholarship.

The interest in the way in which they are intermingled is, however, far from new. To cite only a few examples, John Cole and Eric Wolf (1974) described how two villages situated on both sides of the border between Austria and Italy developed, in the same physical environment, completely different cultural practices and social organization; Peter Sahlins (1989) analyzed how the creation of the border between France and Spain in the seventeenth century generated, via the distinction between the two territories, a sense of national differentiation nourished by local disputes; Ronald Frankenberg (1957) studied the conflicting relationships in a village situated at the border between England and Wales, showing that the boundaries between the residents were not only determined by the colonial, including linguistic, domination of the latter by the former, but also by class distinctions and inequalities related to capital-intensive agriculture; and Abner Cohen (1965) examined how the birth of the Israeli state transformed kinship practices and land distribution, thus establishing new boundaries in Arab villages situated at the border as a result of the dispossession of part of their territory.

More recently, studies have explored the making of identities and networks among minorities of migrant origin in the United States, often on the basis of a common experience of racialization and discrimination. They concern in particular Salvadorans (Menjívar 2000), West Indians (Waters 2001), Chinese (Ngai 2004), and Mexicans (De Genova 2005), the latter having received considerable attention in relation to the southern border of the country (Vélez-Ibáñez & Heyman 2017). In parallel, research on Europe has been conducted on ethnic group formation among immigrants in Britain and Germany (Castles 1984) as well as in Switzerland (Wimmer 2013), in some cases with an emphasis on the experience of specific groups such as Poles in London (Garapich 2016), Libyans in Milan and Berlin (Fontanari 2019), and, in a sort of symmetrical perspective, Andalusians, whose status has changed from that of migrants in Northern Europe in search of work to being forced hosts for African immigrants (Suárez-Navaz 2004). This renewal of attention to connections between borders and boundaries thus seems to respond to Paul Silverstein's call for more research into "the dialectical relationship between state racial formations and migration studies" (Silverstein 2005: 376). The present volume participates in this mobilization.

It offers however certain differences. First, taking advantage of the fact that English has two words when most languages only have one—such as French with *frontière* and Spanish with *frontera*—we have chosen to establish a distinction between borders and boundaries, the former corresponding to territorial and legal limits, the latter to social and symbolic ones. We are aware that it is a convention, but we think that it is heuristically useful, even when it involves showing, in concrete contexts, the blurring of the two or the obscuring of one by the other. We do not reify the concepts, but use them as tools to uncover certain logics that would be less evident otherwise. They are for us critical instruments. Second, playing with this distinction, we could say that we have attempted to cross national borders as well as disciplinary boundaries. Indeed, our case studies are taken from five continents: Africa, Asia, Europe, North America, and South America. And the authors of this volume come from history, sociology, anthropology, law, and political science.

* * *

The first part of this book examines the political and moral economies at work in the connections between borders and boundaries on a global scale as well as within national contexts. By political economies we mean the production, circulation, and appropriation of goods and services, whereas by moral economies we mean the production, circulation, and appropriation of values and affects. Both dimensions have considerable consequences on the way immigration is approached and migrants are treated by states as well as societies.

In that regard, the contrast is striking between the opportunities open to wealthy Russians, Chinese, or Saudis who can buy a residence permit or citizenship status from a microstate in the Mediterranean or the Caribbean, as discussed by Kristin Surak, and the fate endured by Filipina domestic workers in Middle Eastern Arab countries, Israel, Singapore, Taiwan, Canada, and Denmark, as studied by Rhacel Parreñas. In the case of rich foreigners, substantial donations to or investments in countries with corresponding regulations allow billionaires to benefit from their acquired identity—for instance, by obtaining a Maltese or Cypriot passport they gain access to the European Union without the legal constraints imposed on those who do not belong to it. But one could add that money is not the only resource providing a free pass to residency rights or citizenship and that small states are not the only ones to offer special privileges to applicants endowed with a particular form of capital. So-called talent, in sports, science, or technology, has the same function in Western countries. In the case of domestic workers, migrant women are bound to their employer, whom they can only leave under very restrictive conditions, which depend on national policies, because doing so would cause them to lose automatically their residency permit and face deportation. Such unfavorable work contracts, for which the Philippine state develops services dedicated to the preparation of its domestic workers before their departure, lead to situations of extreme dependence and precariousness. The lack of freedom and intimacy as well as the absence of minimal wage and social protection are assimilated by some to a form of indenture, notably in the case of the United Arab Emirates, where the situations of these women can be particularly appalling.

Differences in the regimes of immigration thus reveal hierarchies in the evaluation of the worth of human lives, borders being regulated in dramatically divergent ways determined by economic or national boundaries and with frequent ethno-racial undertones. This is what Ayşe Parla shows in the case of Turkey, where the state distinguishes migrants of Turkish origin and Turkish culture, especially those of Bulgarian descent, from other foreigners. However, society at large does not completely recognize these blood kin as equal to purebred nationals, despite their efforts to perform their belonging to Turkey. The multiple boundaries drawn both across and within borders, which induce attitudes that go from hostility against Kurds to racism toward Africans, are hardly surprising in a country that has not yet recognized the Armenian Genocide, which occurred more than a century ago. That the state establishes distinctions between legitimate and illegitimate migrants is common practice across the globe. In the French case, the state goes as far as to explore and police the intimacy of relationships between men and women, as Mayanthi Fernando demonstrates, analyzing situations that involve binational couples who are tested on their affective and sexual bonds before the foreign partner can obtain a residence permit. Of particular importance here is her analysis of Muslim men, who are taught how to respect gender equality within the space of the family. The specter of deceit in the first case (foreign nationals) and of communalism in the second one (Muslim men) haunts public discourses and policies, adding moral and religious boundaries to the already strictly controlled national borders.

The second part of the volume moves deeper into the ethnic and racial discriminations produced by legal texts and social norms. It does so notably by considering historical precedents to the current moment, thus allowing us to avoid the pitfalls of presentism.

In the United States, the Trump administration's "Muslim ban" thus offers interesting similarities with previous exclusionary measures adopted at the end of the nineteenth and the beginning of the twentieth century. The best known is the 1882 Chinese Exclusion Act, which was the first of its kind directed against a class of aliens, as reminded by Mae Ngai. The act was voted for by Congress and, when it was contested a little later, the Supreme Court ruled that it was a matter of national security and that the government consequently had a sovereign right to refuse and deport foreigners. This decision paved the way for future exclusionary measures. The legislation was enacted in a context of racist violence against Chinese, which it contributed to fueling and legitimizing. It also inspired the passage in 1917 of the Immigration Act, also known as the Asiatic Barred Zone Act, which, as Sherally Munshi explains, was a euphemistic way to designate what was in fact a "Hindu ban," the geographic definition of those excluded avoiding a racial language even in the disguised form of national delineation. Blatant racism was, however, overtly expressed at the time in the congressional debates. Thus, in the exclusion of both Chinese and Hindus, the alleged control of national borders was no less than the endorsement of racial boundaries by the state.

Opening a perspective on both American continents, Michael Hanchard analyzes the historical formation of states under racial regimes from the colonial to the postcolonial times. In a context of the permanent revision of borders through wars of liberation or conflicts with neighboring countries, the definition of racial boundaries in Brazil and Gran Columbia was haunted by the dual question of natives and slaves, including when the latter were freed. The case of the Haitian Revolution was intolerable for Western powers since, for the first time, a black nation-state was created, which made borders and boundaries coincide in an unprecedented way as citizenship and race became coextensive. Moving to a more abstract terrain, Tugba Basaran revisits the founding principle of the recognition of individuals as persons before the law. Although it is included in the 1948 Universal Declaration of Human Rights, it is not implemented everywhere for everyone, in particular where foreigners are concerned, whether in contexts of war, such as in Guantanamo for the United Sates, or in context of immigration, such as in Nauru for Australia. These extreme cases, which are underlain by the construction of racial boundaries, show that the control of borders often relies on border-enforcing legal practices that do not conform to usual territorial legislation and produce lives outside the law.

The third and last part considers borders from a spatial perspective, either as the line separating two territories or, more indefinitely, as the demarcation of an area of sanctuary, for military objectives in no-man's land, and finally for economic purposes in free zones. The authors show that both lines and areas are the result of processes of border-making.

These processes can be used to protect. This is what Linda Bosniak illustrates with the development of sanctuary practices in the United States and elsewhere in response to increasingly drastic and repressive immigration policies. Thus, certain cities declare themselves to be sanctuaries in the tradition of ancient asylum sites in which various classes of people could find refuge, and thus today where illegal immigrants cannot be arrested. The arguments used to justify these practices are diverse, from humanitarian principles and pragmatic self-interest to broader ideas of justice and even radical claims of a right to stay for those who have settled in their host country. At the same time as these movements produce internal borders delimiting sanctuaries where the federal state cannot enforce its law, they construct legal boundaries between those who have access to certain measures, like the DREAM Act of 2001, for alien minors, and others.

In contrast with this logic of protection, the making of borders and boundaries can proceed from logics of dispossession and oppression. The no-man's-land on the northern edge of the Gaza Strip described by Ilana Feldman illustrates the fate of a small town affected by both long-term occupation by the Israeli state and repeated deadly attacks by its army. Episodes of destruction have multiplied since the creation of Israel in 1948. The Nakba, as it is called in the Arab world, not only established a border between the new state and the Occupied Territories, it also created boundaries among Palestinians, notably between natives and refugees, who were dislodged from their land and depended on the assistance of the United Nations. With time, the ordeal of the cycle of ruination and rebuilding has been redoubled by the increasing difficulty in crossing the border and the institution of a new boundary between those who benefit from a permit and those who do not. The tragic history of this town epitomizes the making of borders and boundaries through the politics of colonization, which in this case involves not only land but also water as Palestinians are denied access to the sea.

In a less dramatic context, the originality of borders and borderlands considered by Paul Nugent in Africa is that, contrary to what is the case in Europe and North America, where the asymmetry of wealth, rights, and benefits between those inside and those outside generates major tension around the question of immigration, they separate countries between which such contrasts do not exist and where movements of population are hardly an object of surveillance. In fact, borders are not so much an obstacle to the circulation of people than a hindrance to the circulation of goods, due to bureaucratic complications and corruption practices. These transnational commercial activities are often organized around ethnic, religious, and even gendered boundaries, as illustrated by the parallel between the Nana Benz of Togo, women involved in the lucrative international textile trade, and the Mourides of Senegal, Wolof men of a Sufi brotherhood historically implicated in contraband of groundnuts, medicines, drugs, and weapons. In recent years, however, borderlands have also become more often zones of insecurity, with the increasing presence of Islamist militant organizations, especially in the Sahel region and northern Nigeria.

* * *

Borders between territories in which a form of sovereignty is exercised have long been objects of dispute and conflict. Boundaries between groups that have relationships with each other have long been a way of producing identities and differences. So what is new today?

The contemporary epoch is characterized, as we try to show in this volume, by a dual movement of hardening of both borders and boundaries, and by an increasing intertwinement of the two. On the one hand there is a closing of borders with a proliferation of institutions, apparatuses, and technologies to secure and police them, from Immigration and Customs Enforcement in the United States to Frontex in the European Union, from walls disfiguring landscapes to radars creating virtual fences, from cameras with body-heat detection devices to biometric and facial recognition technologies. This border industrial complex is mostly installed in the Western world, although it also is developing now in the Global South, and it is highly selective in its targeting of aliens—Muslims and Latinos in the United States, Africans and Middle Easterners in Europe, Palestinians in Israel. The religious, ethnic, and racial boundaries thus produced are in large part the legacy of an imperial and colonial past as well as a reflection of present transnational inequalities. The dual irony of these policies is, first, that they are largely independent of the evolution of immigration flows and continue to be loudly vindicated even when there is a decline in the number of people crossing borders; and, second, that they are defended by both populist parties in the name of nationalist ideas and by liberal politicians with the paradoxical argument that these programs will prevent the rise of xenophobic ideologies when they actually legitimize them. On the other hand, there is a strengthening of boundaries with a multiplication of forms of stigmatization, exclusion, oppression, segregation, and brutalization. While such processes have existed in the past, sometimes in much more tragic forms, they have recently manifested themselves with extreme expressions of violence facilitated by the radicalization of racist and intolerant ideologies and the expansion of deadly or maiming weaponry, in particular in Africa and the Middle East, but less visible practices are at work everywhere—for instance, the disproportionate incarceration of African Americans in the United States and growing demonstrations of Islamophobia in Europe.

In this disquieting context, of which we have tried here to analyze various aspects from diverse perspectives on different continents, thinking together borders and boundaries through their complex interactions is not just an academic exercise. It is a way to face some of the most pressing issues of our time—issues which, for many, entail questions of life and death. This is why borders and boundaries are not merely territorial and social limits external to individuals; they are deeply inscribed in their bodies. Undocumented Guatemalans in the United States, Afghans in Western Europe, and Zimbabweans in South Africa all know that they are at any moment at the mercy of an identity check, and the mere sight of a uniform generates among them profound reactions of fear. African American parents in the United States as well as Arab parents in France teach their children to avoid responding to misbehavior or provocations by the police, and to overdo conformity to dominant cultural norms, thus inculcating extreme docility and correctness, just as black parents used to do with their children in South Africa a few decades ago. Borders and boundaries thus produce profoundly incorporated forms of differentiation and inequality. The embodiment of borders and boundaries is a major feature of our time.

This evolution of both borders and boundaries, and the overlap between the two, involves the very foundation of politics, if we consider with Hannah Arendt that "Man exists in politics only in the equal rights that those who are most different guarantee for each other" (Arendt 2005: 94). Nowhere is this existence in politics more at stake than in the delineating of borders and boundaries, and in the treatment of those who are on one side or the other of these lines drawn between humans.

Acknowledgments

The present volume has a long and singular genesis. Indeed, the workshop held in May 2017 at the Institute for Advanced Study, which served as the basis for this collective enterprise, concluded a year of intense intellectual exchanges among scholars working on borders and boundaries. It also brought together social scientists researching this theme who had previously benefited from fellowships in the School of Social Science. A special dynamic resulted from this encounter, of which this book bears witness—or so we hope. But this workshop was also the expansion of a previous collective scientific project in France, involving forty researchers studying French external borders and internal boundaries, which I had initiated in 2006. It had led to the publication of an edited volume and the convening of two conferences with Eric Fassin and Claudio Lomnitz in Paris and at Columbia University. The final steps of this endeavor have also benefited from the grant associated with the Nomis Award I received to develop a research program on crises, which includes a section on borders and boundaries. Regarding the workshop that gave birth to the present volume, I am thankful to the Fritz Thyssen Foundation for its support. I also express my gratitude to the staff of the School of Social Science at the Institute for Advanced Study for their invaluable help, in particular Laura McCune for the organization of the meeting and Munirah Bishop for the revision of the manuscript. Finally, I am indebted to David Castle for his warm support for this project from the start, and to the anonymous readers for their productively critical comments.

Notes

1. Executive Order No. 13769, January 27, 2017 (available at: https://www.whitehouse.gov/presidential-actions/executive-order-protecting-nation-foreign-terrorist-entry-united-states/, accessed August 3, 2019).
2. Loi no. 2017-1510 renforçant la sécurité intérieure et la lutte contre le terrorisme, October 30, 2017 (available at: https://www.legifrance.gouv.fr/eli/loi/2017/10/30/INTX1716370L/jo/texte, accessed August 3, 2019).

3. An analysis of polling data, including a study by the Pew Research Center in May 2016, showed that, among Trump supporters, the three major concerns were immigration (which "threatens US values"), Islam (inasmuch as it thought to "encourage violence"), and ethnic and racial diversity (see Lopez 2016). Various other studies conducted around the time showed that 73 percent of Republicans and 13 percent of Democrats were favorable to the idea of a wall along the border with Mexico, that the "Muslim ban" received the approval of 76 percent of Republicans and 26 percent of Democrats, and that there was a considerably higher proportion of people who thought that black people were "less intelligent," "more lazy," "more rude," "more violent," and "more criminal" than whites among Trump supporters than among those who supported other candidates for the Republican nomination, namely Ted Cruz and John Kasich (ibid.).
4. Black and Arab youths are stopped by the police 20 times more often than other members of the population in France according to a study conducted in May 2016 by Défenseur des Droits, an independent administrative authority in charge of verifying the respect of human rights and making recommendations to the government in case of their violations (see DDD 2017).
5. According to a periodically updated webpage of the UN International Organization for Migration, deaths in the Mediterranean are currently on average between 3,000 and 5,000 each year (see http://missingmigrants.iom.int/region/mediterranean). In parallel, deaths on the US–Mexico border are officially around 400 per annum according to official sources, but possibly more than double that according to the American Civil Liberties Union (https://www.nnirr.org/drupal/stopping-migrant-deaths). In both cases, these statistics are conservative since numerous bodies are never found, and numbers have increased with the tougher enforcement of the border. There were 113,000 migrant arrivals in Europe via the Mediterranean in 2018 (UNIOM 2018). By comparison, in 2017, the most recent year with available data at the time of writing, 147,000 citizens from the United States obtained their first residence permits in the European Union (https://ec.europa.eu/eurostat/statistics-explained/index.php?title=Residence_permits_-_statistics_on_first_permits_issued_during_the_year&oldid=427234#First_residence_permits_by_citizenship, accessed August 22, 2019).
6. Deportations of Roma people from Italy in 2009 and France in 2010 generated protests, in particular from the European Commissioner for Human Rights. Such actions have much more to do with the symbolic strengthening of ethnoracial boundaries than with the effective reinforcement of national borders since, being members of the European Union, Roma people often return to the countries that have deported them (Guild 2011).

References

Alvarez, Robert. 1995. "The Mexican–US Border: The Making of an Anthropology of Borderlands." *Annual Review of Anthropology* 24: 447–70.
Anzaldúa, Gloria. 1987. *Borderlands/La Frontera: The New Mestiza*. San Francisco: Aunt Lute Books.

Arendt, Hannah. 2005 [1993]. "Introduction into Politics." In *The Promise of Politics*, 93–199. New York: Schocken Books.

Balibar, Étienne. 2002 [1996]. "What is a Border?" In *Politics and the Other Scene*, 75–86. London: Verso.

Barth, Fredrik (ed.). 1998 [1969]. *Ethnic Groups and Boundaries: The Social Organization of Culture Difference*. Long Grove, IL: Waveland Press.

Borneman, John. 1992. "State, Territory, and Identity Formation in the Postwar Berlins 1945–1989." *Cultural Anthropology* 7(1): 45–62.

Brubaker, Rogers. 2015. *Grounds for Difference*. Cambridge, MA: Harvard University Press.

Castles, Stephen, with Heather Booth and Tina Wallace. 1984. *Here for Good: Western Europe's New Ethnic Minorities*. London: Pluto Press.

Cohen, Abner. 1965. *Arab Border-Villages in Israel: A Study of Continuity and Change in Social Organization*. Manchester: Manchester University Press.

Cole, John, and Eric Wolf. 1974. *The Hidden Frontier: Ecology and Ethnicity in an Alpine Valley*. New York: Academic Press.

DDD (Défenseur des droits). 2017. "Enquête sur l'accès aux droits, Vol.1: relations police/population—le cas des contrôles d'identité." Available at: https://www.defenseurdesdroits.fr/sites/default/files/atoms/files/rapport-enquete_relations_police_population-20170111_1.pdf (accessed August 3, 2019).

De Genova, Nicholas. 2005. *Working the Boundaries: Race, Space and "Illegality" in Mexican Chicago*. Durham, NC: Duke University Press.

El-Lahib, Yahya, and Samantha Wehbi. 2012. "Immigration and Disability: Ableism in the Policies of the Canadian State." *International Social Work* 55(1): 95–108.

Essed, Philomena, and David Theo Goldberg (eds). 2002. *Race Critical Theories. Text and Context*. Malden, MA: Blackwell.

Fassin, Didier. 2012 [2010]. "Introduction: frontières extérieures, frontières intérieures." In Didier Fassin (ed.), *Les nouvelles frontières de la société française*, 5–24. Paris: La Découverte.

Fontanari, Elena. 2019. *Lives in Transit: An Ethnographic Study of Refugees' Subjectivity across European Borders*. London: Routledge.

Frankenberg, Ronald. 1957. *Village on the Border: A Social Study of Religion, Politics and Football in a North Wales Community*. London: Cohen and West.

Fravel, Taylor. 2008. *Strong Borders, Secure Nation: Cooperation and Conflict in China's Territorial Disputes*. Princeton: Princeton University Press.

Garapich, Michal. 2016. *London's Polish Borders: Transnationalizing Class and Ethnicity among Polish Migrants in London*. Stuttgart: Ibidem Verlag.

Goldberg, David Theo, and John Solomos (eds). 2002. *A Companion to Racial and Ethnic Studies*. Malden, MA: Blackwell.

Green, Sarah. 2013. "Borders and the Relocation of Europe." *Annual Review of Anthropology* 42: 345–61.

Guild, Elspeth. 2011. "Le traitement des Roms dans l'Union Européenne." *Cultures et Conflits* 81/82: 192–4.

Hollifield, James, Philip Martin, and Pia Orrenius (eds). 2014 [1994]. *Controlling Immigration: A Global Perspective*. Stanford: Stanford University Press.

Lamont, Michèle, and Virág Molnár. 2002. "The Study of Boundaries in the Social Sciences." *Annual Review of Sociology* 28: 167–95.

Lopez, German. 2016. "Polls Show Many—Even Most—Trump Supporters Really Are Deeply Hostile to Muslims and Nonwhites." *Vox*, September 12. Available at: https://www.vox.com/2016/9/12/12882796/trump-supporters-racist-deplorables (accessed August 3, 2019).

Menjívar, Cecilia. 2000. *Fragmented Ties: Salvadoran Immigrant Networks in America*. Berkeley: University of California Press.

Mezzadra, Sandro, and Brett Neilson. 2013. *Border as Method, or, The Multiplication of Labor*. Durham, NC: Duke University Press.

Newman, David. 2007. "The Lines that Continue to Separate Us: Borders in Our 'Borderless' World." In Johan Schimanski and Stephen Wolfe (eds), *Border Poetics De-Limited*, 27–57. Hannover: Wehrhahn.

Ngai, Mae. 2004. *Impossible Subjects: Illegal Aliens and the Making of Modern America*. Princeton: Princeton University Press.

Pessar, Patricia, and Sarah Mahler. 2003. "Transnational Migration: Bringing Gender In." *International Migration Review* 37(3): 812–46.

Pratt, Anna. 2005. *Securing Borders: Detention and Deportation in Canada*. Vancouver: University of British Columbia Press.

Prentice, Deborah, and Dale Miller (eds). 1999. *Cultural Divides: Understanding and Overcoming Group Conflict*. New York: Russell Sage Foundation.

Rudolph, Christopher. 2005. "Sovereignty and Territorial Borders in a Global Age." *International Studies Review* 7(1): 1–20.

Sahlins, Peter. 1989. *Boundaries: The Making of France and Spain in the Pyrenees*. Berkeley: University of California Press.

Schultz, Kenneth. 2015. "Borders, Conflict, and Trade." *Annual Review of Political Science* 18: 125–45.

Silverstein, Paul. 2005. "Immigrant Racialization and the New Savage Slot: Race, Migration, and Immigration in the New Europe." *Annual Review of Anthropology* 34: 363–84.

Stolcke, Verena. 1995. "Talking Culture: New Boundaries, New Rhetorics of Exclusion in Europe." *Current Anthropology* 36(1): 1–24.

Suárez-Navaz, Liliana. 2004. *Rebordering the Mediterranean: Boundaries and Citizenship in Southern Europe*. New York: Berghahn Books.

Telles, Edward, and Christina Sue. 2009. "Race Mixture: Boundary Crossing in Comparative Perspective." *Annual Review of Sociology* 35: 129–46.

UNIOM (UN International Organization for Migration). 2018. "Mediterranean Migrant Arrivals Reach 113,145 in 2018; Deaths Reach 2,242." December 21. Available at: https://www.iom.int/news/mediterranean-migrant-arrivals-reach-113145-2018-deaths-reach-2242 (accessed August 3, 2019).

Vélez-Ibáñez, Carlos, and Josiah Heyman. 2017. *The US–Mexico Transborder Region: Cultural Dynamics and Historical Interactions*. Tucson: University of Arizona Press.

Waters, Mary. 2001. *Black Identities: West Indian Immigrant Dreams and American Realities*. Cambridge, MA: Harvard University Press.

Wilson, Thomas, and Hastings Donnan (eds). 2012. *A Companion to Border Studies*. Malden, MA: Wiley-Blackwell.

Wimmer, Andreas. 2013. *Ethnic Boundary Making: Institutions, Power, Networks*. Oxford: Oxford University Press.

Winant, Howard. 2000. "Race and Race Theory." *Annual Review of Sociology* 26: 169–85.

Ypi, Lea. 2018. "Borders of Class: Migration and Citizenship in the Capitalist State." *Ethics and International Affairs* 32(2): 141–52.

Zolberg, Aristide. 2008 [2006]. *A Nation by Design: Immigration Policy in the Fashioning of America*. Cambridge, MA: Harvard University Press.

PART I

Political and Moral Economies

2

What Money Can Buy
Citizenship by Investment on a Global Scale

Kristin Surak

Citizenship, in T.H. Marshall's (1950) foundational account, is the great equalizer. In a society compartmentalized by class and status, it becomes a sharp tool for use against entrenched powers, enabling disadvantaged segments of the population to obtain basic rights. Marshall's native Britain illustrated the progression. From the extension of first civil rights in the eighteenth century, through the acquisition of political rights in the nineteenth, to finally the achievement of social rights in the twentieth, previously marginalized classes acquired an equal positioning with the privileged. If this was not a guarantee of complete equality, at least it provided a similar starting point for many—on Marshall's scorecard, a triumph indeed.

Prompting his foray into citizenship was a deeper concern with transformations in inequality, namely whether the degree of parity that citizenship secures is compatible with class inequities. Marshall asked: how can capitalism, reliant upon inequality as an incentive, exist together with modern citizenship, an institution that hinges on the equality of members? The answer he found was partially damning. Citizenship, effectively, "provided the foundation of equality on which the structure of inequality could be built" (ibid.: 43). Crucial was its connection to the rise of the modern contract, entered into by two individuals, free and equal in status, if not in power. Within this configuration, though, lay a moment of hope, for citizenship in its increasingly elaborated form—particularly with the addition of social welfare rights—simultaneously provided a more equal footing for people to escape the class distinctions of their birth. The end result was a still-stratified class system within high capitalism, but one more flexible than before: "The preservation of economic inequalities has been made more difficult by the enrichment of the status of citizenship" (ibid.: 77). In effect, legal status was a key resource for unsettling once resolute class boundaries.

Marshall's analysis set the tone for analyses of citizenship, equality, and inequality to come, yet not without limits. Though pathbreaking, it presents an excised version of its unit of analysis: the nation-state is viewed in isolation and without its imperial holdings. The most fundamental exclusionary function of citizenship—that of keeping foreigners outside its full embrace—does not enter into his account. His Britain is one without permeable borders. Viewed from a wider optic, the nation-state he examines is a relatively wealthy and institutionally secure one, able to provide the rule of law and social provisions. For those born within its compass, life chances are good—indeed, far better than for those from war-torn, poor, or authoritarian countries. For many in the world, citizenship may be more confining than enabling. As one of the leaders of the investment migration industry described it to a journalist from *Malta Today*:

> Citizenship is inherently unjust. The whole system of citizenship and immigration laws is a completely unjust system. There are only two institutions we have carried over from feudal times that [are based on] birthright concepts: the right to inherit and to citizenship. But what makes you a better person from someone else just because you had the luck to be born in Malta? ... [In comparison to refugees violently kept away at Europe's borders,] the talented and rich have access, and that is equally unjust. (Vella 2016)

He then went on to validate citizenship by investment programs, which enable moneyed individuals, typically from outside the North Atlantic, to apply for a second citizenship in exchange for an economic contribution to a country.

> But at least in an unjust system, at least there is a way that certain people can get access. And at least it benefits the countries that are hosting them. And it benefits the countries that are sending them. At least there is a small door within this very unjust system where a certain little bit of equalization [can occur]. Your life chances are largely determined—[in fact] almost everything is determined—by where you are born and what citizenship you carry. (ibid.)

His argument points to the limits of the transformations Marshall traced. The equalizing potential of citizenship may loosen class boundaries within a state.[1] Yet the border remains, and may even be reinforced by the consolidation of state power that facilitated greater centralization and inclusion in the first place. If class boundaries within a state become more fluid, enabling those at the bottom to secure better life chances, migration controls will still prevent those outside from accessing such opportunities. Indeed, state borders are powerful exclusionary mechanisms. According to one estimate, international migration to OECD countries would increase by a factor of five were immigration controls removed (Pritchett 2006: 72). As advocates of the No Borders network note, immigration regimes and border controls do not merely reflect unequal rights but actively produce inequality, both within and between states, as a pillar supporting capitalist social relations dependent on expropriation and exploitation (Anderson et al. 2009: 11).

The intersection of borders and boundaries—here of states and class—offers intriguing material for reconsidering questions of citizenship and inequality. In a world in which countries enclose themselves with policed borders, to understand the relationship between citizenship and class requires looking both within and between states. The sections that follow will lay out the duplex structure of inequality producing wealthy people with "bad passports," review the mobility options available to them, examine the nature of putatively unjust systems of border controls and wealth accumulation, and reflect on its wider implications.

Global Inequalities

Global wealth is increasingly concentrated in the hands of a small elite. In 2016, the world's richest 1 percent held over half of all global wealth, up from 44 percent five years earlier (Shorrock et al. 2016: 4). Within this select set, the most affluent segment reveals even greater wealth concentration. Over 16.5 million high net worth individuals (HNWIs)—people with investable assets valued between $1 million and $30 million—held 20 percent of global wealth. Ultra-high net worth individuals (UNHWIs), with assets over more than $30 million, numbered just 210,000 yet possessed 13 percent of global wealth (Wealth-X and Arton Capital 2014: 10).[2]

While the North Atlantic continues to produce the most millionaires and billionaires, the past 30 years have seen a marked growth in new wealth beyond the region. In 2000, only 7 percent of UHNWIs came from emerging economies, yet they accounted for nearly a quarter of the group's growth 15 years later (Shorrock et al. 2016: 20).[3] The trend points to the diversification of the geographic origins of new wealth. Of the top 20 markets giving rise to HNWIs, nearly half are non-Western: Japan, China, India, South Korea, Saudi Arabia, Russia, Brazil, Kuwait, and Hong Kong (Capgemini 2016: 9).[4] With the exception of Japan, most regularly appear on "emerging market" lists as places offering enormous profit potential. Figured in local currency terms, emerging economies have contributed more to the increase in global wealth than high-income European and Asian economies (Shorrock et al. 2016: 16).

Notable on the Capgemini list is the number of countries that offer relatively limited mobility (see Capgemini 2016). While a German can show up on the doorstep of 177 countries and enter, a passport from Russia grants visa-free access to only around 100. This may be low, yet it is far better than Kuwaiti papers, which guarantee visa-free access to only 82 countries, while Chinese papers gain their holder immediate entry to only 50.[5] Citizens of relatively freer countries, as ranked by the Freedom House Index, also enjoy better visa-free travel. The inequities of access serves as a reminder that not all citizenships are the same when it comes to the package of rights and benefits they guarantee.

The stakes are high, as noted in the above quote, for though we have little choice in where we are born, no status has a greater impact on one's life

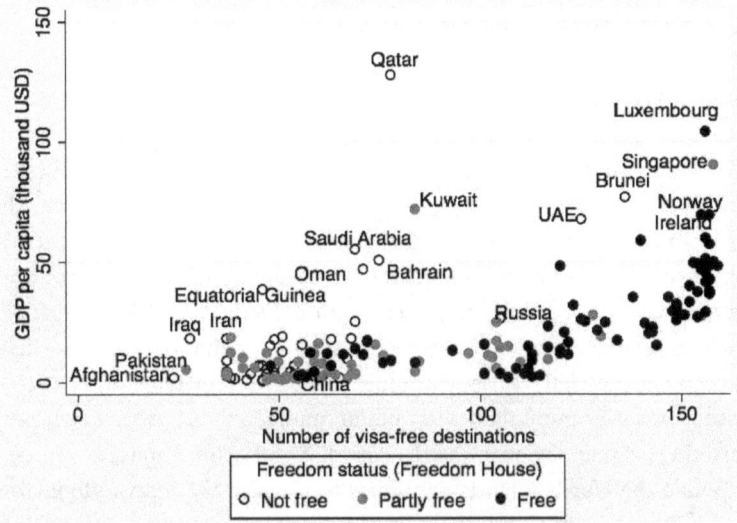

Figure 1

chances than one's country of birth (Korzeniewicz & Moran 2009: 100). According to the World Bank, a woman in Burundi will live, on average, to the age of 59 on an income of around $200 per year, while her counterpart in Finland will likely survive over 84 years on a far more generous income of $38,000.[6] No other measure, on its own, is as influential. It comes as little surprise that the most impoverished decile in low-income countries fares far worse than its counterpart in wealthier states. Notably, however, wealth does not insulate the rich from the consequences of "citizenship penalt[ies]" (Milanovic 2016: 131). In Burundi, the most affluent decile also occupies a lower position in terms of global income distribution than its correlates elsewhere. The difference represents a "citizenship premium" for those born in countries higher up the global income ladder (ibid.: 131–4). Of course, moving to a more prosperous country may offer a solution, but border controls ensure that the population of global movers remains confined below the actual demand for cross-border mobility (Pritchett 2006). The result, as Appiah observes, is that "all individuals in the world are obliged, whether they like it or not, to accept the political arrangements of their birthplace, however repugnant those arrangements are to their principles or ambitions—unless they can persuade somebody else to take them in" (Appiah 1998: 41). Political borders transform citizenship into a "birthright lottery" (Shachar 2009).

The upshot of this are obstacles for the moneyed classes in emerging markets, who are unable to access the mobility options available to counterparts from places wealthier and more Western. Indeed, the wealthy are a highly mobile set. A survey concerning 2,000 HNWIs in six world regions carried out by Barclays found that nearly half had lived in more than one country—a staggering proportion given that migrants account for only 3 percent of the world's population. Topping the motives behind elite mobility were climatic factors, economic security, retirement options, business moves, and educational opportunities (Barclays 2014: 10–11).[7] If we think of "cosmopolitan elites" as a well-heeled globetrotting class for whom borders have little meaning, the nouveaux riches from outside the West—facing the same border controls as their less privileged compatriots—may struggle to get their foot in the door.

The result is a duplex structure of inequality. The first axis lies at the inter-state level. Not all citizenships are the same when it comes to mobility options and the package of rights they guarantee, as a number of studies have shown. Yet below the inequality between countries rests the inequality within them, namely the increasing concentration of wealth and the rise of nouveaux riches. At a structural level, it is the confluence of inter-state and intra-state inequality that produces wealthy people with limited travel options and in search of solutions.

Citizenship by Investment

The quotation introduced earlier is clear in condemning the inherent arbitrariness of citizenship as a powerful sorting mechanism. But after lamenting the unjustness of the system, the speaker goes on to defend a workaround. A leader of the investment migration industry, he obliquely refers to the option, available in several countries, to acquire citizenship through monetary grants. Currently five countries in the Caribbean (Antigua, Dominica, Grenada, Saint Kitts, and Saint Lucia) and two in the Mediterranean (Cyprus and Malta) host citizenship by investment (CBI) programs that supply a formal channel for naturalization to those who can afford it. Of course, any state can extend citizenship on whatever grounds it chooses, and it may do so in exchange for money. But CBI programs are more formalized than brute cash-for-passport exchanges. Unlike discretionary citizenship grants, the programs are bureaucratic. Typically, a designated unit within the government implements the scheme, specifying the minimum price points and possible forms of investment. The government will also assess and approve individual investment options, license service providers, set standards for due diligence, and even confer with external agencies on the suitability of candidates.

But little more is requested beyond the paperwork. Residence requirements are kept to a minimum, if they exist at all. Indeed, the demand for physical presence—even if only to pick up a passport—can be considered an unwelcome burden that may limit the competitiveness of the "product." Most investor citizens have little inclination to settle in their new countries: they are looking for travel options, or what many term an insurance policy.

The price varies based on what citizenship secures, which for many comes down to mobility options. In the Caribbean, prospective naturalizers typically either donate between $100,000 and $200,000 to the government, or invest between $300,000 and $450,000 in approved real-estate projects, and in exchange receive a passport that grants them visa-free access to around 120 countries, including—crucially—the Schengen Area of Europe. An Egyptian businessman with companies in Europe, for example, might write off citizenship in Dominica as a work expense that enables him to quickly travel to the investment site without waiting weeks for visas.

The Mediterranean countries are dearer. The Maltese government requires a donation of €650,000, in addition to the purchase of bonds and other investments, amounting to around €1 million in total. In Cyprus, the cost is an eye-watering minimum of €2.5 million, though additional family members incur no further charges. These higher price tags secure greater benefits as well: both Malta and Cyprus are members of the European Union, and Maltese citizens can travel visa-free to the US as well. A Russian oligarch, for example, might use a Cypriot passport to spend more time at her mansion in London while putting her children through private schooling in England.

Borders, Boundaries, and an Unjust World

But are the wealthy naturalizers, often born in countries with authoritarian regimes, perhaps under a weakened rule of law or even torn by war, the victims of an unjust system as the opening quotation suggests? The answer can be supplied only in broad strokes as comprehensive survey evidence on the clients participating in citizenship by investment programs is nonexistent.[8] However, if the naturalizers resemble the run-of-the-mill affluent in their home country, the dominant patterns of wealth creation can indicate how they achieved their lofty status. Examining the origins of their wealth suggests that rich naturalizers did not simply draw a bad straw in the birthright lottery. On the contrary, for most it was birth in their country of origin at a specific historical juncture that enabled them to amass substantial assets in the first place. That is, political borders contained the political-economic transformations that facilitated the creation and accumulation of capital that catapulted them into the ranks of global UHNWIs. Effectively, borders produce structural differentiations that offer economic advantages, and disadvantages (Sahlins 1988: 258–9), generating or reinforcing class boundaries. A general picture can be sketched from the two leading countries supplying investment migrants: China and Russia.

In China, entrepreneurs account for the bulk of billionaires (Freund 2016: 28). But hard work alone does not explain their achievements—if it does anywhere—in a world defined by connections. "Insider privatization" determined the deregulation of state-owned enterprises in the 1980s, securing for cadres and well-placed managers early advantages in what would become the world's greatest experiment in marketization. The 1990s saw growth driven further by the legalization of large private businesses and the designation of Special Economic Zones, attracting "foreign" investment from Taiwan and Hong Kong. But the Communist Party kept the market tightly controlled, limiting foreign ownership and requiring that ventures be run jointly with nationals. The result was a boon for well-connected citizens who reaped stunning gains. By 2001, then president, Jiang Zemin, encouraged the increasing—and increasingly wealthy—business class to take its place alongside workers, cadres, and soldiers as a fundament of socialism, but with "Chinese characteristics." Over the years of economic reform, privately held wealth exploded, from slightly more than the national income in 1980 to 500 percent of national income in 2016 (Novokmet et al. 2017: 25). With marketization and privatization, the share of state assets—that is, public property—as a proportion of national wealth dropped from about 70 percent in 1978 to 30 percent in 2015 (Piketty et al 2017: 4). Inequality has followed: while China once boasted inequality levels similar to the egalitarian Nordic countries in the 1970s, they are approaching US rates today. Meanwhile, as of 2015, the wealthiest 10 percent now hold about 67 percent of national wealth (ibid.: 6).

Yet most entrepreneurs remain dependent on the state for capital and business opportunities. Carefully cultivated personal connections with officials and other businesspeople continue to be crucial for getting ahead, and those without them remain shut out (Osburg 2013; see also Goodman 2008). In turn, officials have become dependent on connections with successful entrepreneurs as well, for it is in cooperation with these drivers of economic growth that they are able to attain their assigned development goals. Meanwhile Beijing continues to protect Chinese markets against foreign ownership, leaving investment opportunities to be monopolized by nationals: it is the Chinese business elite who have benefited most. Whereas China accounted for only 4 percent of global wealth in 2000, by 2016 it accounted for 15 percent (Shorrock et al. 2016: 16).

In the case of Russia and several former Soviet states, the fall of communism offered the IMF, World Bank, and US Treasury the opportunity to implement neoliberal market reforms: so-called shock therapy. Boris Yeltsin drove through—in many cases by decree—the rapid privatization of state assets, facilitating the accumulation of vast quantities of wealth by well-placed bosses and apparatchiks. In a context of unstable property rights, insider status allowed the most nimble to win government contracts and licenses, and later shares of firms and natural resources, in what was even then called a rigged bidding system. The result? A handful of the well-connected gained substantial ownership of key firms at astoundingly low prices. Energy, telecommunications, oil, and metals would nurse a new generation of oligarchs. Freund (2016: 28) estimates that between half to all billionaires in Russia, Ukraine, Georgia, and Kazakhstan acquired their fortunes by leveraging political connections to exploit natural resources.

As political ties determined access to the spoils, inequality soared. In the transition from communism to capitalism, the share of the income held by the wealthiest 10 percent increased from 25 percent in 1991 to more than 45 percent in 1996. More dramatic was the increase in the wealthiest 1 percent's share of income, which rocketed from around 5 percent in 1989 to over 26 percent by 2008 (Novokmet et al. 2017: 33). Disaggregating the growth, Novokmet et al. (ibid.: 26) find that the marked rise in private wealth within Russia has come largely at the expense of public wealth.

In light of this historical context, we might return to the assertions of injustice in the opening quotation. To what extent are the wealthy in developing economies suffering under inequalities in citizenship? A cursory examination of the Chinese and Russian cases suggests that the borders that many investment migrants attempt to work around are often the very ones that enabled them to amass great wealth in the first place. In many instances, the entrepreneurial or oligarchic elites would not have accumulated the vast financial resources required to seek out other options had they not been born in their country of origin at a particular historical conjuncture—one marked by mass privatization, marketization, and increasing economic inequality within them. For the winners, the accrued capital becomes a resource for transcending political borders once they become inconvenient, and investment migration options help secure these routes. In many cases, the nouveaux riches are simply looking for better mobility options than those offered by their country of birth, business opportunities, or an insurance policy if an authoritarian government cracks down or turns against them. This is the market for citizenship by investment, a product of borders on which market players seek to capitalize.

An Investor Citizenry

What are the implications? Globally, the number of investor citizens is small, with around 10,000 individuals naturalizing through these channels each year (see Surak n.d.).⁹ Countries running popular programs may see around 2,000 or so new citizens using the provisions annually. For a microstate like Saint Kitts, with a resident population of only 55,000, the proportions are significant. According to the available records, it naturalized nearly 11,000 investors between 2006 and 2016, the time when the program took off. Individuals working with the scheme suggest that the true figure is even higher. What are the implications for the countries offering CBI programs?

For microstates, the potential economic benefits are great. Malta amassed over €1 billion in revenue in the first four years of its scheme. With its longer-standing program, Cyprus has accrued over €2 billion. These figures can be compared with the GDP of each country, approximately €10 billion and €20 billion respectively. In the Caribbean, Antigua and Grenada collect around 15 percent of GDP through CBI programs, but they have been dwarfed by their neighbor, Saint Kitts, which has traditionally accounted for much of the sales in the Caribbean and has in some years obtained nearly 40 percent of its GDP through citizenship by investment. Many questions might be asked about whether these sizeable injections have benefited local economies. Travel around the islands reveals the trophy projects on display, like solar panels at the airport in St. John's, Antigua, and funds have been used for social initiatives such as scholarship programs and entrepreneurial training. In some cases, the schemes have funded the construction of popular resorts that employ hundreds of locals and attract tourist dollars to the islands, furthering economic development. In others, promised hotel or port projects have never gotten off the ground or have proceeded at the slow pace of a white elephant. Several Caribbean countries confirm that they have used program proceeds to pay off loans, an expenditure that improves the economic health of a country but leaves no visible traces. Malta is accruing its revenues in a fund, though at the time of writing, none of the money had been spent, leaving the public works projects promised at the launch of the program yet to get off the ground. (There is now talk of repaving all of the roads in the country.)

Economic citizens may care about these outcomes for they do have a stake in their new country. Those who secure their new nationality by investing in real estate or businesses will be concerned about their adopted country's economic prospects, and even those who donate to the government retain an interest in its foreign relations, for regional superpowers determine the value of investor citizenship (Surak 2016). When Saint Kitts lost visa-free access to Canada in 2014, applications for investor naturalization dropped as well. Yet citizenship acquired through CBI represents membership in its thinnest form, what Joppke has termed "citizenship lite" (Joppke 2010). Stripped away are concerns with identity and a sense of belonging. Gone are expectations of social welfare benefits, social protection, and resource redistribution. The obligations of membership, already on the decline across the board (see Spiro 2008), are nonexistent as well. No military service, no jury duty, and of course no substantial taxes are expected of the new citizens. In the main, its substance is reduced to access to travel documents and benefits in other countries.

Arguably, a similar rationale holds for many people who take advantage of ancestry options to naturalize (see Cook-Martin 2013). Italy allows anyone who can prove descent through an Italian male to apply for citizenship, and more than 1 million people have taken advantage of the provision. Furthermore, no visit to the country is required—the rite of passage can take place in an Italian embassy anywhere in the world (Tintori 2012). Indeed, many people, not merely the rich, are great strategizers when it comes to citizenship options: members of the middle class from outside the West acquire dual nationality to offset perceived deficits in their home-country membership—a form of compensatory citizenship (Harpaz 2015). It is those who have the most to gain economically from a second passport who make use of the option. Migrants from less developed countries are more likely to obtain additional citizenship through naturalization than are those from more prosperous ones (Dronkers & Vink 2012; Jasso & Rosenzweig 1986: 303). In contrast, migrants from high-income countries tend to naturalize once they develop family or lifestyle ties to a new country, rather than as a hedge against economic risks (Vink et al. 2013).[10] Studies have shown that members of the middle and upper-middle classes seeking economic opportunities and mobility options will employ ancestry routes (Cook-Martin 2013; Harpaz 2015), "birth tourism" (Balta & Altan-Olcay 2016), or investment residence visas (Ley 2010; Ong 1999) to secure access to opportunities in wealthier states.[11] The HNWIs above them may not be so different.

Thus as strategizers, investor citizens perhaps distinguish themselves more in terms of degree than in kind. Yet for them, the deal depends on a thorough separation of state and nation. Wealthy naturalizers seek the benefits the state secures—and largely those it secures not within but outside its borders (see Surak 2016)—and show little to no interest in its imagined community. The result is hardly a mushrooming international diaspora of, for example, hyphenated Saint Lucians. Unlike their fellow citizens "at home," these non-present, virtual citizens are members of the state but not the nation. A month after Saint Kitts hosted the regional investment migration summit in 2018, it also put on its first international diaspora conference, aimed at harnessing the economic and human capital of its local progeny who have made good in the United States and Great Britain. No place was made for its economic citizens abroad. Yet the governments of microstates might count themselves lucky if the affluent did see this as a boundary worth crossing, allowing affective ties to emerge. At present, a one-off contribution is enough to make an investor citizen. Harnessing communal ties might transform this momentary injection of foreign direct investment into a more continuous flow of, effectively, remittances. When hurricanes hit the islands, now almost an annual occurrence, economic citizens might be rallied for charitable giving to special relief funds. Yet such a scenario remains hard to imagine for those involved. The governments hope that, at best, a few of these "expats" might come and spend time—and money—on the islands.

What is the impact of investor citizenship on inequality within countries of origin? Contra Marshall, does CBI reinforce class disparities rather than unsettling them? One might presume that elites, as they circumvent the state borders that once facilitated their wealth accumulation, might thereby impede economic growth. And indeed, many evade foreign exchange controls to pay for their new passport, draining resources from a country that might otherwise be reinvested in it. But given the small numbers and relatively low costs involved, the effect is likely to be close to zero. If, for example, Chinese nationals represent half of the global market in citizenship by investment, which Bloomberg projects has a turnover of $2 billion annually, they are investing around $1 billion abroad every year for such programs. What appears to be a sizeable figure, however, represents less than 1 percent of the more than $150 billion in overseas investments that left China in 2016 (Reuters 2016). Foreign transfers are even more endemic among Russians: oligarchs hold about as much wealth outside the country as the rest of the population does within it (Novokmet et al. 2017: 18, 26). If a duplex structure of inequality drives demand for investor citizenship, it is not clear that these programs alone significantly exacerbate it within countries of origin; enough is done without them (cf. Shachar 2017: 804).

At stake is what money can buy. An analogous case can be seen in the competition for globally mobile talent, whether scientific, artistic, entrepreneurial, or athletic (see Shachar 2006, 2011). Richer countries establish special provisions to lure the best and brightest to their territory, offering a package with which poorer countries cannot contend. But selection is not only positive; it is also negative. These more prosperous or more peaceful places also screen out the less desirable, who would enter if they could but are held at bay in offshore detention, third-country waiting zones, or at airport gates because they cannot get a visa to enter. As the authoritarian turn in Turkey deepens, two neighbors in Istanbul may hope to gain citizenship in Portugal. But it is the one who can prove Sephardic Jewish ancestry who can readily acquire a Portuguese passport, without even living in their adopted country. Hierarchies of worth channel mobility and membership through naturalization, not just in cases of citizenship by investment. If much of the discourse on citizenship in the Western world celebrates its promise of equality, access remains fundamentally unequal. The porosity of borders varies based on the value ascribed to different human beings—whether labor migrants, refugees, those reuniting with family, or investors. This serves as an opportunity to reinscribe social boundaries, which can leave the less "worthy" waiting on the doorstep or push the talented or the wealthy to the head of the line, securing them benefits beyond those available to their less fortunate compatriots.

There are also great inequalities in the package of benefits that citizenship secures, something that the residents of economically challenged microstates know very well. Locals on the island of Saint Kitts, home to the oldest CBI program, may be critical of how the scheme is managed, but few seem ready to denounce the concept of investment citizenship itself.[12] Many will condemn how the program is run and question the use or whereabouts of funds. Those with strong party alignments will celebrate how the present government is handling it in comparison to the unscrupulous previous government—or vice versa. But common across these positions is the baseline sentiment that the island needs the money and few other options are available. As a DJ at a local Afro-nationalist radio station put it succinctly:

Personally, I don't have a problem with citizenship by investment because it provides a much needed economic boost. After colonialism, we just had sugar and a bit of early tourism, but that was fragile. [Citizenship by investment] offsets the financial burdens and challenges that we have.

The independence gained by small islands has come with financial struggles. Those that retain colonial connections as dependencies have better access to transfer payments from the metropole than their neighbors, a key line of support if an island is resource-poor and heavily reliant on imports (see Baldacchino 2010).[13] Under such circumstances, it is of little surprise that shortly after the country's independence the cabinet ministers of Saint Kitts established a committee to look into non-traditional sources of funding for the country. From this point of view, the key concern is not pocketing a profit by selling citizenship, but securing much-needed revenue for the country, even if of a meager trickle-down sort. These complexities need to be kept in mind when assessing the inequalities that structure CBI programs.

Capital, as is often observed, is far more mobile than people. But here we see a twist: individuals attached to capital can ride it to new destinations. Citizenship by investment provides an option for the wealthy to sidestep the borders that incubate much wealth accumulation and the exacerbation of class boundaries once they become inconvenient. For the VIP class, memberships have their privileges.

Notes

1. The vast literature on second-class citizenship and "illegal" migration excavates the limits of such inclusivity.
2. Asset figures used for calculating HNWIs and UHNWIs typically under report wealth by excluding primary residences and collectables such as art. They also do not report wealth held offshore. According to one estimate, already a decade old, HNWIs held around $12 trillion in tax havens (Palan et al. 2010: 5). More recent analyses report that as much as 10 percent of global GDP is held offshore (Alstadsaeter et al. 2017).
3. The Credit Suisse report (Shorrock et al. 2016) counts individuals with wealth between $1 million and $50 million as high net worth.
4. Hong Kong issues its own passports, which allow for much greater visa-free travel than those of mainland China. The statistics I quote provide only the general contours of a more complex configuration. Most quantitative studies of the wealthy do not make clear how the nationality of their respondents is assessed, nor do they take into account multiple nationalities or residences.
5. Of course, there are limits to these figures. Visa-free access to the United States is, for many, far more desirable than visa-free access to Uruguay, while a wealthy Kazakh businessperson may be satisfied with the regional visa-free access her passport grants. In addition, the rights that visa-free access brings can vary greatly. The Quality of Nationalities Index takes a basket of such factors into account. Generally, countries outside the West do not rank as highly as those within it.

6. See https://data.worldbank.org/indicator/SP.DYN.LE00.FE.IN?locations= BI-FI and https://data.worldbank.org/indicator/NY.ADJ.NNTY.PC.CD?locations=BI-FI (accessed August 15, 2019).
7. The study, however, lumps together respondents from highly developed and less developed countries. My ongoing research suggests that wealthy individuals from mid- to less-developed countries who participate in citizenship by investment and residence by investment programs are motivated by security concerns, educational advantages, business opportunities, and lifestyle options.
8. Indeed, government figures can be difficult to access given the potential controversies surrounding the programs.
9. The size of the phenomenon depends also on program caps and the availability of alternatives. Demand for second passports in Latin America, for example, has been muted due to easy access to Spanish or Italian citizenship through ancestry routes for a whiter wealthy class. Investor citizenship is also a phenomenon of the nouveaux riches. Often families with inherited wealth have already worked out options to secure citizenship for their descendants in the North Atlantic. Giving birth in the US is a common solution, while others within the former British Empire have made use of easy travel to London to secure the same.
10. Harpaz (2015: 2097) also finds that people in highly developed nations eligible for ancestry routes respond mainly to changes in the difficulty of acquiring them—whether on the side of the sending or receiving state. In contrast, those in less developed countries are more responsive to changes in the benefits gained from a second passport. In the West, long-distance naturalizers adopt a "specific-sentimental" approach, while those outside it take a "general-instrumental" strategy.
11. Investment residence visas differ from citizenship by investment in that a substantial period as a resident or permanent resident is required before the person can naturalize as a citizen. See Surak (2016) for a full discussion.
12. I made two fieldwork trips to Saint Kitts in 2016 and 2018 and spoke to over twenty locals, beyond those involved directly in the citizenship by investment program, about their opinions of the program. They included workers in small shops, cab drivers, people selling home-bottled juice on the street, and museum employees, among others. Most I met in the capital, Basseterre, but because the island is compact—it takes an hour to circumnavigate Saint Kitts by car—many people who work in Basseterre live elsewhere. Though the sample is small, it was striking that only one person came out strongly against the sale of citizenship in itself.
13. Indeed, the island of Anguilla, once on track to become a part of an independent Saint Kitts, seceded to remain a British Overseas Territory.

References

Alstadsaeter, Annette, Niels Johannesen, and Gabriel Zucman. 2017. "Tax Evasion and Inequality." National Bureau of Economic Research Working Paper 23805.

Available at: https://gabriel-zucman.eu/files/AJZ2017.pdf (accessed July 23, 2019).

Anderson, Bridget, Nandita Sharma, and Cynthia Wright. 2009. "Editorial: Why No Borders?" *Refuge: Canada's Journal on Refugees* 26(2): 5–18.

Appiah, Kwame Anthony. 1998. "Citizenship in Theory and Practice: A Response to Charles Kesler." In Noah M.J. Pickus (ed.), *Immigration and Citizenship in the Twenty-First Century*, 41–49. Lanham, MD: Rowman and Littlefield.

Baldacchino, Godfrey. 2010. *Island Enclaves: Offshoring Strategies, Creative Governance, and Subnational Island Jurisdictions*. Montreal: McGill-Queens University Press.

Balta, Evren, and Özlem Altan-Olcay. 2016. "Strategic Citizens of America: Transnational Inequalities and Transformation of Citizenship." *Ethnic and Racial Studies* 39(6): 939–57.

Barclays. 2014. "The Rise of the Global Citizen?" *Barclays Wealth Insights* 18.

Capgemini. 2016. "Capgemini World Wealth Report 2016." Available at: https://worldwealthreport.com/resources/world-wealth-report-2016/ (accessed July 23, 2019).

Cook-Martín, David. 2013. *The Scramble for Citizens: Dual Nationality and State Competition for Immigrants*. Stanford: Stanford University Press.

Dronkers, Jaap, and Maarten Peter Vink. 2012. "Explaining Access to Citizenship in Europe: How Citizenship Policies Affect Naturalization Rates." *European Union Politics* 13(3): 390–412.

Freund, Caroline. 2016. *Rich People, Poor Countries: The Rise of Emerging-Market Tycoons and Their Mega Firms*. Washington, DC: Peterson Institute for International Economics.

Goodman, David (ed). 2008. *The New Rich in China: Future Rulers, Present Lives*. London: Routledge.

Harpaz, Yossi. 2015. "Ancestry into Opportunity: How Global Inequality Drives Demand for Long-Distance European Union Citizenship." *Journal of Ethnic and Migration Studies* 41(13): 2081–104.

Jasso, G., and M.R. Rosenzweig. 1986. "What's in a Name? Country-of-Origin Influences on the Earnings of Immigrants in the United States." *Research in Human Capital and Development* 4: 75–106.

Joppke, Christian. 2010. "The Inevitable Lightening of Citizenship." *European Journal of Sociology* 51(1): 9–32.

Korzeniewicz, Roberto Patricio, and Timothy Patrick Moran. 2009. *Unveiling Inequality: A World-Historical Perspective*. New York: Russell Sage Foundation.

Ley, David. 2010. *Millionaire Migrants: Trans-Pacific Life Lines*. Chichester: Wiley-Blackwell.

Marshall, T.H. 1950. "Citizenship and Social Class." In *Citizenship and Social Class and Other Essays*, 1–85. Cambridge: University of Cambridge Press.

Milanovic, Branko. 2016. *Global Inequality: A New Approach for the Age of Globalization*. Cambridge, MA: Belknap Press.

Novokmet, Filip, Thomas Piketty, and Gabriel Zucman. 2017. "From Soviets to Oligarchs: Inequality and Property in Russia, 1905–2016." Wealth and Income Database Working Paper No. 2017/09. Available at: http://piketty.pse.ens.fr/files/NPZ2017WIDworld.pdf (accessed July 23, 2019).

Ong, Aiwah. 1999. *Flexible Citizenship*. Durham, NC: Duke University Press.
Osburg, John. 2013. *Anxious Wealth: Money and Morality among China's New Rich*. Stanford: Stanford University Press.
Palan, Ronen, Richard Murphy, and Christian Chavagneux. 2010. *Tax Havens: How Globalization Really Works*. Ithaca, NY: Cornell University Press.
Piketty, Thomas, Li Yang, and Gabriel Zucman. 2017. "Capital Accumulation, Private Property, and Rising Inequality in China, 1978–2015." Wealth and Income Database Working Paper No. 2017/6. Available at: https://wid.world/document/t-piketty-l-yang-and-g-zucman-capital-accumulation-private-property-and-inequality-in-china-1978-2015-2016/ (accessed July 23, 2019).
Pritchett, Lant. 2006. *Let Their People Come: Breaking the Gridlock on International Labor Mobility*. Washington, DC: Center for Global Development.
Reuters. 2016. "China's Outward Investment Tops $161 Billion in 2016: Minister." *Reuters*, December 26. Available at: https://www.reuters.com/article/us-china-economy-investment/chinas-outward-investment-tops-161-billion-in-2016-minister-idUSKBN14F07R (accessed July 23, 2019).
Sahlins, Peter. 1988. "The Nation in the Village: State-Building and Communal Struggles in the Catalan Borderland during the Eighteenth and Nineteenth Centuries." *Journal of Modern History* 60(2): 234–63.
Shachar, Ayelet. 2006. "The Race for Talent: Highly Skilled Migrants and Competitive Immigration Regimes." *New York University Law Review* 81: 148–206.
—— 2009. *The Birthright Lottery*. Cambridge, MA: Harvard University Press.
—— 2011. "Picking Winners: Olympic Citizenship and the Global Race for Talent." *Yale Law Journal* 120(8): 2088–139.
—— 2017. "Citizenship for Sale?" In Ayalet Shachar, Rainer Baubock, Irene Bloemraad, and Maarten Vink (eds), *Oxford Handbook of Citizenship*, pp. 789–816. Oxford: Oxford University Press.
Shorrock, Anthony, Jim Davies, Rodrigo Lluberas, and Antonios Koutsoukis. 2016. "Global Wealth Report 2016." Credit Suisse Research Institute report. Available at: http://www.db.zs-intern.de/uploads/1479892972-GlobalWealthReport2016.pdf (accessed July 23, 2019).
Spiro, Peter J. 2008. *Beyond Citizenship: American Identity after Globalization*. Oxford: Oxford University Press.
Surak, Kristin. 2016. "Global Citizenship 2.0: The Growth of Citizenship by Investment Programs." Investment Migration Council Working Papers No. 2016/3. Available at: https://investmentmigration.org/download/global-citizenship-2-0-growth-citizenship-investment-programs/ (accessed July 23, 2019).
—— n.d. "Commodifying Sovereign Prerogatives: How to Sell Citizenship." Unpublished manuscript.
Tintori, Guido. 2012. "More than One Million Individuals Got Italian Citizenship Abroad in Twelve Years (1998–2010)." *RSCAS Citizenship News* (blog), 2012. Available at: http://eudo-citizenship.eu/news/citizenship-news/748-more-than-one-million-individuals-got-italian-citizenship-abroad-in-the-twelve-years-1998-2010 percent3E.
Vella, Matthew. 2016. "'Citizenship Is Inherently Unjust' Says Passport King Christian Kalin". *Malta Today*, May 1. Available at: https://www.maltatoday.com.

mt/news/interview/64647/watch__citizenship_is_inherently_unjust_says_passport_king_christian_kalin#.WyUdcy2ZNTY (accessed July 23, 2019).

Vink, Maarten Peter, Tijana Prokic-Breuer, and Jaap Dronkers. 2013. "Immigrant Naturalization in the Context of Institutional Diversity: Policy Matters, but to Whom?" *International Migration* 51(5): 1–20.

Wealth-X and Arton Capital. 2014 "A Shrinking World: Global Citizenship for UNHW Individuals." Available at: https://www.artoncapital.com/documents/publications/Arton-Capital-Wealth-X-Report-web.pdf (accessed July 23, 2019).

3
Monitoring International Labor Precarity
The State Management of Migrant Domestic Workers

Rhacel Parreñas

An estimated 10.2 million Filipinos reside overseas, comprising an estimated 5 million expatriates, slightly over 4 million temporary migrant workers, and slightly over 1 million undocumented workers (CFO 2013). As expatriate Filipinos include the second-generation children of immigrants in countries such as Australia, Canada, and the United States, one can argue that temporary migrant workers constitute the majority of those departing the country. Everyday more than 6,000 migrant workers depart the Philippines. While they work in more than 160 countries, the vast majority—more than two-thirds—are employed in the Middle East. They include an almost equal number of men and women, with the latter concentrated in domestic work. Not unlike other high-sending countries, the Philippines carefully manages and monitors the outmigration of workers. With migrant employment deeply entrenched in the country's development strategy, predeparture orientation programs have become a central tool used by the Philippines and other traditional sending countries such as Indonesia, Nepal, and Sri Lanka to protect migrant workers. These programs provide migrant workers with information intended to ease their incorporation into destination countries and empower them to maximize their labor opportunities.

While the Philippines requires all migrant workers to participate in a Pre-Departure Orientation Seminar, those considered "vulnerable populations" must additionally complete the Comprehensive Pre-Departure Education Program, with domestic workers being the only group labeled as such. Consequently, domestic workers must complete one to five days of predeparture orientation seminars in contrast to the two hours required of all other migrant workers. Although they come from rural areas from the most northern to the most southern tip of the Philippines, all predeparture orientation seminars for domestic workers are held in the three office buildings of the Overseas Workers' Welfare Administration (OWWA) in Metro Manila. None offers an easy commute as they are far from metro stations and only accessible by public bus or "jeepney" for prospective migrant domestic workers, none of whom are likely to have access to their own private transportation. Approximately 3,000 prospective migrant domestic workers participate in these seminars daily; most stay in facilities provided by recruitment agencies and travel through the heavy traffic of Manila for at least three hours to get to and from the seminar.

Every weekday morning one can catch a glimpse of hundreds of them lingering outside of OWWA buildings, patiently waiting for the facilities to open so they can clear the security required of them to enter the government facility. The buildings where these seminars are held are not the most modern of structures but instead are old, dark, and damp. One visibly sees the lack of government resources in the absence of lights in some of the hallways, the elevators that prospective migrants are barred from using (even if they happen to be working), the need for toilet paper in the rest rooms, and the lack of central air-conditioning. Safety does not seem to be a concern; white plastic chairs fill almost every inch of classrooms, preventing doors from fully opening and not giving participants—almost all of whom are women—much room to move. A room with a maximum capacity of 60 would usually have 100 attendees in it. I sat through 100 hours of these seminars intended for domestic workers bound for the Middle East.

The organizers do not paint a rosy picture but instead present a bleak outlook of a life defined by overwork, isolation, and physical violence. For instance, the risk of rape is one frequently acknowledged, with descriptions of various scenarios of sexual harassment and assault. Near the end of one seminar, the teacher began to describe to the 80 or so female participants in the room an actual incident of rape experienced by a former domestic worker. He then proceeded to ask the class what they would do if they found themselves in the same situation. It was then that a woman seated next to me raised her hand and began to share with the class a detailed description of her rape by an air-con repair man while she worked in Lebanon. The rape had occurred two weeks before her scheduled return to the Philippines.

Though most migrant domestic workers venture outside the Philippines repeatedly and serially to various destination countries, I was surprised to learn that the traumatic experience of rape did not dissuade the woman next to me from returning to the Middle East. I learned that the woman actually chose not to tell her employers of the incident because it would have foreseeably delayed her return to the Philippines and forced her to wrangle with a "he said, she said" battle in a court in Beirut. As soon as she arrived in Manila, she chose not to return home immediately but instead went straight to a recruitment agency, where she reapplied for a job as a domestic worker in another country. This time she was bound for Saudi Arabia.

A question that I have pondered is: how could this woman repress the trauma of rape and want to place herself in yet another highly vulnerable situation once again? What also left me astounded was the reaction of other participants, none of whom seemed to be dissuaded by her disturbing story. As if he had been reading my mind, the instructor then asked if anyone in the room was having second thoughts about venturing to the Middle East. No one initially responded. Then, seemingly in unison, everyone in the room suddenly screamed, "No!" One student then explained: "We know that not all of us will have that experience. Each one of us has a destiny and that is not all of our destinies." Closing the discussion, another student then chimed in: "That is why it is important we all pray we have a good destiny."

The advice shared by this last student sounded eerily familiar, as it is actually a message repeatedly promoted by the Philippine government in these seminars. When addressing the challenges of migrant domestic labor, instructors in predeparture orientation seminars usually tell students to cross their fingers, think positive thoughts, or pray. As another instructor advised his class on how to cope with the challenges of domestic work in the Middle East:

Class, number one: pray for your employer. Your employer is the key to your success. So pray for your employer. People ask if employers are rapists. Too negative. Positive thoughts. Pray you have a nice employer. OK with work and OK with food. Number two: pray that your employer is wealthy because they can afford [the minimum monthly wage of] $400. Number three: pray your employer is religious. More likely they are good. If your employer is not good, you better study the house and escape routes. [Loud laughter.] Number one: prayer, prayer for employer.

The Philippines seems to be facing the conundrum of deploying a significant number of their citizens in the occupation of domestic work while knowing that this makes them highly vulnerable. A source of this vulnerability is the challenge of regulating the occupation, one acknowledged by the Philippine state when it instructs prospective migrants to "pray" for a good employer. In the predeparture seminars, teachers do not attempt to empower domestic workers by advising them on how to control their labor or embrace their expertise as household workers and accordingly determine how they should do their work, manage the pace of their labor, and set the hours of their work. Instead, the government merely warns domestic workers of the vulnerabilities they face, thereby identifying domestic work as a "vulnerable occupation."

One can say that the Philippine state has also done little to regularize domestic work. This is despite its efforts to raise standards of employment, which the country did when it raised the minimum wage for all overseas migrant domestic workers from $200 to $400 in 2006. Yet, reflecting the low value given to this work, the Philippine state has not revisited this wage rate for more than a decade. Moreover, due to the limited regulation of the occupation, the enforcement of this wage rate remains a challenge. As acknowledged by the Philippine state, the challenge of enforcement has indeed resulted in the absence of labor standards. When the state advises prospective migrants to "pray" for a "good employer," the state reminds them that domestic work is an informal occupation and labor standards and conditions accordingly vary across households.

In this chapter, I call attention to the precarity of migrant domestic work, explaining how state policies at both ends of the migration spectrum limit the control of domestic workers over their labor and migration and, as acknowledged by the Philippine state, leave them vulnerable to physical abuse, including rape. The precarity of migrant domestic workers results from state policies that restrict their rights and protections. In the Middle East, migrant domestic workers are excluded from labor protection as they are barred from full participation in the labor market. Their residency is contingent on their live-in employment with their employer-sponsor, whose permission they must then secure in order to transfer or quit their jobs. Their employer, for instance, must approve their departure from the country. The precarity of belonging for migrant domestic workers emerges from the border politics of receiving states that constrain the incorporation of migrant domestic workers, as well as the complicity of sending states in the exclusionary terms of governance confronting domestic workers. Receiving states may authorize the labor migration of domestic workers and accordingly grant legal residency to them, but they fail to fully recognize their labor. Instead, they restrict the rights and protection of domestic workers and subject them to a relationship of unequal dependency with employers. Across the globe, the legal residency of migrant domestic workers is contingent on their live-in, continuous employment with a sole employer, their inability to freely change employers, and the restriction of their employment to domestic work. Aggravating the precarity wrought by these conditions is domestic workers' ineligibility for permanent residency and their exemption from labor protection in the vast majority of receiving states.

My purpose here is to describe and analyze the precarity of domestic workers, and establish how this precarity emerges from the restrictive conditions of membership, that is from the borders imposed, by receiving states, and the complicity of sending states to their citizenry's exclusion. It provides a multi-scalar discussion of the regulation of domestic work, beginning with the recent efforts of the International Labour Organization to formalize the occupation, followed by the state via an overview of the legal status of migrant domestic workers in key destination countries across the globe, as well as a close examination of the policies that control the outmigration of domestic workers in the high-sending state of the Philippines. The chapter also looks at inconsistencies in rules governing the labor of domestic workers across households, focusing on the case of the United Arab Emirates (UAE), which is a key destination of migrant domestic workers from not only the Philippines but also Indonesia, Ethiopia, India, and Sri Lanka.

The Global Regulation of Domestic Work

Domestic work, according to the International Labour Organization (ILO), refers to "work performed in or for a household or households." Domestic workers include housecleaners, elderly caregivers, and nannies. In its efforts to establish formal recognition and a standard of employment for domestic work, in 2011 the ILO successfully passed the Domestic Workers Convention, otherwise known as Convention 189.[1] Convention 189 had positive effects, leading to the enactment of legal reforms for the greater protection of domestic workers in many countries including, for instance, Singapore which has since instituted a mandatory weekly day off (HRW 2013).

Convention 189 calls for universal standards of employment, which include the implementation of a minimum age of employment, the enactment of state provisions for the protection of domestic workers against abuse, the state recognition of the right of domestic workers to privacy, the use of a written contract in domestic work, the implementation of fair labor conditions including a 24-hour rest day per week for domestic workers, fair wages, guaranteed proper and regular remuneration, a safe working environment, social security protection, and among others the right to legal protection and mediation. Recognizing the dependence of member states on migrant laborers, Convention 189 also calls for the entitlement of migrant domestic workers to a valid work contract and repatriation as well as freedom of movement in the form of residential flexibility and access to their travel and identity documents.

The approval and subsequent ratification of Convention 189 signals a significant advancement in the recognition of domestic work. However, it only provides opaque guidelines for the ILO's member states. By only providing abstract recommendations, it subsequently falls short in enforcing the formal recognition of domestic work. For example, it fails to mandate a minimum wage for domestic workers. The convention declares "each Member shall take measures to ensure that domestic workers enjoy minimum wage coverage, *where such coverage exists*, and that remuneration is established without discrimination based on sex."[2] Minimizing its intervention in national policies, the convention only mandates the enforcement of a minimum wage "where such coverage exists" and notably does not oblige states to provide such coverage. Considering that domestic work falls outside labor law protections in numerous countries, the terms of the convention fail to enforce the recognition of domestic work by member states. Take for instance the case of Singapore, where domestic workers are not protected by the Employment Act, resulting in their not being entitled to the minimum wage and overtime pay.

Convention 189 also does not offer explicit standards for "fair terms of employment." For example, the convention notes that "each Member shall take measures to ensure that domestic workers, like workers generally, enjoy fair terms of employment as well as decent working conditions and, if they reside in a household, decent living conditions that respect their privacy."[3] But as Article 6 shows, the convention does not explicitly define but instead intentionally keeps the terms of decency abstract, which in turn allows member states to avoid legislation and the enforcement of labor standards. Take for instance the provision of privacy, which member states are required to enforce but without minimal standards, resulting in the possibility of its enforcement via the provision of a closet for domestic workers. This is likely to be the case in Singapore, where domestic workers are usually given what is referred to as a "bomb shelter," best described as a windowless pantry off of the kitchen in most apartments. A pantry one could argue provides sufficient, but not necessarily the most humane, privacy.

Exclusionary State Policies and Domestic Work

ILO Convention 189 provides nation-states with guidelines for the treatment of the estimated 67 million domestic workers around the world (ILO 2013), but its political reach is limited by the autonomy of member states. We see this limit in nation-state policies that promote a labor migration program for domestic workers. Countries may acknowledge the need of their citizenry for paid domestic labor and accordingly grant the allocation of a working visa for such workers, but they still fail to fully recognize these workers as laborers and instead subject them to a relationship of indenture with their employers. Those destinations include but are not limited to Gulf Cooperation Council member states such as Saudi Arabia and the UAE (Sabban 2012); the Scandinavian nations of Denmark and Norway (Stenum 2011); the country of Israel (Liebelt 2011); and various destinations in Asia including Singapore (Paul 2011), Taiwan (Lan 2006, 2007), Malaysia (Chin 1998), and Hong Kong (Constable 2007).

In nearly all countries with an active labor migration program for domestic workers, the legal residency of migrant domestic workers is contingent on the sponsorship of an employer (Parreñas 2015). What this means is that domestic workers can only legally reside and work in the host society if continuously employed by a resident sponsor. In other words, migrant domestic workers are not free workers who can freely participate in the labor market. Instead, they are bound to work only for their sponsor.[4] The bound status of domestic workers puts them in a relationship of unequal dependency with their employer/sponsor, and some would argue that it places them in a position of indenture. This would be true if they are unable to change jobs, which is unfortunately the case in many countries across the globe.

Nation-states often make it very hard for the migrant domestic worker to change jobs. For example, in Singapore, agencies charge domestic workers two months' pay if they change employers; in Singapore, the UAE and most other Middle Eastern countries, domestic workers also cannot change employers without the permission of their employer; in Denmark, *au pairs* can only change employers twice within a two year period; in Israel, they can only change employers three times within a 63 month period, after which they must remain with their current employer in order to avoid deportation; in Taiwan, domestic workers can only change employers if their current employer is no longer fit to employ them, such as if they relocated to another country, died, or declared bankruptcy; in the United States, domestic workers with a nonimmigrant visa (which would include a B1, A3, or G5) are ineligible to change employers; and in Canada, they historically had to work for an employer for two continuous years to qualify for permanent residency and must complete this requirement within a four year period, which then discouraged them from ever changing employers (Pratt 2012). All these examples not only indicate the limited freedom of domestic workers to change employers but also the potential power of employers. Indeed, employers have the power to not only fire but they can also deport domestic workers at will.

Exacerbating the power of employers is the designation of domestic workers as a permanently deportable group of workers. With the exception of those in Canada and Italy, migrant domestic workers are ineligible for permanent residency. This means that their legal residency perpetually ties them to a sponsor who has the power to deport them at will. The absence of labor protection also magnifies the power of employers. In most countries, domestic workers are exempt from standard labor laws, resulting in fairly low standards of employment including the denial of privacy, absence of a minimum wage, and exclusion from overtime pay. These include the top destination countries of the UAE, where domestic worker immigration was handled by the Ministry of the Interior instead of the Ministry of Labor until January 1, 2015; Singapore, where domestic workers now have the right to a weekly day off but remain exempt from the Employment Act; and Taiwan, where domestic workers are not covered by the Labor Standards Law.

Indicative of Convention 189's relative degree of influence, policies in countries across the globe have slowly shifted toward greater recognition of the labor rights of domestic workers, such as mandatory days off in Singapore, and, in the UAE, the shift of responsibility for migrant workers to the Ministry of Labor plus the enactment of a labor law for domestic workers in September 2017. Yet, as Abigail Bakan and Daiva Stasiulis (2005) have observed in Canada, the enforcement of these laws is likely to remain a challenge. Regardless, there also remains a limit to the degree of acceptance of domestic work as real work. While extrinsic conditions of domestic work such as wage rates and workload vary across states, we see a consistency in the refusal of governments to legally incorporate migrant domestic workers as independent workers, instead maintaining their status as bound laborers. Taking the case of the UAE, while the country recently enacted a labor law that raises standards of employment for domestic workers and guarantees them a weekly rest day, privacy, and among others 30 days of vacation per annum, the new law does not question the conditional residency status of domestic workers and maintains their bound relationship to an employer/sponsor.

The Migrant Protection Policies of the Philippines

The absence of labor standards coupled with the minimal protection of domestic workers in most countries of destination raise the question of whether sending countries have taken steps toward instituting protective measures for the welfare of domestic workers. While some scholars have argued that sending states do little to protect migrant workers (Guevarra 2010; Rodriguez 2010), others have acknowledged that high migrant-sending countries including Ethiopia, Indonesia, and the Philippines do not only closely monitor the outmigration of domestic workers but have also implemented robust programs for the purpose of protecting them from potential abuse, albeit with admittedly limited reach (see Fernandez 2013; Lan 2006). Fernandez (2013), for instance, describes how protective programs in Ethiopia reduce the capabilities of prospective migrants by forcing their dependence on recruitment agencies, a problem that likewise plagues migrants departing the Philippines.

Illustrating Philippine state efforts to "protect" migrant domestic workers, prospective Filipino migrants must navigate and clear premigration requirements at three government offices, including the Philippine Overseas Employment Administration (POEA), which registers the outmigration of a worker; the Technical Education and Skills Department Authority (TESDA) which ensures the migrant worker meets the basic skill level of their designated job; and finally the Overseas Workers Welfare Administration (OWWA), which oversees the cultural sensitivity and language training of migrant workers. Notably, all prospective migrants from the Philippines must go through each of these three government agencies. However, their experiences are not uniform. Domestic workers, as the only group identified by the state as a "vulnerable migrant population," undergo greater scrutiny. The labeling of migrant domestic workers as a "vulnerable group" points to government awareness of the high risks involved in their migration, raising the question of what, according to the government, these risks are, and what advice it extends to migrant domestic workers to address these risks.

The different treatment of domestic workers and other prospective migrant workers, purportedly for their protection as a vulnerable group, emerges in the requirements set forth by each of the three government agencies that must clear their migration. To protect domestic workers from unscrupulous employers, the POEA requires them to use government-certified recruitment agencies, who are meant to vet employers. Yet doing so increases their reliance on the market in their selection of an employer and consequently weakens their social networks, which sociologist Pierrette Hondagneu-Sotelo (2001) has identified as the primary resource used by domestic workers to create and raise standards of employment in their otherwise isolated and unregulated occupation. While other migrant workers are also made to use recruitment agencies, they do so not at the expense of their networks (Kathiravelu 2016).

The requirements set forth by the second government office that oversees the migration of domestic workers, TESDA, likewise illustrates the greater scrutiny domestic workers undergo. Unlike other prospective labor migrants, they must complete skills training for a minimum of 216 hours with TESDA in order to qualify for migration. They must specifically acquire training in four core skill sets, namely housecleaning, laundry and ironing, preparing hot and cold meals, and serving food and beverages. While this requirement potentially suggests the recognition of domestic work as real work, the inconsistency in training suggests otherwise. TESDA usually outsources this training, resulting in inconsistent standards across training centers. In one of three training centers I visited, domestic workers had to carry buckets of water up and down three flights of stairs as part of their endurance training. None of the other schools required this of prospective migrants. This inconsistency in standards of training should not come as a surprise as it merely reflects the absence of standards in the occupation.

The Philippine government's general attitude toward domestic work and overall perception of the risks confronting migrant domestic workers become particularly apparent in the orientation required of them, which is the final hurdle that domestic workers must complete in order to secure their departure from the Philippines. Facilitated by the OWWA, the Pre-Departure Orientation Seminar (PDOS) is an occupation- as well as country- or region-specific seminar that gives migrants an overview of cultural awareness, employment rights, financial planning, and travel logistics. Sitting through 100 hours of these seminars for domestic workers bound for the Middle East provided me with insights into the particular demographic of this group of workers. As many have never flown on a plane, the PDOS devotes at least an hour to travel logistics, informing prospective migrants on what they should do upon arrival at an airport, telling them how to identify the appropriate counter where they can check in for their flight, explaining to them why they should not worry when their bags are taken from them to be placed in the cargo hold, illustrating to them what a boarding pass is, and warning them to not take the blanket provided by the airline with them when they get off the plane. Indeed, migrant domestic workers bound for the Middle East represent the poorest of the poor of the Philippines. The majority have not completed high school, reside in a hut with a thatched roof in a remote rural area, and have worked as street peddlers, domestic workers, or contingent factory workers prior to migration.

Instituted in 1982, coincidentally as the country saw an increase in the migration of domestic workers, the PDOS does not only give us a glimpse of the demographic of migrant domestic workers but also reveals in a multitude of ways how the state perceives domestic work. Attending a PDOS is required not only of domestic workers but all migrant workers departing the Philippines. For occupations other than domestic work, the PDOS extends to no more than two hours, but for domestic workers it extends to a minimum of one to five days, depending on the country of destination, with domestic workers bound for the Middle East needing to complete at least three days of the seminar.

During the PDOS, which for domestic workers includes the Comprehensive Pre-Departure Education Program for Household Service Workers, domestic workers first learn of the absence of labor protection in the country of destination. This point is clearly delivered in the enumeration of the vulnerabilities they are likely to face upon migration. The vulnerabilities they are told that they will likely experience include the loneliness wrought by the isolation of domestic employment, the likelihood of an absence of freedom, and the risk of physical abuse including rape. When addressing these vulnerabilities, domestic workers are usually told to toughen up. For instance, warned about the loneliness they might feel if denied a day off, domestic workers are advised to not jump out of a window but instead to think of their children back in the Philippines and their children's need of them to stay alive as they rely on the remittances they send back to them for their survival. To empower them against these challenges, domestic workers are advised instead to carry a printed photograph of their children. To underscore the significance of doing so, PDOS participants are often chastised for not having an actual photographic print of their children in hand when asked by the teacher to share one with the class. They are told that an image on a cell phone is not sufficient—though they are not told that this is because their employer will likely confiscate their phone upon their arrival in their country of destination.

As part of the PDOS, domestics are also given time to reflect on the reasons that have led them to going abroad. They are allotted a few minutes to write down their goals for migration. Then, they are told to fold that piece of paper, keep it in a safe place, and then take it abroad with them. The teacher then explains that there will be a moment when they are abroad, when they are feeling overworked, battered, isolated, and homesick, and they will feel like giving up, even contemplating suicide. They are advised that it is during that moment that they must take out that piece of paper and read it out loud to themselves, because doing so will remind them of their reasons for migration and will "give them the strength to not give up." As described earlier, rape is another topic that all the seminars I attended addressed. Teachers usually address the topic of rape with real-life examples, ones that distressed returnees from the Middle East had actually experienced. They would then follow with an open discussion on what participants should do to minimize the risk of rape, thwart an attacker, and, if abused, flee a household.

While the state acknowledges the vulnerabilities of migrant domestic workers, it does not offer any preventive measures against their potential abuse, and as we can see with the case of Joanna Demafelis—whose corpse was discovered in late 2017 after it had been abandoned in a freezer in Kuwait for more than a year—even the possibility of their murder.[5] Instead, the state remains complicit in accepting the lack of standards and the absence of regulation of domestic work, merely warning prospective migrants that this is the case. Seminar attendees were frequently asked

"Can you take it?" (*Kaya mo ba?*). This raises the question of what labor conditions domestic workers should expect upon migration. In a variety of ways, the abuse of domestic workers is normalized during their PDOS training. Not to be granted a day off or prevented from communicating with one's family in the Philippines are just some of the conditions that domestic workers are told they might confront. Days off and communication, they are told, should not be taken as their rights, but instead they should be seen as a privileges that they will earn after gaining the trust of their employer. Though abuse is normalized in the predeparture seminars, it is however also an avenue used by the state to teach prospective migrants of the basic rights that the Philippine government has established for them via bilateral agreements with receiving countries. Domestic workers learn of the monthly minimum wage of $400, their right to privacy, eight hours of rest and three meals per day, and free toiletries and work attire. Yet these rights are not sufficiently underscored but are instead overshadowed by narratives of abuse.

Establishing the state's failure to see domestic work as real work, the predeparture seminars instill the values of deference and servility. Prominent in seminars is the reminder of the unequal power relationship between employers and domestic workers, which is captured in the narrative shared by one teacher:

> If you are a cell phone, you are an open line. Everything depends on your employer—your work, your rest. They are awake at 2 a.m. You can ask for permission to sleep and they will say no. You can't tell your madam, "It is 10 p.m., go to sleep now." [Laughter in the room.] You have no freedom. If you have no day off, you will look out the window and wave at people. Homesickness is often caused by isolation.

Domestic workers can expect not only the denial of a day off, but also a relationship of servility in which employers can control their most minute actions and behavior including when they should be awake and asleep. Cementing the deference and servility expected of them, domestic workers are also told to avoid eye contact with male employers and use "sir" and "ma'am" when referring to employers.

Acknowledging the vulnerabilities confronting migrant domestic workers, sending states such as the Philippines have implemented a robust set of programs intended to deter their placement with an abusive employer, provide them with the adequate skills needed to meet employer expectations, and finally educate them not only of their basic labor rights—even if minimal—but also inform them of the high likelihood of their abuse. These programs are not exclusive to the Philippines but found in other high-sending countries of domestic workers, most notably Indonesia, from which the largest number of domestic workers originate (Xiang & Lindquist 2014). These state programs do little to protect domestic workers from abuse as they acquiesce to the exclusionary conditions of membership that limit labor market flexibility, see the absence of labor standards as par for the course when it comes to domestic work, and lastly promote the subservience of domestic workers.

The Household and the Unregulated Labor of Domestic Work

How is the minimal regulation of domestic work manifest on the ground? I address this question by looking at the case of the United Arab Emirates (UAE). I base my discussion on my interviews with 85 Filipino domestic workers and 35 employers conducted in non-consecutive periods in 2014, 2015, and 2016. Suggesting improvements in the employment conditions of domestic workers, the UAE passed Federal Law No. 10 on September 26, 2017, implementing a mandatory weekly rest day for domestic workers, a guaranteed thirty-day paid vacation per annum, a maximum twelve-hour workday, and the remuneration of wages no later than ten days after the end of the month. These laws address the common problems of overwork and withheld salaries that plague domestic workers. However, these improvements do not completely dislodge the perception of domestic work as a private household responsibility. Employers maintain their despotic power over domestic workers as they remain subject to the *kafala* system that binds their residency to continuous employment by their sponsor, whose permission they still need to secure in order to change employers.

The prevailing view of domestic work as not real work results in the inconsistency of labor standards across households, and work conditions become dependent on the personal whims of employers. Reflecting Cameron Macdonald's (2011) observations of domestic workers in Boston, the labor of domestic workers in the UAE are mere extensions of the work of their female employers in the household. Standards of employment accordingly vary. Schedules differ for instance, with some domestic workers expected to clean only while their employers are asleep, and some requiring domestic workers to clean under their watchful eye. Junna, for example, is required to clean the house between 4 a.m. and 6 a.m. daily, while her counterpart across town Elanie only cleans in the afternoon under the observation of her stay-at-home female employer. How domestic workers are expected to do their job also differs across households. For example, it is not unheard of for some employers to dictate the order in which domestic workers must wash dishes, with some expecting domestic workers to clear plates of food before placing them in the sink and others requiring them to soak plates before washing them with soap. Others have a more hands-off approach and leave domestic workers to do their job as they see fit. These variations in standards indicate that employers ultimately determine job conditions and wield a higher status vis-à-vis domestic workers. As other scholars have noted, the hierarchy between employers and domestic workers usually demarcates an invisible boundary that shapes interactions between them, establishing spatial limits for domestic workers in the household (Ray & Quayum 2009; Rollins 1985), restricting their access to food (Hondagneu-Sotelo 2001), and, as I just described, controlling the minute actions of domestic workers and the temporal distribution of their job performance.

The minimal regulation of domestic work visibly results in a lack of labor standards, as we see in the varying degrees of freedom that employers grant domestic workers. Some employers grant domestic workers a day off and others do not; some allow them to leave the house without a chaperone and some only allow them to leave if accompanied by one. These variations will likely remain even after the passage of new domestic worker labor laws. Taking the case of Singapore, for example, employers still do not grant the mandatory day off for domestic workers that came into force on January 1, 2013. In the UAE, employers can still actually restrict the physical mobility of domestic workers and force them to rest at home during their day off.

We also see variations in the ability of domestic workers to communicate with the outside world. It is not unusual for domestic workers initially to be denied access to a cell phone. Indeed, it is common practice for agencies to confiscate cell phones from domestic workers upon their arrival in the UAE, which they do by inspecting their belongings and surrendering phones to their employer. Unless they manage to smuggle a phone into their employer's household or secretly have a neighbor, or in one case a garbage collector, purchase a phone and SIM card for them, domestic workers have to earn the trust of their employers to gain the ability to communicate with those outside the household, including their own family in the Philippines.[6] Gaining their trust, according to interviewees, is not easy as they recognize that they are technically strangers who have been placed in their employer's home without personal ties. Among interviewees, only a few were given immediate access to a cell phone; others had to creatively convince employers. For instance, one purposefully got lost in a mall, then told her employer she would have been easy to find if she had access to a cell phone. While most employers eventually learn to trust their domestic workers and accordingly grant them freedom of communication, with some even generously purchasing them the latest smart phone every year, many still monitor the communication of their domestic workers with the outside world.

The absence of labor standards and consequent result of varying standards across households results in vastly uneven work responsibilities for domestic workers across households. It is an inconsistency acknowledged by the Philippine state when it advises domestic workers to "pray" for a good employer. Job responsibilities of domestic workers can include mopping floors, dusting furniture, making beds, doing the laundry and ironing, cooking, and caring for children, elderly, or the disabled. While those employed in Emirati households are likely to share the burden with coworkers, the "all-around" work that they do, like their counterparts who work alone, is still likely to extend to more than sixteen hours per day. Overwork plagues most domestic workers. Quitting is notably not a convenient option as domestic workers are still subject to the *kafala* system that requires them to secure the permission of their employer before they can leave their employ, which is a condition that in turn leaves them susceptible to forced labor. The unequal dependency that defines domestic work only reinforces the higher status of employers and magnifies the social boundaries controlling their intimacy.

Conclusion

In this chapter, I have examined how the state management of the migration of domestic workers gives rise to precarious labor conditions. I have established not only the absence of labor standards in the occupation but underscored how state policies subject domestic workers to an unequal relationship of bound servitude with employers who are given the despotic power to fire as well as deport migrant domestic workers at will. This relationship of inequality is exacerbated in nation-states that require domestic workers to secure the permission of their employers to quit their job, which is the case in Singapore and most destinations in the Middle

East, including the UAE. With its focus on the state, this chapter provides a multi-scalar analysis of domestic work, illustrating how state policies enable the abusive conditions frequently associated with domestic work while illustrating the analytic significance of situating our understanding of everyday workplace relationships in the context of the larger structural forces that inform them. It tells us that we cannot view the abuse of employers as isolated incidents that we can attribute to the bad behavior of some individuals. Instead, we need to realize that state policies enable such behavior when they maintain the view of domestic work as a private responsibility, promote the subservient position of the worker vis-à-vis their employer, and legally subject domestic workers to a relationship of indenture with their employers.

My intention is to add to our knowledge of the politics of borders and boundaries in a multitude of ways. By illustrating how states shape conditions of employment for domestic workers, my discussion shows how border politics extend beyond the crossing of borders to reach intimate household spaces. The limited rights of migrant domestic workers undoubtedly enable workplace abuse. This is clearly established in the frequent reporting of their abuse, and even murder, in the media. The exclusionary terms of membership that confront migrant domestic workers are notably not universally imposed against migrants. Receiving states selectively include and exclude migrant workers, enforcing boundaries that distinguish the rights extended to migrant workers. Professional workers, for instance, are extended greater rights, including in the UAE, where they are granted eligibility to petition family members and transfer employment without needing to secure their current employer's permission. In contrast, undocumented workers are criminalized and live with the threat not only of deportation but also incarceration.

My analysis advances our understanding of border politics when it situates the operations of state border control in a "transnational social field" (Basch et al. 1993), concretely linking the policies advanced by both receiving and sending countries of migration. Discussions of migrant exclusion frequently focus solely on the terms of membership extended by receiving countries and do not account for how sending countries are not only complicit but also facilitate the subjugation of their migrant citizenry. As I have described, the Philippines promotes the servitude and servility of domestic workers, culturally agreeing with the border politics employed by receiving countries from Canada to Hong Kong and the UAE. The cultural collusion that we see between sending and receiving states when it comes to domestic work, particularly the shared perception of this labor as not real work, points to how the common devaluation of this labor across nations comes at the cost of the exclusionary terms of membership for migrant domestic workers and ultimately their heightened risk of abuse and exploitation.

Notes

1. Domestic Workers Convention (hereafter Convention 189). Available at: http://www.ilo.org/dyn/normlex/en/f?p=NORMLEXPUB:12100:0::NO::P12100_INSTRUMENT_ID:2551460 (accessed July 22, 2019).
2. Convention 189, art. 11, emphasis added.
3. Convention 189, art. 6.
4. An exception in this regard is Italy.
5. For the Demafelis case, see Wang and Murphy (2018).
6. Most employers give domestic workers permission to speak to their family in the Philippines at least once a month, but some fail to do so.

References

Bakan, Abigail, and Daiva Stasiulis. 2005. *Negotiating Citizenship: Migrant Women in Canada and the Global System*. Toronto: University of Toronto Press.

Basch, Linda, Nina Glick Schiller, and Christina Szanton Blanc. 1993. *Nations Unbound: Transnational Projects, Postcolonial Predicaments, and Deterritorialized Nation-States*. New York: Routledge.

Chin, Christine. 1998. *In Service and Servitude: Foreign Female Domestic Workers and the Malaysian "Modernity" Project*. New York: Columbia University Press.

Constable, Nicole. 2007. *Maid to Order in Hong Kong: Stories of Filipina Workers*, 2nd ed. Ithaca, NY: Cornell University Press.

CFO (Commission on Filipinos Overseas). 2013. "Stock Estimates of Overseas Filipinos as of December 2013." Available at: https://www.cfo.gov.ph/downloads/statistics/stock-estimates.html (accessed May 19, 2018).

Fernandez, Bina. 2013. "Traffickers, Brokers, Employment Agents, and Social Networks: The Regulation of Intermediaries in the Migration of Ethiopian Domestic Workers to the Middle East." *International Migration Review* 47(4): 814–43.

Guevarra, Anna. 2010. *Marketing Dreams, Manufacturing Heroes: The Transnational Labor Brokering of Filipino Workers*. New Brunswick, NJ: Rutgers University Press.

Hondagneu-Sotelo, Pierrette. 2001. *Domestica: Immigrant Workers Cleaning and Caring in the Shadows of Affluence*. Berkeley: University of California Press.

HRW (Human Rights Watch). 2013. "The ILO Domestic Workers Convention: New Standards to Fight Discrimination, Exploitation and Abuse." Available at: https://www.hrw.org/sites/default/files/related_material/2013ilo_dw_convention_brochure.pdf (accessed July 22, 2019).

ILO (International Labour Organization). 2013. "Domestic Workers across the World: Global and Regional Statistics and the Extent of Legal Protection." Available at: https://www.ilo.org/wcmsp5/groups/public/---dgreports/---dcomm/---publ/documents/publication/wcms_173363.pdf (accessed July 22, 2019).

Kathiravelu, Laavanya. 2016. *Migrant Dubai: Low Wage Workers and the Construction of a Global City*. New York: Palgrave Macmillan.

Lan, Pei-Chia. 2006. *Global Cinderellas: Migrant Domestics and Newly Rich Employers in Taiwan*. Durham, NC: Duke University Press.

——— 2007. "Legal Servitude, Free Illegality: Migrant 'Guest' Workers in Taiwan." In Rhacel Parreñas and Lok Siu (eds), *Asian Diasporas: New Formations, New Conceptions*, 253–278. Stanford: Stanford University Press.

Liebelt, Claudia. 2011. *Caring for the "Holy Land": Filipina Domestic Workers in Israel*. Oxford: Berghahn Books.

Macdonald, Cameron. 2010. *Shadow Mothers: Nannies, Au Pairs, and the Micropolitics of Mothering*. Berkeley: University of California Press.

Parreñas, Rhacel Salazar. 2015. *Servants of Globalization: Migration and Domestic Work*, 2nd ed. Stanford: Stanford University Press.

Paul, Anju Mary. 2011. "Stepwise International Migration: A Multistage Migration Pattern for the Aspiring Migrant." *American Journal of Sociology* 116(6): 1842–86.

Pratt, Geraldine. 2012. *Families Apart: Migrant Mothers and the Conflicts of Labor and Love*. Minneapolis: University of Minnesota Press.

Ray, Raka, and Seemin Quayum. 2009. *Cultures of Servitude: Modernity, Domesticity and Class in India*. Stanford: Stanford University Press.

Rodriguez, Robyn. 2010. *Migrants for Export: How the Philippine State Brokers Labor to the World*. Minneapolis: University of Minnesota Press.

Rollins, Judith. 1985. *Between Women: Domestics and Their Employers*. Philadelphia: Temple University Press.

Sabban, Rima. 2012. *Maids Crossing: Domestic Workers in the UAE*. Saarbrücken: LAP Lambert Press.

Stenum, Helle. 2011. "Abused Domestic Workers in Europe: The Case of Au Pairs." Directorate-General for Internal Policies, European Parliament. Available at: https://ec.europa.eu/anti-trafficking/sites/antitrafficking/files/abused_domestic_workers_in_europe_the_case_of_au_pairs_0.pdf (accessed July 22, 2019).

Wang, Amy B., and Brian Murphy. 2018. How a maid found dead in a freezer set off a diplomatic clash between the Philippines and Kuwait. *Washington Post*, April 3. Available at: https://www.washingtonpost.com/news/worldviews/wp/2018/04/03/how-a-maid-found-dead-in-a-freezer-set-off-a-diplomatic-clash-between-the-philippines-and-kuwait/?noredirect=on.%20Verified%20on%20August%2016,%202019 (accessed August 22, 2019).

Xiang, Biao, and Johan Lindquist. 2014. "Migration Infrastructure." *International Migration Review* 48(S1): S122–S148.

4
When Migrants Claim Blood Kinship
Constructing Hierarchies of Human Worth

Ayşe Parla

In the summer of 2016, some citizens of Turkey learned from the news headlines that they had been assigned "race codes"—in Turkish, *soy kodu*—in classified government records. When the Turkish Republic was founded in 1923, these same citizens had already been legally marked as belonging to one of the three officially designated minorities in Turkey: Greek, Armenian, and Jewish. Nearly a century later, members of these legally designated minorities found out that each minority group had also been assigned a distinctive number: the Greeks had been assigned the number 1, the Armenians number 2, and Jews number 3.

This secret "race code," as it was officially referred to, had been buried in the mazes of bureaucracy and carefully guarded by government officials for nearly a century, but it became public knowledge in 2016 through a leak. The vice president at the Istanbul City Council of the Ministry of National Education happened to refer to the race code in an official explanation written in response to the query of a lawyer who was trying to register his client's child in an Armenian minority school.[1] The vice president replied that for the student in question to be able to register at the said school:

> the vital (registry) records of the parents of the said student need to match their secret race code. The race code of our Armenian citizens is number 2. Therefore, it is only if the parents' vital records confirm their secret race code as 2 (which they currently do not), the said-student may register in the aforementioned school.[2]

Garo Paylan, an Armenian MP for the People's Democratic Party, a left-wing, pro-minority opposition party,[3] called upon the minister of internal affairs to give an explanation to the public regrading the official's scandalous reference to the "secret race code." The minister initially tried to dismiss the MP's challenge by stating that the code was implemented not just for Armenians or members of other legally designated minorities. In fact, all citizens in Turkey, the minister proclaimed, were assigned a secret code in government records. In other words, he justified the clandestine practice of marking citizens in terms of a racial category by assuring the public that no untoward exception was being made for minorities.

This declaration was met with further outrage among concerned citizens. Kurdish and Alevi citizens of Turkey—who are not legally categorized as minorities but who have historically been persecuted and who continue to be marginalized, the former for not belonging to the majority (Turkish) ethnicity and the latter for not belonging to the majority (Sunni) sect of Islam—sardonically wondered in public what their own secret race code might be. Eventually, the minister had to revise his initial trivializing declaration: now he promised that the execution of the race code was going to be repealed as far as the record keeping of the Ministry of National Education was concerned. The lawyer who had been instrumental in spilling the century-kept state secret was skeptical. "Because this was semi-official practice," the lawyer cautioned, "the only way to really put an end to the racial code regulation would be through a circular that explicitly prohibits the use of the race code."[4]

It seems unlikely that the Turkish public will know any time soon the full scope of the purposes to which the secret race code was put and to what extent it has been utilized in realms beyond that of the regulation of minority school registration. The public is also unlikely to know for sure whether the race code will continue to have any relevance in the decision-making process of other governmental bodies. The line of inquiry I want to pursue in this essay, although inspired by this awkwardly pernicious story of a governmental practice of stamping the citizenry according to a race code, follows a different path. If the "race code" is the outed secret whose exact function was never quite made clear, this chapter takes to task another, related categorization that has persisted as an open secret for regulating the borders of the Turkish nation-state since its inception. Specifically, I tackle the category of *soydaş*, a term related to the troubling phrase *soy kodu*.

Sometimes translated in migration scholarship on Turkey as "ethnic kin," or as "co-nationals," but more aptly captured as "racial kin" or "consanguines" (Gündoğan forthcoming), *soydaş* is an agglutinated word that is composed of a root, *soy*, and a suffix, *-daş*.[5] The root *soy* covers a range from race, ethnicity, lineage, and blood to family, ancestry, kin, and descent. The suffix *-daş* means having something in common, being a fellow, or sharing the same. But there is an emotional component of belonging inherent to the suffix *-daş* as well, which functions as a crucial landing point for the structures of feeling around this word for speakers of Turkish. The suffix *-daş* covers a range of affiliations from "sharing," as in *kardeş* (sibling), "having in common," as in *dindaş* (of the same religion), "fellowship" as in *yoldaş* (comrade, sharing the same path), and *vatandaş* (citizen, sharing the same homeland). And while it carries a cultural and affective sense of blood kinship, similarity, affinity, national spirit, the term *soydaş* also has legal ramifications: it refers to those migrants who are considered to be "of Turkish origin" and who have historically comprised the only category to qualify as a migrant (*göçmen*) and thus admitted within the borders of the Turkish nation-state. Interrogating this critical term provides a revealing yet hitherto neglected window onto the limits of belonging in contemporary Turkey. By focusing on the border and boundary work that the category *soydaş* accomplishes, we get yet another glimpse into the construction of what Fassin (this volume) calls "hierarchies in the evaluation of the worth of human lives," this time not from the point of view of the most marginalized but from the point of view of those migrants considered to be racial kin of the nation-state.

The Border and Boundary Work of Soydaş

Frustrated with her status as a labor migrant in Turkey without a work permit or citizenship, İsmigül, who had migrated with her family from Bulgaria in 1998 and who identified as ethnically Turkish, would often say in consternation and protest: "We work and we wait. We wait and wait. Still, no citizenship, no work permit. We, too, have Turkish blood in our veins."

During my decade-long fieldwork among ethnically Turkish migrants who have migrated from Bulgaria to Turkey, I have recurrently witnessed this simultaneous emphasis on labor and consanguinity whenever these migrants appeal to officials for legalization. Rather than rely on the act of labor alone in grounding their entitlement—as, for example the *sans papier* movement in France famously did (McNevin 2006)—Turkish migrants from Bulgaria resort to the language of blood-based kinship to ground their entitlement to legalization and to mark their distinction from other undocumented migrants in Turkey who hail from increasingly diverse geographies spanning the Middle East, former Soviet Union, and sub-Saharan Africa. "Once, I confronted them [the officials]," İsmigül said. "'Those from the Philippines are getting work permits now,' I said to the clerk at the Ministry of Foreigner Affairs. 'Why not us? And we are Turks, we are *soydaş*.'" But being *soydaş* is not an unequivocally embraced status, either. "Why do we keep being called *soydaş*?" İsmigül would ask after she acquired the citizenship she coveted and pursued for over a decade: "I just want to be citizen, simple as that."

Following Didier Fassin's distinction between borders as historically and legally determined demarcations that separate people on territorial and political grounds, and boundaries as symbolic, internal differentiations based on ethno-racial, cultural, and class grounds (Fassin 2011; see also Fassin, this volume), this chapter explores how the term *soydaş* embodies the paradoxical interplay between border and boundary. On the one hand, as a cultural category with legal implications, *soydaş* is the designation that enables the cross-border movement of ethnically Turkish migrants living outside of national borders. Whether they migrate primarily for economic motives or to escape political turmoil in their countries of origin, being identified as *soydaş* grants migrants entry into Turkish territory based on a strong notion of national kinship based on blood. On the other hand, the category *soydaş* performs its own acts of exclusion even for those who can claim the identification of consanguinity: once they have crossed the national border, *soydaş* come up against various internal boundaries that constantly remind them that they will always be just slightly different from the norm. In the case of migrants from Bulgaria, they may be held to task for the regionally specific way they speak the Turkish language; their habits of dress, which, especially in more conservative regions of Turkey, are considered to be too "skimpy" (*açık saçık*); their culinary choices, which include pork, a forbidden food according to majority Muslim norms; or because of different gender norms, which often involve women being more outspoken in public and equal participants in the household economy. At the same time that the term *soydaş* refracts "citizen" through the ethno-racial logic of national belonging in Turkey, it also exposes the unspoken limits of putative sameness. Interrogating this critical term thus provides a different vantage point on the limits of belonging in contemporary Turkey through a focus on the inclusive exclusion of even those considered to be racial kin.

Göçmen (Migrant): An Exceptionally Restrictive Definition

It has been now widely documented in the scholarship on nationalism and citizenship that most nation-states have explicit or implicit criteria that favor certain migrants over others, even if the state describes its nationalism in civic rather than ethnic terms, or purports to abide by the principle of *jus solis* (territorial citizenship) rather than *jus sanguinis* (blood-based citizenship). Moreover, even when they are not couched in terms of the more blatant language of blood kinship, discourses around integration often smuggle in assumptions around who is more suited to assimilate into what are upheld as key national values and norms. That these discourses inform migration policy even in those countries considered liberal, progressive, or inclusive has been revealed by critical scholars of migration and citizenship in Europe and the United States. To cite a few examples: women refugees from North Africa and the Middle East have been preferred over men from the same region for better fitting the idea of "pure" victimhood (Ticktin 2011) in France, or as Mayanthi Fernando shows in her contribution to this volume, the sexual and affective intimacies of binational couples become the subject of state interrogation to determine suitability for French citizenship. In the case of the United States, refugees from Cuba who claim that they wish to escape communism have met with greater rates of acceptance compared to those fleeing military state violence in Latin America. Meanwhile, as Mae Ngai and Sherally Munshi show in this volume, the 1882 Chinese Exclusion Act and the Asiatic Barred Zone Act legalized the exclusion of Chinese and Hindus from US territory, which purports to be the quintessential land of the melting pot.

It is not much of a novelty, therefore, to point out that migration policy around the globe utilizes certain criteria of desirability or deservingness, even though those criteria may vary, with gender or political background or religion becoming the basis of welcome or rejection. My contention is that the Turkish case poses its own brand of ethno-racial nationalism within the existing global spectrum of hierachizing migrant desirability: it legally defines the general category of *göçmen* (migrant) in such a limited way that in practice migrant becomes synonymous with *soydaş*, even though the law does not explicitly use the latter term. This legal codification of ethno-racial sentiment, or *de jure* discrimination, is what I argue gives Turkey's migration regime its bitterly distinctive flavor.

Since the founding of the Turkish Republic in 1923 and up until the introduction of the Yabancıları Koruma Kanunu ("Law on the Protection of Foreigners") in 2014, there was no unified legislation to regulating migration into Turkey. Instead, officials drew on the İskan Kanunu ("Settlement Law") of 1934 in ad hoc ways. However, the lack of unified legislation, and the decisive clause defining who is considered a migrant has remained constant: the first version of the Settlement Law as well as its most recent version in 2006 defines *göçmen* as someone "of Turkish race/lineage and who has ties to Turkish culture."[6] All other migrants who arrive in Turkey and do not fulfill this criteria of racial kinship are legally referred to as "foreigners" (*yabancılar*). Furthermore, the Settlement Law stipulates that "those who are not of the Turkish race and do not have ties to Turkish culture, or, those who are of the Turkish race and who have ties to Turkish culture but have been deported, and those who are seen as a national security threat will not be accepted as immigrants."[7]

In a recent and important overview of migration and settlement policies in Turkey's changing political landscape, sociologist and migration scholar Sema Erder (2014) has singled out the Settlement Law as a foundational and under-studied legal text, one that critically indicates the content and scope of citizenship in Turkey. Through meticulous analysis of the range of regulations that fall under its rubric—from the right to use land to the distribution of property—Erder suggests that the Settlement Law reflects a general fear of "the foreigner" in Turkey's political culture and a concomitant instinct to close inward. Indeed, veteran sociologist İsmail Beşikçi, imprisoned for years for his research and writing on Kurds in Turkey, had earlier named the Settlement Law "a racist exile law" (Beşikçi 1977), one that was primarily used to assimilate what was deemed an unruly and threatening Kurdish population.[8] In an important and prescient article on the subject, political scientist and migration scholar Kemal Kirişçi quotes an MP speaking during the parliamentary debates that accompanied the drafting of the Settlement Law in 1926: "Any person who calls himself a Turk in the Turkish Republic, their Turkishness should be clear and transparent to the state. Here, the state does not want to harbor the slightest suspicion of the Turkishness of any Turk" (quoted in Kirişçi 2000: 16). As political scientist Mesut Yeğen (2004) has further elaborated, the Settlement Law stipulated that Kurdish groups deemed troublesome were to be uprooted from the regions they resided in—designated as Zone 3 and as the most dangerous—to areas that were more ethnically "mixed," and thus safer—designated Zone 1—so as to ensure their proper "integration" and acquisition of Turkishness. In Sema Erder's gloss again, the Settlement Law thus marked a new mode of governance: if the pervasive strategy of the Ottoman Empire could be described as "mix in order to govern," the Turkish nation-state seemed to follow a principle of "eliminate in order to govern" (Erder 2014: 88). The Settlement Law was thus intended to regulate borders and boundaries simultaneously: it literally remapped internal boundaries by displacing and resettling populations deemed threatening, and it defined the external border as permeable only for those who were to be brought into the fold of the new nation-state.

Navigating between the Scylla of exceptionalism and the Charybdis of normalization, the peculiarity of Turkey's migration governance may be situated in comparative perspective as follows. It is no novelty of the Turkish context that a particular group of migrants are categorically privileged as *soydaş* and given preferential treatment when crossing national borders and in their access to citizenship. Other well-known examples of such policy preferences for those designated as co-ethnics include, for example, the "repatriate immigration" of Russian Jews to Israel (Remennick 1999); second- or third-generation Japanese émigrés to Brazil who return to Japan (Tsuda 2003); Hungarian labor migrants in Romania to Hungary (Fox 2009); the settlements of Greeks from the former Soviet Union under a special, more favorable regulation that differs from the constitutional regulations that other migrants in Greece are subjected to (Baldwin-Edwards & Kyriakou 2004); the acceptance of those with German ethnicity as citizens in Germany (Münz and Ohlinger 2003);[9] and the migration of "colonists" or *pied noir* back to France, Portugal, and the Netherlands (Smith 2003). Furthermore, there often exists a special terminology to designate the legally privileged status of these migrants in these diverse contexts as well: *Aussiedler* (individuals of German descent) in Germany, and *palinnostoundes* (repatriates) in Greece are two obvious examples (see Voutira 2004).

But in Turkey, in addition to there existing a special, culturally inflected term—*soydaş* (racial kin)—for those deemed to be ethnically and racially closer, the blanket, legal term for "migrant"—*göçmen*—itself is not neutral. That is to say, the law does not even attempt at neutral wording and instead codifies racial affinity in the very definition of migrant. This de jure codification of the privileging of racial kin also results in an interesting reversal: the hierarchy of desirability common to most other migration regimes, where (political) refugees are considered more deserving than (economic) migrants, is, in this instance, flipped.[10] In Turkey, migrants acquire a higher status than refugees precisely because of the already historically particular and favorable connotations of the term *göçmen*.

Is the exceptionally restrictive definition of the term *göçmen* merely a technical glitch, one might wonder? Until 1990, when Turkey was still primarily a country of emigration, the use of the word *göçmen* in public usage was reserved primarily for people associated with Turkishness. In fact, the older generation often utilized the older Arabic word *muhacir*, which is also the term that has historically been used to designate the Muslim Turkish refugees fleeing back to receding Ottoman territory, especially after the Balkan Wars of 1912. While considered an older incarnation of *göçmen*, the term *muhacir* additionally has a more pronounced religious reference to Islam and carries a strong geographic reference to the Balkans as the place of origin. Whether spoken of as *göçmen* or as *muhacir*, the corollary in the public imaginary was someone who was ethnically Turkish, who was Muslim, and who most likely came from the Balkans. However, with increasing transnational flows into Turkey after 1990, first from the former Soviet Union, followed by sub-Saharan Africa, Afghanistan, and most recently Syria, the term *göçmen* is increasingly deployed in news coverage and popular usage in its more familiar sense as anyone who crosses national borders. It is now also almost invariably used with the qualifier *kaçak* (clandestine, illegal). But even as the range of the inclusiveness of the term *göçmen* has expanded in public usage, the laws that regulate migration continue to limit the term to its original restrictive definition, which only includes those of Turkish descent and culture. In the next section, I discuss the wider ramification of such a legally restricted definition in designating who is considered a migrant toward a reconsideration of the terms and limits of belonging in Turkey's citizenship regime.

The Disavowal of Race as a Relevant Category of Belonging

The common wisdom is that race is an irrelevant category in the analysis of politics and social life in Turkey. As the popular argument goes, there has never been a sizeable black population in Turkey to empirically meet the conditions for the emergence of racism. A distinctively Turkish version of the argument of US exceptionalism, this particular rejection of the relevance of race beyond a singular contextual and historical manifestation is an extremely well-rehearsed, tightly sealed conviction in Turkey. Even blatant public incidents of racism directed at the increasing numbers of sub-Saharan African migrants, and now directed at Syrian refugees, have not shaken that conviction. African youths are spat on if they dare take a seat instead of standing up on public buses; seasoned residents gang up on new black residents to evict them from their neighborhood; a police officer who got suspicious of a Nigerian migrant simply for walking on the street at night "accidentally" shot him during interrogation.[11] In her ethnographic research among Ugandan women in Turkey, Emel Coşkun (2018) shares the chilling testimonies of women engaged in informal work in manufacturing and textile production. The foremen would use a Turkish variant of the n-word in conjunction with a sexist swear term so often that the working women got curious about what the phrase meant, assuming it to be common everyday vocabulary. Women from sub-Saharan Africa also are subjected to acts of racism on the street on a daily basis: Ugandan women living in the migrant hubs of Kumkapı and Aksaray complained the most about the harassment they faced by adolescents, Coskun notes; they reported being sworn at and spat upon, and on occasion they faced people who pulled out knives. The rape and murder of two Ugandan women in the past three years, Jesca and Beatrice, both at the hands of acquaintances who were only brought to trial after feminist lawyers stepped in to take over cases that were being covered up, is only one manifestation of the systematic sexual violence to which African migrant women in Turkey are exposed.

But none of those instances of racism, whether one chooses to define racism as discriminatory behavior based on individual/group prejudice or as institutionalized impunity and inequality, seem to crack the collectively upheld myth in Turkey that the problem of racism belongs elsewhere. The comments of a popular host of a top-rated TV show in Turkey, Acun Ilıcalı, recently raised the profile of the race question once more. During a particularly contentious episode of the popular reality show *Survivor*, Pascal Nauma, a well-known African-French retired footballer, accused one of his competitors in the show of having used the "n-word." Nauma, who has lived in Turkey for many years, is famous for his eccentric behavior both on and off the field, and his popularity owes as much to his professional skills as to his public persona; he once declared that not only did he feel that Turkey is his home, but also that he is a Turk. However, Nauma confronted the fact, in front of a public glued to the show, that there are limits to "being a Turk". It turned out that one could not simultaneously claim to be a Turk and to call out racism in Turkey.

In the debate section of the episode where tensions ran high, Pascal Nauma listed his grievances against what he explicitly articulated as the racism of one of his competitors. The competitor, Nauma said, had referred to the color of his blanket with the n-word. The competitor had then casually remarked that Pascal—in reference to whom the competitor again used the n-word—should clean up the mess on the floor. The competitor had then gone on to complain that the workers—here using the n-word again—hired by the host of the show were being overpaid and ripping the host off.

At this point, Acun Ilıcalı, the show's multi-millionaire host, whose close friendship with Pascal Nauma is well known to the show's fan base, felt the need to intervene. "Pascal," he said, addressing him and the millions of devoted watchers. "As you well know, there is no racism in Turkey. So even if a Turk uses the n-word, it only shows that he does not know what the word means." Pascal Nouma was quick to retreat. He accepted Ilıcalı's correction: "Of course, of course, Acun," he said, "In fact during all my years in Turkey, I only met two people who are like that [i.e., racist]." In subsequent press commentary, Ilıcalı felt the need to confirm that the terms of the debate were properly rectified: "Pascal was not accusing his fellow competitor of racism, really," he explained. "Pascal was simply trying to express a point about crudeness and disrespect."

But it is not just the realm of popular and public culture where the vehement denial of the fact that race is a pertinent category in social life is routinely enacted. Similar disavowals also dominate the scholarship on Turkish nationalism and the Turkish state. Such disavowals seem to be performed with greater ferocity precisely at a time when growing numbers of scholars are bringing forth evidence of the racist underpinnings of the founding ideology of the Turkish nation-state, and arguing for the continuing relevance of that republican legacy in contemporary Turkish society and state policy. The pushback against this critical scholarship takes different forms but predominantly converges around strategies of trivializing instances of racist policy and ideology. In his thorough and astute analysis of the defensive strategies deployed by those who defend Turkish republican history and ideology against charges of racism, political scientist Murat Ergin (2008) points out that their strategies of trivializing such charges rely on the contention that any racist state discourse or policy that may have surfaced in the history of Turkey was merely "aberrational." State-funded research of enormous scope in the 1930s, for example, which involved tens of thousands of subjects whose cranial measurements were taken so as to prove the "Europeanness" and whiteness of the Turks (see Maksudyan 2005), gets brushed aside as an anomaly, a perk of Ataturk's adopted daughter whose "anthropological" research was closely supervised and encouraged by the founding father himself. Subsequent instances of institutionalized discrimination—such as the Varlık Vergisi ("capital levy") of 1942 that was imposed on the already drastically reduced number of non-Muslim citizens (Aktar 2006) and the subsequent deportation of those who could not pay up to labor camps in the Southeastern city of Erzurum, where several died or became permanently sick—is also dismissed as an unfortunate but exceptional moment, and one—it is carefully noted—that bore no resemblance to the labor camps in Nazi Germany.[12] Other cases of legalized discrimination—such as the citizenship laws that were implemented during the first two decades of the republic, and which exempted "ethnic Turks" from customs fees and made Turkishness a prerequisite for becoming a government employee, doctor, dentist, or nurse (Çağaptay 2014)—are reduced to transient moments in the history of the republic. The perspective that trivializes the relevance of race as a category of discrimination in state discourse and practice contends that such policies did not endure, despite the absence of Armenians, Greeks, and Jews in the upper ranks of the military and state bureaucracy to this day. In sum, for those who deny the relevance of race as part of the founding ideology and practices of the Turkish state, there is at most an admittance that there have been bouts of excessive nationalism, some official pronouncements of national pride and superiority, or even an occasional "ethnicist" emphasis during the country's founding years. But none of this, the argument goes, is to be conflated with racism, either at the level of group prejudice or of instutionalized structures of inequality.

In her scathing analysis of the "Janus-faced nature" of the Israeli state, anthropologist Nadia Abu El-Haj (2010) argues that it is only by attending to the simultaneously colonial *and* neoliberal nature of the Israeli state that one can capture its distinctively racist manifestations. One could arguably propose that *all* nation-states are Janus-faced in their formal claim to inclusive citizenship whilst also substantively engaging in exclusionary practices. Indeed there exists by now excellent critical literature on the role of race even within nation-states that boast being the bastions of civic citizenship, including Tugba Basaran's critical rethinking of the uneven application of the founding principles of the 1948 Universal Declaration of Human Rights (Basaran, this volume). But the nuance that Abu El-Haj brings to this critical scholarship is to underscore the successful self-fashioning of Zionism as a nationalist, anticolonial movement in search of an independent state. In contradistinction to South Africa, for example, where white rule was justified explicitly in terms of biological-racial difference, Israel's success in denying its racial character lies, according to Abu El-Haj, in being able to "represent itself as but another nation-state in the national order of things, all of which began in violence" (Abu El-Haj 2010: 74).

I see strong parallels between the Israeli and Turkish states in terms of the disavowal of race as a relevant category of state formation. Inspired by Abu El-Haj's analysis of the normalizing move enacted by the Israeli state to justify violence, I want to suggest that the success with which, in turn, the Turkish state continues to elude acknowledgement of its racial underpinnings owes much to its self-fashioning as a state that was founded upon a struggle for independence and one waged against imperial powers at the turn of the twentieth century. This particular self-fashioning goes a long way in erasing or justifying with great success the foundational acts of violence that eliminated the non-Muslim population and reengineered a population that was predicated on Turkishness. Yet the statistics alone give a soberingly straightforward indication of the violence that the remaking of the population during the founding of the Turkish nation-state entailed. At the beginning of World War I, in what was still the Ottoman Empire, the total population of the Ottoman provinces including Anatolia, the Balkans, and Syria was 16 million, of which about 20 percent was non-Muslim. Within the latter group, the great majority were Greeks and Armenians, with some members of other Christian communities as well (Courbage & Fargues 1998). In 1915, the Armenian Genocide decimated the Armenian population. On the heels of this event, in 1923, the Turkish Republic was founded. Then, in 1924, the forced exchange of the Greek population in Turkey with the Muslim population in Thrace virtually eliminated the Greek presence. By 1927, the total population, now reduced to 13 million, was less than 3 percent non-Muslim. That the processes of Muslimization and Turkification continued well after the founding of the republic is reflected by the fact that, by 1950, the percentage of non-Muslims in Turkey had dropped below 1 percent. By 1980, it was 0.2 percent, while today it is estimated to be around 0.01 percent.

The ideal of a homogeneous Sunni and Turkish citizenry was achieved not only through genocide and displacement but also through the active recruitment of migrants who were deemed to be ethnic and religious kin, and therefore desirable. The turn of the twentieth century, in particular the Balkan Wars of 1912/13, were times of mass migration from the Balkans to an Ottoman Empire on the brink of collapse. Muslim populations that had been settled in strategic boundary regions during the expansionist phases of the empire now fled as these previously conquered territories were lost to various emerging nation-states in the Balkans. Laws regarding minorities and their (remaining) property were also meant to enable the transfer of property confiscated from those who were designated as religious minorities to the *muhacir* fleeing the Balkan Wars (Üngör & Polatel 2011). Historian Raymond Kevorkian (2011) similarly argues that parallel processes were at work in the displacement of Armenian deportees and in "making room" for the *muhacir*. While the Muslimization and Turkification of Anatolia involved the settlement of ethnically Turkish migrants from the Middle East as well (Dündar 2001), migrants from the Balkans seem to have been strongly preferred by both the late Ottoman government and the founders of the early Turkish Republic. The preference for *muhacir* from the Balkans has led historian İlhan Tekeli (1990) to describe the migrations at the end of the nineteenth and beginning of the twentieth centuries as migrations of Balkanization.

Records of an investigation by the government into a complaint about the mistreatment of a migrant from Bulgaria by the Yalova municipality in the early twentieth century reveals an officially sanctioned preference for those considered "blood kin." The response to the complaint is worded in the following terms: "While a population increase is being planned for your province with migrants of clean Turkish blood coming from Bulgaria, his excellency would certainly not condone the loss of such Turkish immigrants who are already settled there" (quoted in Çağaptay 2009: 92).

While the scope of the term *göçmen* technically includes all migrants of Turkish origin, the implementation of the rule has its own internal hierarchy: migrants from the Balkans have outperformed other groups identified, such as Iraqi Turkmen and Uighurs, as well as other groups from Afghanistan identified as Turkic. Notwithstanding this internal hierarchy of migrant desirability, figures of those granted citizenship during the foundational years of the republic show that the combination of Sunni Islam and a claim to Turkishness seem to have trumped all as the most secure combination for qualifying for immigrant status.

My historical detour also demonstrates that contemporary appeals to racial kinship utilized by migrants from Bulgaria are not just another instance of the trend identified in the migration literature as the "reethnicization of citizenship" (Joppke 2005) or the intensification, since the nineties, of "transborder membership politics" (Kim 2016). Rather, citizenship in Turkey has always been deeply ethnicized and racialized. If anything, the period since the 1990s has witnessed a countertrend: the *soydaş*, who could rely on not only being granted citizenship but also count on being settled with property, can no longer quite do so. The decline in the privileges that accrue from being designated *soydaş* and what that loss implies for racial citizenship is what I turn to next.

The Waning Privilege of Being Soydaş

Since the 1990s, the state policy of favoritism toward *soydaş* from Bulgaria has been in decline. There are no longer enthusiastic official proclamations welcoming the homecoming of *soydaş*, as was the case most recently with a big exodus from Bulgaria in 1989. I explore elsewhere (Parla 2019) in ethnographic detail the shifting constellation of ethno-national appropriation, political instrumentalization, and labor market exploitation that accounts for the relative decline in the privilege that accrues from being a migrant from Bulgaria. Here, I want simply to underscore the following: there is indeed a shift in state policy that is inclined to keep the *soydaş* as a loyal transnational constituency instead of legalizing them in Turkey. Nonetheless, despite this shift in policy, the legal definition of a migrant as someone with Turkish origins continues to carry the greatest legal purchasing power and is thus the main premise on which migrants from Bulgaria make their demands for legalization. Such demands are often accompanied by performances of over-identification as *soydaş*, as evident in İsmigul's words quoted above. These performances entail constant boundary marking by asserting one's distinction from and deservingness in relation to other undocumented migrants in Turkey. "Naturally the state will prefer us, and not those foreigners from Afghanistan, Africa, Uzbekistan, what not," İsmigül declared on another occasion. My interlocutors would also perform racial kinship to condemn and distance themselves from the Kurdish population in Turkey, whose demands for cultural and political rights they saw as unreasonable and treacherous.

The term *soydaş* enacts internal boundary maintenance as well. One migrant, who had arrived in 1989 and was pursuing a PhD in Istanbul, had gently warned me more than once not to conflate the various migrations of Turks from Bulgaria to Turkey, saying that the 1989 immigrants were distinctive because they were political migrants, thereby implying that they were more deserving of citizenship than post-1990 migrants who came in search of jobs. Another migrant from Starazagora, Bulgaria, who was proud of the general occupational success of the 1989 immigrants in Turkey, expressed concern that the post-1990 immigrants were less educated, had fewer skills, and came to Turkey "only for the money." The latter, he thought, were giving the better-educated, highly skilled 1989 immigrants like him a bad name. Another migrant from the Kırdjali region of Bulgaria who worked as a clerk in Istanbul was perhaps the most unflinchingly harsh in her assessment of the post-1990 migrants: they are *kansız*, she told me, literally "without blood." It is as if those who did not join the 1989 migration wave have lost their entitlement to being blood relatives of the Turkish nation-state.

Finally, the status of *soydaş* itself is twofold. On the one hand, it provides the only leverage by which the *soydaş* from Bulgaria can make legal claims for inclusion and distance themselves from the rest of the undocumented migrants in Turkey, those who are not called migrants in legal terms but designated *yabancılar* (foreigners). On the other hand, my *soydaş* interlocutors viewed themselves as having a second-class status, one with which they voice chronic dissatisfaction. The category *soydaş* creates a peculiar boundary, one that both enables legal privilege and represents a degree of cultural capital, but one that also subtly indicates distance from unmarked belonging. While nowhere as insulting as the racist slurs directed at other, ethnically non-Turkish migrants, or the derogatory labels non-Muslim minoritized citizens are subjected to, the category of *soydaş* still smacks of second-class citizenship regardless of its historical legacy of inclusiveness and a nod to sameness. All delineations of boundaries within groups, even when they seem more favorable, can be morally contaminated in the face of nationalist and economic priorities. Yet, given the lack of alternatives for legalization and for a broader sense of belonging, it is still the best option for those who are trying to legalize their status in their struggle for dignified living and working conditions in Turkey.

It should come as no surprise that within a nationalist cosmology that defines belonging in ethno-racial and religious terms, those who cannot claim unmarked belonging develop strategies to acquiesce to or resist the terms of their belonging. Survivors of the Armenian Genocide are bound to carry on in a post-genocidal geography defined by legalized dispossession on the one hand and institutionalized and normalized denial of genocide on the other (Ekmekcioglu 2016; Suciyan 2015; Üngör & Polatel 2011). Members of the Jewish minority, Turkey's "tolerated minority" (Brink-Danan 2011) who were nonetheless subjected to pogroms in 1934, faced additional taxes levied on minorities, and continue to be targets of sudden outbursts of anti-Semitism, have routinely had to enact what Paul Silverstein (2004) has called "performative citizenship." Similar to Algerians with French citizenship who reside in France, Jews in Turkey who are Turkish citizens often demonstrate in overtly visible ways that their allegiance to the values of the Turkish state is absolute. While being non-Muslim constitutes the most visible marker of otherness, other minorities, even if they are not legally designated as such, have also been the target of state violence. For example, even if they are not categorized as foreign, the Muslim Alevi population in Turkey has been subjected to a strict policy of domestication on account of not being Sunni (Tambar 2016). As for the mostly Sunni Muslim Kurdish population, who have been deemed troublesome but also assimilable, the Turkish state refused until the 1990s to acknowledge them as a separate ethnicity, using the designation "mountain Turks" to identify them and refusing demands for cultural rights such as education in their native language. Only when Kurds are willing to be assimilated into or prioritize Sunni Islam (an option never available to Alevi Kurds) have they been welcomed into the fold of Islamic religiosity and ethnic nationalism. And when they have chosen to pursue the path of struggle instead of assimilation, the Kurds have faced some of the most punitive measures enacted in the name of the Turkish state. It is only within this hierarchy of otherness produced by Turkey's citizenship regime that the significance of the cultural and legal category of *soydaş* can be fully understood and so too the zeal with which those who can claim that category write themselves into the nationalist narrative of belonging.

Conclusion

In December 2008, an unprecedented and controversial petition grabbed public attention in Turkey. Initiated by a group of intellectuals and journalists, the campaign was called "I apologize to my Armenian brothers and sisters," and it called for a public apology for "the Great Catastrophe that the Ottoman Armenians had been subjected to in 1915."[13] As the number of signatures soared and a nationalist backlash intensified, Canan Arıtman, a deputy from the main opposition, the People's Republican Party (which historically represents the mainstream secular, Kemalist state tradition in Turkey) attacked Abdullah Gül, the country's president at the time and a former member of the conservative, Islamist and ruling Justice and Development Party. Arıtman charged President Gül with failing to take proper action against the petition. Aritman also accused the petition's supporters of denigrating national pride by signaling to the international community that Turkey had accepted the allegations of genocide. She went on to suggest that President Gül was rubber-stamping the campaign because of his Armenian origins: "Abdullah Gül should act as the president of the entire Turkish nation, not solely as the president of those who share his own ethnicity. Investigate the origins of the president's mother and you will see what I mean."[14]

Arıtman elicited criticism from both the Left and Right, including her own party, for being out of line. But despite the unfavorable reception of Arıtman's attack, President Gül soon released a press statement, denying the claim that his family had Armenian roots. The president declared, "Our meticulously kept family tree from past to present, existing official documents of origin, as well as the past and present fellow townsmen of Kayseri, attest to his impeccable Turkish and Muslim lineage" on both sides. In the same breath that Gül cited genealogical evidence of his Turkishness and Muslimness, he also sought to assure the nation that he "respect[ed] all of [its] citizens' ethnic origins, different beliefs and family ties. I see all these differences as both a fact and as the enrichment of a country with an imperial past." He concluded by emphasizing again equality among citizens: "No one is superior to another … I am proud of my country for having reached this level of tolerance." President Gül went on to sue deputy Artıman for slander and won symbolic pecuniary compensation.

If a former president not only insists on proving his own "pure," namely Muslim-Turkish origins, but also sues someone for slander for insinuating that he may be anything else, what of ordinary citizens? And what of the Turkish migrants from Bulgaria who are trying to legalize their status as they live in Turkey and work for a living? The compulsion to prove origins trickles down from the presidential palace to legal bureaucratic spaces where a group of ethnically privileged but economically precarious migrants make their best—and often only—bid for belonging by claiming the status of consanguinity. What I have tried to show in this chapter is that if those who are overtly discriminated against constitute the more conspicuous facade of the limits of belonging in Turkey, those who are selected for inclusion also provide a revealing perspective on Turkey's differentiated citizenship regime. In order to lay bare the full implications of differentiated citizenship practices and the religious and ethno-racial terms of belonging on which the Turkish state is predicated, we need to take to task both the boundaries drawn to exclude those who are deemed irredeemably foreign and the borders opened on behalf of those who are deemed to be (almost) the same.

Notes

1. According to current legislation, only those who can prove their Armenian identity can be enrolled in Armenian minority schools in Turkey.
2. Journalist Ferda Balancar reported on the case in the Armenian weekly *Agos*, providing a copy of the leaked document from which the quote is taken. See Balancar (2013).
3. Also relevant for the purposes of this chapter are the following statistics: of the thousands of MPs who have served since the founding of the Turkish Republic in 1923, Garo Paylan is one of only nine Armenians to be elected and one of only twenty-five MPs that belong to one of the three legally designated minorities.
4. For coverage of this incident, including the leaked official document from which the quote is taken, see Balancar (2013).
5. Previous iterations of the word used in publications during the early years of the republic, as well as in parliamentary discussions, was *ırkdaş*. The root *ırk* leaves no leeway for interpretation, as it exclusively means "race." But even without such evidence of deployments of the literal term for race, I would insist on thinking about *soy* and *ırk* ("ethnicity" and "race") together, given that the former often becomes a euphemism for the latter, as Etienne Balibar and Immanuel Wallerstein (1991) have forcefully argued. My approach is also similar to the integrative approach propounded by Andreas Wimmer (2008), who consciously rejects a definitional ontology of ethnicity, and proposes that we view race and racial identification as a subset of ethnicity and expose how ethnicity gets variously and contingently operationalized.
6. İskan Kanunu ("Settlement Law"), No. 885/1926, No. 2510/1934, No. 5543/2006.
7. İskan Kanunu ("Settlement Law"), No. 5543/2006, art. 4. In a parliamentary meeting when the most recent version of the Settlement Law was being debated, one expert insisted on the problematic nature of the formulation that equalizes migrants with those who are of Turkish origin. The expert's proposal of an alternative formulation, namely, "they will not be accepted as migrants of Turkish origin," was rejected (Erder 2014: 165).

8. Beşikçi (1977) detailed how the Settlement Law was primarily used to colonize what was deemed an unruly and threatening Kurdish population. His book was instantly banned upon publication. See also Martin van Bruinessen (2005) for an excellent discussion of the significance of this work within Beşikçi's larger oeuvre.
9. I thank Didier Fassin for raising the critical point that by contrast there is no right to return for Palestinians chased from their home in 1948.
10. This formulation is indebted to an insightful question posed to me by Nihan Kayalı during a talk at UCLA's Center for the Study of International Migration.
11. These observations are based on work with the Migrant Solidarity Network in Turkey, during which I came to personally witness and hear testimonies of discrimination faced by black migrants. The trial of the police officer who shot Festus Okey, a Nigerian migrant who had applied for asylum, became a high-profile case after the Migrant Solidarity Network started to pursue it by becoming a party to the case, which the court had been stalling for years on account of missing evidence.
12. German-Turkish journalist Recep Maraşlı (2016) has claimed, based on archival documents he accessed in what used to be the concentration camp of Sachsenhausen, that the Istanbul police chief and the Minority Bureau chief officer, both of whom would later be in charge of the deportation of Armenians and Jews to the labor camp in Aşkale, visited the camp in Germany for several days on an official mission, during which they were given a detailed tour of the premises, and, according to the testimony of the camp doctor during his trial, expressed their intention to put to use what they learned from the Nazis in Turkey.
13. For coverage of the campaign, see Anon. (2008). Also note that the term "genocide" was avoided even in this campaign, which was unprecedented in rallying the public around the hitherto unsayable.
14. This and subsequent quotations on the exchange between Arıtman and Gul are taken from NTV news coverage (https://www.ntv.com.tr/turkiye/gul-dava-acti-aritman-israrli,5eKOLaouXECJvUUbrqLpRQ (accessed August 19, 2019).

References

Abu El-Haj, Nadia. 2010. "Racial Palestinianization and the Janus-Faced Nature of the Israeli State." *Patterns of Prejudice* 44(1): 27–41.

Aktar, Ayhan. 2006. *Varlık Vergisi ve "Türkleştirme" Politikaları* [Wealth tax and "Turkification" policies]. Istanbul: Iletişim.

Anon. 2008. "Aydınlardan Ermeni Kardeşlerimden Özür Diliyorum Kampanyası" ["I apologize to my Armenian brethren" campaign by intellectuals]. *Bianet Haber Merkezi* [Bianet News Center], December 5. Available at: http://m.bianet.org/kurdi/insan-haklari/111276-aydinlardan-ermeni-kardeslerimden-ozur-diliyorum-kampanyasi (accessed August 28, 2019).

Balancar, Ferda. 2013 "90 Yıldır Soy Kodu İle Fişlemişler. [They were flagged with a race code)]. *Agos*, August 1. Available at: http://www.agos.com.tr/tr/yazi/5384/90-yildir-soy-kodu-ile-fislemisler (accessed August 22, 2019).

Baldwin-Edwards, Martin, and Giannis Kyriakou. 2004. "Statistical Data on Immigrants in Greece: An Analytic Study of Available Data and Recommendations for Conformity with European Union Standards." Athens: Mediterranean Migration Observatory, UEHR, Panteion University.

Balibar, Etienne, and Immanuel Wallerstein. 1991. *Race, Nation, Class: Ambiguous Identities*. London: Verso.

Beşikçi, İsmail. 1977. *Kürtlerin `Mecburi İskan'ı* [The mandatory settlement of the Kurds]. Ankara: Komal.

Brink-Danan, Marcy. 2011. *Jewish Life in Twenty-First-Century Turkey: The Other Side of Tolerance*. Bloomington: Indiana University Press.

Çağaptay, Soner. 2009. *Türkiye'de İslam, Laiklik ve Milliyetçilik: Türk Kimdir?* [Islam, secularism, and nationalism in Turkey: who is a Turk?]. İstanbul: İstanbul Bilgi Üniversitesi Yayınları.

Çağaptay, Soner. 2014. "Race, Assimilation, and Kemalism: Turkish Nationalism and the Minorities in the 1930s." *Middle Eastern Studies* 40(3): 86–101.

Coşkun, Emel. 2018. "Criminalisation and Prostitution of Migrant Women in Turkey: A Case Study of Ugandan Women." *Women's Studies International Forum* 68: 85–93.

Courbage, Youssef, and Philippe Fargues. 1997. *Christians and Jews under Islam*, trans. Judy Mabro. London: I.B. Tauris.

Dündar, Fuat. 2001. *I·ttihat ve Terakki'nin Müslümanları I·skân Politikası (1913–1918)* [The Muslim settlement policy of the union and progress (1913–1918)]. Istanbul: Iletişim.

Ekmekçioğlu, Lerna. 2016. *Recovering Armenia: The Limits of Belonging in Post-Genocide Turkey*. Stanford: Stanford University Press.

Erder, Sema. 2014. "Türkiye'de Değişen Siyasal Konjonktür, Değişen Göç ve İskan Politikaları" [Turkey's changing political conjuncture and changing migration patterns and settlement policies]. In Ahmet İçduygu, Sema Erder, Ömer Faruk Gençkaya (eds), *Türkiye'nin Uluslararası Göç Politikaları (1923–2023): Ulus-Devlet Oluşumundan Ulus-Ötesi Dönüşümlere* [Turkey's international migration policy (1923–2023): from nation-state formation to transnational transformation], 77–138. Istanbul: Koç Üniversitesi Göç Araştırmaları Merkezi.

Ergin, Murat. 2008. "'Is the Turk a White Man?' Towards a Theoretical Framework for Race in the Making of Turkishness." *Middle Eastern Studies* 44(6): 827–50.

Fassin, Didier. 2011. "Policing Borders, Producing Boundaries: The Governmentality of Immigration in Dark Times." *Annual Review of Anthropology* 40: 213–26.

Fox, John. 2009. "From National Inclusion to Economic Exclusion: Transylvanian Hungarian Ethnic Return Migration to Hungary." In Takeyuki Tsuda (ed.), *Diasporic Homecomings: Ethnic Return Migration in Comparative Perspective*, 186–207. Stanford: Stanford University Press.

Gündoğan, Azat Zana. forthcoming. "Divergent Responses to Urban Transformation Projects in Turkey: Common Sense and State Affinity in Community Mobilization." *Urban Geography*.

Joppke, Christian. 2005. *Selecting by Origin: Ethnic Migration in the Liberal State*. Cambridge, MA: Harvard University Press.

Kevorkian, Raymond. 2011. *The Armenian Genocide: A Complete History.* London: I.B. Tauris.

Kim, Jaaeun. 2016. *Contested Embrace: Transborder Membership Politics in Twentieth-Century Korea.* Stanford: Stanford University Press.

Kirişçi, Kemal. 2000. "Disaggregating Turkish Citizenship and Immigration Practices." *Middle Eastern Studies* 36(3): 1–22.

Maksudyan, Nazan. 2005. *Türklüğü Ölçmek: Bilimkurgusal Antropoloji ve Türk Milliyetçiliğinin Irkçı Çehresi 1925-1939* [Measuring Turkishness: science-fictional anthropology and the racist face of Turkish nationalism]. Istanbul: Metis Publishing.

Maraşlı, Recep. 2016. "Varlık Vergısı ve Aşkalenin Mimarları Nazilerden Ders Almış" [The architects of the capital levy and of Askale learned from the Nazis]. *Avlaremoz*, November 13. Available at: http://www.avlaremoz.com/2016/11/13/varlik-vergisi-ve-askalenin-mimarlari-nazilerden-ders-almis-recep-marasli/ (accessed August 22, 2019).

McNevin, Anne. 2006. "Political Belonging in a Neoliberal Era: The Struggle of the Sans-Papiers." *Citizenship Studies* 10(2): 135–51.

Münz, Rainer, and Rainer Ohlinger (eds). 2003. *Diasporas and Ethnic Migrants: Germany, Israel and Post-Soviet Successor States.* London: Frank Cass.

Parla, Ayşe. 2019. *Precarious Hope: Migration and the Limits of Belonging in Turkey.* Stanford: Stanford University Press.

Remennick, L.I. 1999. "'Women with a Russian Accent' in Israel." *European Journal of Women's Studies* 6(4): 441–461.

Silverstein, Paul A. 2004. *Algeria in France: Transpolitics, Race, and Nation.* Bloomington: University of Indiana Press.

Smith, Andrea L. (ed.). 2003. *Europe's Invisible Migrants.* Amsterdam: Amsterdam University Press.

Suciyan, Talin. 2015. *The Armenians in Modern Turkey: Post-Genocide Society, Politics and History.* London: I.B. Tauris.

Tambar, Kabir. 2016. "Brotherhood in Dispossession: State Violence and the Ethics of Expectation in Turkey." *Cultural Anthropology* 31(1): 30–55.

Tekeli, Ilhan. 1990. "Osmanlı İmparatorluğundan Günümüze Nüfusun Zorunlu Yer Değiştirmesi ve İskan Sorunu" [The issue of forced migration and settlement from the Ottoman Empire until today]. *Toplum ve Bilim* 50: 49–72.

Ticktin, Miriam. 2011. *Casualties of Care: Immigration and the Politics of Humanitarianism in France.* Berkeley: University of California Press.

Tsuda, T. 2003. *Strangers in the Ethnic Homeland: Japanese Brazilian Return Migration in Transnational Perspective.* New York: Columbia University Press.

Üngör, Uğur, and Mehmet Polatel. 2011. *Confiscation and Destruction: The Young Turk Seizure of Armenian Property.* London: Continuum.

van Bruinessen, Martin. 2005. "Ismail Beşikçi: Turkish Sociologist, Critic of Kemalism, and Kurdologist." *Journal of Kurdish Studies* 5: 19–34.

Vouitra, Eftihia. 2004. "Ethnic Greeks from the Former Soviet Union as 'Privileged Return Migrants'." *Espace, Populations, Sociétés* 3: 533–44.

Wimmer, Andreas. 2008. "The Making and Unmaking of Ethnic Boundaries: A Multilevel Process Theory." *American Journal of Sociology* 113(4): 970–1022.

Yeğen, Mesut. 2004. "Citizenship and Ethnicity in Turkey." *Middle Eastern Studies* 40(6): 597–615.

5
Family Resemblances
Binational Marriage, Muslim "Communalism," and the Patriarchal State

Mayanthi Fernando

Jean-Luc and Lisa are sitting on a couch, Jean-Luc dressed in a white polo shirt and Lisa in a green Congolese dress. Jean-Luc, animated, does most of the talking; he has one arm around Lisa, and uses the other to gesticulate as he tells their story to the interviewer. Lisa, her own arms folded across her chest, remains largely impassive, looking to the side.

"There were six of them," Jean-Luc begins. "They banged on the door. It was in the morning."

"8 o'clock," Lisa says.

"Around 8 o'clock," Jean-Luc continues. "They banged on the door. I opened the door. Police! They barged right in. My wife was still sleeping."

Lisa nods slightly, lips pursed, stone-faced. If Jean-Luc's anger bubbles hot and voluble, Lisa's seems more contained, seething. She blinks furiously throughout as Jean-Luc talks.

"I said, 'My wife is still sleeping!' They entered the bedroom where my wife was still asleep. I said to them, 'At least wait until I wake up my wife. She has hypertension, you're going to scare her, that's going to make her blood pressure go up even more. Let me wake her up.' So they let me wake her, but I had to leave the door open. We're on the seventh floor! They didn't want her to get away. I said, 'Listen, my wife isn't going to fly away, we're on the seventh floor, and you've also got your men at the entrance to the building. Let her at least get dressed.' He [the officer] refused, and he pushed open the door with his foot. I said, 'But my wife is naked! You can't seriously want to look at my naked wife.' 'She'll get dressed in front of us,' he said. I pushed the door shut, I got really angry, I told him to stand aside. [He said to me]: 'If this continues, we're cuffing you and taking you with us.'"

At this point, Lisa sighs audibly and looks down.

Jean-Luc goes on: "I said, 'But I don't want you to see my wife naked!' After that, they came in. They didn't even wait for her to get her things. They just told her to get dressed, take whatever she could on her person, and follow them. I said: 'Where are you taking her?' 'That's not your business' [an officer replied]. I said to them, 'But it is my business! You're taking my wife away, I'd like to know where.' And immediately he said the detention center in Lyon."

Jean-Luc looks at Lisa for confirmation.

"Yes, the detention center in Lyon," she says, still looking down.

"To the detention center in Lyon," Jean-Luc affirms. "I said, 'Why?!' And he said, 'Your wife doesn't have her papers. We're taking her there first, and then she'll be sent back to the Congo.'"

Thus begins *Les Amoureux au ban public*, a 2011 documentary by scholar and activist Nicolas Ferran on binational couples and their encounters with the immigration bureaucracy in France.[1] The film takes its name from an association—Les Amoureux au Ban Public, or ABP—set up in 2007 and formalized in 2010.[2] ABP provides legal advice and support to such binational couples and advocates for couples' right to love and live together regardless of national borders, based on the right to marriage and family life recognized under Article 8 of the European Convention on Human Rights (Neveu Kringelbach 2013: 6). In the film, Jean-Luc and Lisa are not the only ones with a harrowing, and often humiliating, story of their homes being invaded by immigration and police officials, their intimate lives subject to bureaucratic scrutiny, and the sincerity of their marriages questioned. Laetitia and Mohamed, a young couple, recount how the police came to their apartment to take Mohamed in for questioning, suspecting a *mariage blanc* (a green-card marriage in American parlance). Alaé and Audrey, another young couple, describe their multiyear ordeal getting Alaé a visa and then a residence permit (*carte de séjour*) for France, which needs to be renewed every year. This means that investigators continue to visit their home, looking through their bedroom and bathroom to verify that they are living together (*une vie commune*, or cohabitation, is a requirement for renewal). During one of those visits, Audrey recounts, she asked the investigators if they really thought that she and Alaé were faking their relationship, given that they had had a child together. An investigator responded that Audrey could have become pregnant by another man to get papers for Alaé. "Our daughter was standing next to me," Audrey says, "and I felt so insulted." She told the investigator that he was out of line and demanded he show some respect. "You're in my home," she said. The agent responded: "Listen, this is how these inquiries go. You married a Moroccan, a Maghrebin. That's how it goes for [people from] those countries."

In another scene, Jeanne, a young woman with dark hair, wearing a pink turtleneck, tells the story of her relationship with Papi, whom she married in Cameroon. When they went to the French Consulate there to have their marriage registered, the consulate requested an inquiry by the chief prosecutor, suspecting a fraudulent marriage. Upon returning to France, Jeanne was questioned about her relationship and asked whether she had "consummated" her union. In an emotional account that simmers with hurt and rage, she recounts in the film how every time she responded to a question, the officer in charge of her case scolded her. "Each time I said something," Jeanne remembers, the officer said, "There you go. That's the proof that he married you for the papers." Jeanne continues: "He presented himself as some kind of protector, as a big brother ... He wanted to help me, to get me out of the terrible clutches of this Cameroonian man who had—it was clear as day!—obviously married me for his papers." The officer asked Jeanne if she had told her parents about the marriage, and when she told him she had not, he wanted to know why. At this point, Jeanne's simmering frustration starts to boil over. "I had to keep justifying my way of dealing with my life to this guy I didn't know," she says. "I remember at one point, I said to him, 'Listen, this is my way of dealing with things.' And he responded: 'No. Now, your way of dealing with things concerns us all. Your life isn't yours anymore, it's all of ours.'"

In yet another scene, Elza, a young white woman in stylish glasses, tells of being visited by police investigators (*police judiciaire*) at the home she shared with Hichem. The couple, who had met at architecture school, had applied for a marriage license after living together for a year; Hichem was at the time *sans-papiers*, without legal papers, since his residence permit had not been renewed. The police violently arrested Hichem—"I saw my future husband cuffed and tied up like an animal," Elza says—and took him to a detention center to await deportation. (A judge later declared his arrest illegal and he was released, then arrested again and eventually deported, "put on a boat to Tangiers.") During this period of Hichem's detention, Elza was interrogated about her relationship. "They asked me questions that were pretty intimate and embarrassing," she remembers. "Like, had I been with other men before? Was I taking contraceptives to make sure I didn't get pregnant, because a child could regularize Hichem's legal status.

Already, that's pretty embarrassing. And then [the police officer] finished by telling me that he really hoped for my sake that I wasn't being hoodwinked, because I fit the profile." At this point, Elza goes from humiliation to anger. She continues: "And when I told the police that it felt like an interrogation, that it was surreal, that, as a citizen of France, they were taking away my right, for the simple crime of having fallen in love with a foreigner, they were taking away my fundamental right—which is to fall in love with whomever one wants, to live with whomever one wants, when one wants, as one wants, without anyone giving us trouble—the officer said to me, 'Mademoiselle, we're not preventing you from being in love. It's just that you should really choose better.'"

My chapter takes these stories in *Les Amoureux au ban public* as the starting point to reflect on the regulation of migrant intimacies as a major part of the border and boundary work of the French state and French society. Didier Fassin notes that the French nation-state, and French republican nationalism, is premised on and reproduces both external borders (legal distinctions between citizens and foreigners) and internal boundaries (social distinctions based on race, ethnicity, and religion) (Fassin 2010a).[3] Moreover, as he and others also note, the very division between external borders and internal boundaries has become increasingly muddied, with racial and religious minorities in France presumed to be foreigners or not-quite-French even when they are, legally, full citizens (Balibar 2007; Fassin 2010b; Fassin & Fassin 2006; Fernando 2014b). Indeed, that muddying is itself a form of boundary work. I intervene in this scholarship to focus on another kind of limit that is not only foundational to secular-liberal nation-states but also, I want to argue, key to the maintenance of those states' national borders and internal boundaries. That is, of course, the limit between public and private, political and intimate. I am particularly interested in marriage, the family, and sex and romance, and how all three domains—usually considered as part of the private sphere—have become central to state practices of border control and boundary work (Cole 2014), as well as to the discourse of French nationalism across the political spectrum.

The centrality to French nationalism of marriage, sex and romance, and family goes hand in hand with the transformation of conventional liberal nationalism into what Sara Farris (2017) calls "femonationalism" and Eric Fassin (2010) "sexual nationalism" (see also Ticktin 2008). With these terms, Farris and Fassin index how women's rights and sexual liberty have come to be seen as the fundamental values that define France (and Europe more broadly), values that need especially to be protected from repressive patriarchal Islamic norms regarding marriage, family, sex, and romance. Muslim marriages and the Muslim family home have therefore become key sites of public consternation and state surveillance (Fernando 2014a; Surkis 2010), as have migrant marriages more generally (Neveu Kringelbach 2013). In recent decades, references to arranged marriages, forced marriages, and fraudulent marriages have come to saturate debates about immigration, and multiple laws have given public officials and police increasing powers to combat marital fraud. A new term—*mariage gris*—has entered the lexicon to distinguish between green-card marriages (*mariages blancs*) and ultra-fraudulent marriages where a nonnational (almost always an African or Arab in media and politicians' accounts) fakes love to dupe his or her unsuspecting French partner into what is, in fact, a green-card marriage. This is what police officials in the film implied had happened to Jeanne and Elza. Thus the French state has become increasingly invested in protecting French national identity and French national values through the policing of migrant and Muslim intimacies, transgressing the limit between public and private that ostensibly underpins secular democracy.

My chapter makes three key points. First, I underscore how norms about intimacy and the family increasingly serve to enforce external borders and internal boundaries in France, determining who can belong legally and socially to the nation. Second, I argue that these seemingly distinct categories—external borders and internal boundaries—are, in fact, entangled, precisely through the question of intimacy, and that they therefore need to be thought about together.[4] Finally, I show how, in policing its borders and boundaries by managing intimate relations between nationals and nonnationals, the French state mirrors the patriarchal Muslim family it seeks, at least in theory, to combat as contrary to French norms. My argument is not simply that France today remains a deeply patriarchal and gender-unequal society; it does, of course, in myriad ways. Rather, my argument is that the state acts like the Muslim patriarch so often figured as the *bête noire* of secular, egalitarian France, the controlling, communalist father (and sometimes brother) against whom much of this border and boundary work is supposed to function.

Family and the Art of Government

Michel Foucault writes that with the emergence of the modern state at the end of the sixteenth century, sovereignty gives way to what he calls governmentality, and good government of the state—"just at this time beginning to be called *police*" (Foucault 1991: 92)—comes to be seen as coextensive with the art of governing the household. Thus the family becomes the model for governing the state:

> The art of government ... is essentially concerned with answering the question of how to introduce economy—that is to say, the correct manner of managing individuals, goods and wealth within the family (which a good father is expected to do in relation to his wife, children and servants) and of making the family fortunes prosper—how to introduce this meticulous attention of the father toward his family into the management of the state. (ibid.: 92)

This is, however, only one shift in the history of governing that Foucault tracks, and the role of the family changes again in the middle of the eighteenth century, even as family and the art of government remain tightly connected. This period sees the emergence of the notion of population, of which the family is now considered an internal element. As a result, Foucault writes, the family goes from being a model for government to becoming "the privileged instrument for the government of the population" (ibid.: 100).

This history of family and government maps onto Foucault's history of sexuality, for the governance of population through the family also means the governance of sex and sexuality. Sex, writes Joan Scott, following Foucault, "became the foundation for the state's regulation of populations, the disciplining of bodies, the surveillance of children and families, distinctions between the normal and the perverse" (Scott 2018: 161). This, in turn, meant that the liberal-democratic distinction between public/political life and private life was always unstable, the private sphere of sex and family always subject to surveillance and intervention. According to French sociologist Frédéric Le Play, writing in the mid-nineteenth century: "private life stamps public life with its character. The family is the foundation of the state" (cited in ibid.: 76). Even as women were relegated to the ostensibly private sphere of domesticity and family distinct from the masculine realm of politics and the market economy, that domestic sphere and the women and children inhabiting it were—as the "privileged instrument for the government of the population," as Foucault put it—subject to surveillance, discipline, and regulation. Unsurprisingly, then, the family remains instrumental to a nation-state's border and boundary work.

Policing Intimacy at the Border

Sara Farris writes, "The family is the social 'space' upon which nations draw the boundaries between the noncitizen and the citizen, the foreigner and the 'native,' those who must demonstrate their allegiance to the nation and those whose allegiance is taken for granted by birthright or cultural elective affinities" (Farris 2017: 110; see also Cole 2014). Indeed, marriage has become a major site of legal regulation in France in the name of stricter immigration controls and in the name of women's rights, and between 2003 and 2006 a series of measures both tightened access to immigration via marriage and enabled mayoral, prefectural, and consular officials to request administrative or police inquiries into the nature of a couple's relationship, on the grounds of suspicion of a forced or fraudulent marriage. As a result, the probation period during which a non-EU spouse is granted only short-term, renewable residence permits was extended from one to up to four years, and the length of time required for foreign spouses to apply for citizenship was extended from two to four years after the date of marriage (Neveu Kringelbach 2013: 9). Moreover, according to Hélène Neveu Kringelbach, by the mid-2000s word was passed down from the Ministry of the Interior to consulates and prefectures that up to half of marriages between French citizens and nonnationals were fraudulent, and prefectures were given quotas for the number of spousal visas they could deliver annually (ibid.: 4). As part of the crackdown on fraudulent marriages, an April 2006 domestic violence law increased the power of public officials to annul arranged or forced marriages; the same law enabled officials to investigate "suspicious" marriages and annul fraudulent ones—that is, marriages contracted not out of love but rather for purposes of immigration or naturalization (Surkis 2010: 540–41). This law followed a May 2005 letter of instruction (*circulaire*) from the Ministry of Justice that details how to identify and investigate suspected cases of "simulated or arranged marriages"—that is, either consensually fraudulent or forced. While the irregular immigration status of a prospective spouse cannot, in theory, be the sole reason for officials to request an inquiry by the chief prosecutor's office, in practice it often is. And a 2003 immigration law enacted to combat marital fraud allows police to interview prospective marriage partners separately if they become suspicious about the true intentions of one or both of the partners (ibid.).

As a result, writes Neveu Kringelback, couples are required to lay bare the details of their intimate lives together in order to prove to suspicious officials the genuine character of their relationship. "At every step," she notes, "couples are now required to demonstrate that they share an everyday life and remain intimate through multiple elements of evidence" (Neveu Kringelback 2013: 9). These range from bureaucratic items like rent receipts, electricity bills, and a common bank account to more intimate objects like photographs of holidays together, print-outs of e-mail or instant-message exchanges if the couple lives apart, and even love letters. A Parisian lawyer showed me some of her case files for clients appealing deportation orders (*obligation de quitter le territoire français*, OQTF), visa denials, and retractions of naturalization based on suspected marriage fraud.[5] Many of the files included these artifacts of conjugal intimacy, and the lawyer told me that she often felt awkward amassing amorous declarations as bureaucratic evidence, slotted into plastic pages in a binder, to be leafed through by a judge. A report by ABP notes that many couples are asked about their sex lives: "Has the marriage been consummated, how often do you have sexual relations, when did you first and last have sex, etc.—these are some of the questions often posed" (ABP 2008: 21). The report goes on to underscore how:

> the suspicion that systematically surrounds binational marriages imposes on couples an existence punctuated by repeated inspections (*contrôles*) meant to verify the truth of their domestic life. The law provides that such inspections can happen before the celebration of a marriage, before the registration of the marriage, before marriages celebrated overseas, before the issuance of a visa for France, before the first issuance of a residence permit, and, after that, every year, at the moment of renewing that temporary residence permit. (ibid.: 19)

At stake in these regulative measures is the reinscription of a normative notion of marriage that emphasizes romantic love—and not, say, financial or immigration considerations—as the basis for sexual and conjugal union.[6] Moreover, these legal measures are, in essence, exercises in national sovereignty, a sovereignty that is enacted by policing the intimate lives of migrants and their French partners.[7] Yet this border work becomes a kind of boundary drawing as well. As Judith Surkis notes, all the various legal measures detailed above "grant public officials increased latitude to monitor migrant intimacies and to scrutinize the marital choices of French citizens who are perceived to be (and hence made into) 'foreigners'" (Surkis 2010: 539). This is particularly true for French nationals of sub-Saharan or North African descent, whose marriages to nonnationals from their "home" countries are especially scrutinized as potentially fraudulent or forced marriages. In other words, the rigorous policing of intimacy between nationals and nonnationals to shore up France's legal and territorial borders in the name of protecting its citizens muddies any clear distinction between external borders and internal, social boundaries. Intimacy is the hinge through which border work is also boundary work.

Gender Equality at Borders and Boundaries

Combatting fraud is not the only reason for the state's surveillance of marriage and family. The family—and in particular the patriarchal Muslim family—has come to be seen as that which prevents the proper integration of immigrants and their French-born descendants. As I noted earlier, republican nationalism now claims sexual liberty and gender equality as the national values that distinguish France (and Europe) from the non-West; thus, gender equality in the home and individual freedom in sexual and romantic pursuits have become key signifiers of proper integration. A July 2006 law on immigration and integration made it mandatory for most non-EU nationals who intend to settle in France to sign a *contrat d'accueil et d'intégration* (CAI, contract for reception and integration) with the state in order to obtain legal residency for up to four years, intended to promote "republican integration" (*intégration républicaine*).[8] Signing the contract has become necessary for renewing a one-year residence permit (*carte de séjour*) or receiving a long-term *carte de résident de long séjour* (Hachimi Alaoui 2012: 124). Article 5 of the law reads: "Civic education includes a presentation of French institutions and values of the Republic, including equality between men and women and secularism" (cited in Farris 2017: 97).

Migrants can learn the values of France through a booklet with a range of information on how to live in France, and through a video shown to newcomers during the introductory integration session. As Farris writes, "the whole integration infrastructure, from the introductory meeting to the civic integration session, repeatedly and explicitly mentions equality between men and women as a key value of French society" (Farris 2017: 97). In the integration booklet, "equality between men and women appears in the very first part of discussing the institutions of France, right after the introductory section recalling the French Revolution and the Declaration of the Rights of Man and Citizen" (ibid.: 97). A paragraph entitled "France, a country of equality" states: "Equality between men and women is a fundamental principle of French society ... Wives are not subordinate to the husband's authority, nor to that of the father or brother with regard to, for example, working or opening a bank account" (cited in Hachimi Alaoui 2012: 128). According to the booklet, husband and wife are equal and should have joint authority over their children, including deciding on their education. Other parts of the booklet refer to the importance of freedom of marriage, and state that forced marriage and polygamy are illegal. Significantly, as Farris underscores, gender equality here pertains to the family, not to the realms of economy or politics. Not only has the family become the privileged focus of migrant integration, but gender equality itself also begins—and ends—with the family.[9]

The Muslim family in particular is thought to be in need of reform, with regard to both recent migrants and those who have resided for years in France and have produced a second and even third generation of descendants. As Myriam Hachimi Alaoui notes, the discourse of gender equality is always coupled with "the question of Islam and its compatibility with laïcité" (ibid.: 128), and the specter of Muslim communalism (*communautarisme*) hovers over all political and public discussions of integration. Posited as the antithesis of republican integration, *communautarisme* means enclosing oneself or one's dependents within one's community, and privileging "particular" ethnic, racial, and religious attachments over "universal" national ones. Many republicans believe that a significant portion of binational marriages are "communal" or "ethnic" marriages in which French citizens marry—or are forcibly married to—spouses from their parents' or grandparents' countries of origin. Thus marriage with a partner from one's own community—in essence, endogamy—is often criticized as *communautarisme* (Neveu Kringelbach 2013: 8) and marrying out of one's community promoted as a sign of integration. Beyond the matter of ethno-racial or religious overidentification, Muslim *communautarisme* troubles republicans because it is thought to sequester women—especially young women—within their communities and to restrict their individual freedom. And, although many decry constraints on professional and educational freedoms for Muslim girls and women, press coverage, political discourse, and legal measures focus most on constraints on their sexual and romantic freedom.

The Problem of Muslim Communalism as a Problem of Intimacy

Interestingly, some Muslim women—women who present themselves as secular and integrated—have been key to confirming popular fears about Muslim communalism. Of particular note is the movement Ni Putes Ni Soumises (NPNS, Neither Whores Nor Doormats), whose leaders—Fadela Amara, Loubna Méliane, and Sihem Habchi—emerged in the 2000s as vociferous critics of Muslim fundamentalism, Muslim communalism, and what they portrayed in their autobiographies as a miserable life for women and girls in the *banlieues* (immigrant suburbs). Much has been written already about NPNS and its success in mainstream politics and media (Benabdessadok 2004; Fernando 2009, 2013; Kemp 2009; Winter 2009). I focus here on the narrative structure of those autobiographies, and on how they define freedom and unfreedom. Many of these autobiographies tell a similar story of the female Muslim protagonist's chafing under the strict rules of a patriarchal father and an acquiescent or sympathetic but powerless mother; of rules that give sons more freedom than daughters; of the protagonist's growing desire for the freedom to be herself; of her eventual liberation—usually with help from non-Muslim allies or organizations—from the confines of her watchful family and community; and, finally, of her blossoming into full personhood through the exercise of her newfound sexual and romantic freedom. In what follows, I attend to Amara's and Méliane's autobiographies to highlight their critique of the constant surveillance of young women's intimate lives by fathers and brothers, a surveillance they define as integral to the patriarchal Muslim family.

Though only the first chapter of Amara's *Ni putes ni soumises* is strictly autobiographical, the authority of her analysis regarding what she calls "the social breakdown in the projects" and the predicament of young women comes from her personal experiences as one of those women. That first chapter covers both the anti-Arab racism she and her family faced (they were, in fact, Berber) and her "ordinary childhood in an immigrant suburb" (Amara 2006: 45). This included a home life marked by gender inequality (women were responsible for household chores) and restrictions placed by her father on her freedom of movement, in contrast to the liberty enjoyed by her brothers. "My father," she writes, "had a rather simple idea of everyone's place in society: men and women were certainly equal before the law, but men belonged to the outside world and women to the private one at home!" (ibid.: 45). And he had inherited this retrograde perspective from North Africa: "Berber fathers like him came from a patriarchal and male chauvinist society" in Algeria (ibid.: 46).

In the next chapter, Amara chronicles a "growing male oppression," as the authority of fathers waned and patriarchy took a new form through the authority of brothers. Amara attributes this to the ongoing unemployment crisis that diminished the status of now-unemployed fathers and created a vacuum that was filled by the next generation of men. Also unemployed and thoroughly excluded from French society, these young men have come to assuage their feelings of powerlessness, emasculation, and "incredible rage" by dominating the only domain they can: young women in the housing projects (ibid.: 68). Amara writes:

> Today ... fathers are absent ... Now the eldest son has taken over; he rules the family. He has physically replaced the father in his protective and repressive roles ... He has assumed responsibility for teaching family values to younger sisters and for policing their conduct outside the home to ensure that they behave. (ibid.: 63)

The older brother took as his mission the protection of his sister's virginity and her family's honor. As a result, "women [in the *banlieues*] saw the freedom they had acquired during the ... antiracist demonstrations of the 1980s [in which Amara participated] become more and more restricted." "Little by little," Amara concludes, "the pressure on young women's daily lives in the projects turned to oppression. Their comings and goings were controlled, and their freedom to leave home was reduced to nothing" (ibid.: 63).

One final step occurred to make patriarchy and the surveillance of women a truly communal—and therefore communalist—affair. The "male power" that Amara describes was, she writes, extended

> from the older brother to all the young men in the projects. Their surveillance was systematically directed against the 'tribe of young women.' Now the honor of each family of the project was in the hands of these young men. Since the honor consisted in preserving women's virginity, these young men became the collective guardians of this treasure. (ibid.: 64)

They assumed that they "had the right to control her life and the company she kept" (ibid.: 64). As a result, a woman's intimate life was no longer her own, but rather the purview of the community at large.

Amara's NPNS colleague Loubna Méliane, the child of a Moroccan father and a French mother, also published her autobiography in 2003. Titled *Vivre libre* (Living free), it focuses squarely on Méliane herself, whom the cover blurb calls a "young girl from the ghetto." Méliane's experiences growing up were much the same as Amara's, though she writes of a general pattern of surveillance that fell on both young women and young men:

> For a boy, it was "don't hang out with the wrong crowd" and for girls it was "don't lose your virginity." In other words, [you had] to respect the traditions of the neighborhood, [and were] watched over permanently by others, be they adults or youth, *rebeus*, *blacks* or *gaulois*,[10] or suffer the consequences of being quickly labeled a delinquent or, for girls, a slut. (Méliane 2003: 9)

She goes on to write of the control that families continued to exercise over daughters even after they reached the age of majority:

> It's not that at 18 years old one had rights. That doesn't exist in our community (*chez nous*). A girl becomes an adult (*est majeure*) the day she's married. Even in France, we are considered the responsibility of the family, and we escape that diktat only on the day we marry. (ibid.: 96)

In Méliane's telling, marriage itself is heavily regulated by an Arab-Muslim girl's family. Méliane, who was married-off briefly by her father to a man not of her choosing—"as they do back home (*comme au bled*)," according to the cover blurb—unsurprisingly focuses on the lack of freedom young women in the *banlieues* have over their romantic and sexual lives. "An Arab girl (*une fille rebeu*)," she writes, "cannot get married without her parents' agreement" (ibid.: 81). She recounts the story of the sister of one of her friends, "from a hyper-traditional Algerian family," who fell in love with a Moroccan; her husband-to-be came to her parents to ask for her hand in marriage but "the family had responded: 'No, we don't want any Moroccans,' and [they] threw him out like a piece of trash … Another of her sisters had done 'worse.' She went off with a White guy and was totally banished from the family". (ibid.: 81)

Méliane ends this tale of three sisters with a success story about her own friend, who, after "a very hard and very difficult" time, managed to get her parents to accept the Moroccan boyfriend with whom she was "madly in love." It took a long time, writes Méliane, "but she [finally] married the love of her life" (ibid.: 82). "Arabs (*les rebeus*) have a real problem with this, that they have to deal with," Méliane concludes, referring to way that "traditional" Arab families meddle in the intimate lives of their children and refuse to allow them to marry for love. And "girls are not the only victims of these traditions, boys don't escape them either. How many boys have had to suffer in having to marry a girl they didn't want? They are also miserable (*malheureux*). Just like we are miserable in being forced to give way. But girls have to fight more to marry whom they want" (ibid.: 82–3).

Later in her autobiography, Méliane, like Amara, turns to the young men of the housing projects who have taken on the role their fathers once had in controlling the behavior of women. She calls them "barbaric young men, male chauvinists in the making (*machistes en herbe*)," who "trample the rights of girls in the projects" (ibid.: 159). And, like Amara, she decries the increasing lack of gender mixing and the subsequent hardening of emotional and amorous aptitudes in a generation of young men:

> Their emotional futures, their capacity to be husbands, or lovers, fathers and citizens, is dramatically obstructed. They allow themselves everything, hiding behind supposed cultural and religious traditions, because they live in frustration, in social and sexual misery. They don't speak of love, they don't know what it is. (ibid.: 159–60)

The consequence of this arc, from the control of women's lives exercised first by fathers and now by all young men in the name of patriarchy, Islam, and community, is that love itself—not just the freedom to love whomever one wants but the capacity to love at all—is increasingly under threat.

Amara's and Méliane's autobiographies outline the norms of companionate marriage and love, of privacy and intimacy, and of freedom and unfreedom that subtend secular republican society. These are the norms against which both women judge their Arab-Muslim communities of origin, confirming for their majoritarian non-Muslim audience its suspicions about Muslim communalism and Muslim patriarchy. What I want to underscore, again, is that the external borders and internal boundaries of France are constructed via normative ideas about the proper configuration of what is private and intimate—and therefore only the purview of the individual heart and mind—and what is public—and therefore can be regulated by the community or society at large. The general criticism of Muslim migrants and Muslim residents is that they sequester women in the domestic sphere, preventing women entry into the public sphere of work and education, and, at the same time, transgress the normative limit around an individual's intimate life, making public that which should be private. In other words, the accusation that Muslim patriarchal communalism denies women's freedom is, at its heart, an accusation that Muslim communalists misunderstand or disrespect secular French norms of public and private.

Conclusion

At first glance, gender seems the key operating distinction between secular French republicanism and Muslim communalism, and Amara and Méliane both highlight the repression of women as the main issue at hand. But, as I note above, the repression of women within Muslim communities is linked to the broader problem of communalist Muslims' disregard for the secular norms of public/private. What Amara and Méliane both find problematic is the inability of women to live their professional, romantic, and sexual lives without surveillance by their family or community of those private and intimate domains. Gender equality does not mean that young men's private and intimate lives should also be surveilled, but rather than no one's should be. Gender equality hinges on the normative arrangement of public/private, where one's private life is one's own, one is free to love whom one wants, and one's community does not get to decide the course of one's romantic, sexual, and married life. Practices like forced and arranged marriages for the sake of endogamy; virginity certificates; the sequestering of young women inside the home; the ostracism of those who choose their own partner or marry exogamously; and the general control over romantic life exercised first by fathers and now by all young men—all are practices associated with Muslim communalism. And these practices are considered problematic not simply because they repress women, but because they repress the freedom that all individuals should be granted from the surveillance and regulation of the intimate domain of sex, romantic love, and marriage.

And yet, ironically, it is precisely those practices so reviled as communalist that the French state consistently engages in to police its borders, and precisely this freedom from surveillance that is repressed by the state and its immigration bureaucracy, all in the name of protecting the French nation and its secular values. Note the subtitle to the ABP's report, mentioned earlier, to describe the couples who have experienced that process: *soupçonnés, humiliés, réprimé*—suspected, humiliated, repressed (ABP 2008). This subtitle could work just as well for many of the chapters in Amara's and Méliane's autobiographies, chronicling the difficulties of living free sexual and romantic lives in the *banlieues*. Likewise, the sentiments expressed by the couples in the film *Les Amoureux au ban public* are certainly those of humiliation in the face of suspicion about and repression of their intimate lives. Moreover, the experiences described by those couples mirror—and even exceed—the forms of surveillance that Amara and Méliane describe in the *banlieues*. Take, for instance, Jean-Luc and Lisa, who open the film with their harrowing story. The police barge into their bedroom, where Lisa is sleeping naked; in other words, the police quite literally intrude into the most intimate sphere of the home and catch Lisa at her most physically intimate. Audrey and Alaé also recount how the inner sanctum of their home is violated, with the police coming numerous times to look through their bedroom and bathroom in order to verify that the couple have, in fact, established an intimate life together.

Other women detail the way their sex lives explicitly become the purview of the police. Recall that Jeanne, who had married Papi, a Cameroonian, was asked whether she had consummated her marriage. Elza, too, was asked "questions that were pretty intimate and embarrassing. Like, had I been with other men before? Was I taking contraceptives to make sure I didn't get pregnant?" And the police surveillance of and intrusion into the intimate details of these women's sex lives is done in the name of protecting them from unscrupulous men and, ultimately, from themselves and their bad romantic choices.[11] As Elza recounts, the officer asking her such intimate questions told her he was doing so for her own good. A child with her partner Hicham could regularize his status, he told her. And he ended by telling Elza that "he really hoped for my sake that I wasn't being hoodwinked, because I fit the profile." According to the officer, he suspected a *mariage gris* and was looking out for Elza, whose good judgment, it seemed, had been clouded by love. Jeanne, too, was presumed to have been duped by her partner Papi. As Jeanne narrates, the officer framed everything she told him about her relationship with Papi as evidence of a *mariage gris*. And, like the officer interrogating Elza, he did so in the name of protecting Jeanne from men who would otherwise take advantage of her: "He presented himself as some kind of protector, as a big brother." Jeanne was thereby conscripted as a wayward sister, incapable of choosing wisely for herself, and thus subjected to familial and communal regulation. The police officer was quite clear about this, if you recall.

When Jeanne protested that she should not have to justify how she lived her life, the officer responded: "your way of dealing with things concerns us all. Your life isn't yours anymore, it's all of ours." The officer explicitly inhabits the role of big brother, guardian of his sister's virtue for the sake of their family and the national community. And he is quite clear that Jeanne's romantic and sexual life is not her own, and that her choice to marry exogamously—outside the national borders and racial boundaries of the majoritarian French community—can only bring disapproval and surveillance by the state-qua-family.

The interaction between Elza and the officer interrogating her perhaps best captures the dynamic I am tracking. There, one sees the tension between, on the one hand, the norms of romantic love, sexual freedom, and companionate marriage that constitute liberal-democratic subjects and, on the other, the communal regulation of love, sex, and marriage that define not only the patriarchal Muslim family (as seen through the eyes of contemporary critics) but also the policing of borders and boundaries by secular modern nation-states. Elza tells the police officer that her fundamental freedoms as an individual and a citizen are being violated: "they were taking away my right, for the simple crime of having fallen in love with a foreigner, they were taking away my fundamental right—which is to fall in love with whomever one wants, to live with whomever one wants, when one wants, as one wants." Here, Elza voices the norms of romance and love, of what constitutes individual freedom, that underpin Amara's and Méliane's critique of Muslim communalism, by now a general sentiment in France. The officer responds: "Mademoiselle, we're not preventing you from being in love. It's just that you should really choose better." The officer thereby voices another set of norms ascribed to patriarchy and communalism—but equally foundational to French nationalism—where women's (and men's) romantic, sexual, and marriage choices are not their own, and where the community's or nation's identity is maintained not only through endogamy but also through the careful surveillance and regulation of individuals' private and intimate lives.

If we remember Foucault's history of the family in relation to governmentality, it is unsurprising that the modern policing of external borders and internal boundaries so often entails the regulation of the intimate sphere of marriage, sexuality, and romantic love. In Foucault's account, the father-headed family initially serves as the model for the art of government but soon becomes the privileged instrument of, and no longer simply the model for, good government. Indeed, as feminist scholars have argued, it is difficult to disentangle the family as model and the family as instrument since governing population—the paradigm of family as instrument—so often reinscribes the patriarchal family as model, both in the structural sense (the state as patriarch) and in the normative one (the norms of the proper family being reproduced tend to be patriarchal). Moreover, the division of life into public and private and the relegation of women to the latter domain, as well as the positioning of women as repositories of the nation's traditions and responsible for its continuation through social and biological reproduction, mean that the regulation of women has been central to the nation-state and modern nationalism. Finally, sex in marriage—part of the family-as-instrument paradigm—remains a site of state investment and, therefore, state surveillance, and not only with regard to migrants and minorities.

In contemporary France, the family continues to serve as model and instrument for governing population, its external borders and internal boundaries maintained by policing intimacy. This produces a certain irony: even as the patriarchal, communalist Muslim family has become a major source of public and political condemnation, portrayed as contrary to French values, the state's regulation of migrant marriages mirrors the very communalist patriarchy so ferociously criticized by pundits, politicians, judges, and the media with regard to Islam. Put another way, even as the state draws its internal boundaries against communalist Muslim fathers and brothers, it simultaneously mimics those very same patriarchal communalists as it seeks to protect the French nation through the policing of its external borders via binational marriages.

Notes

1. *Les Amoureux au ban public*, dir. Nicolas Ferran (2011), 70 mins. All translations in this chapter are my own.
2. The name of the organization—Les Amoureux au Ban Public (Lovers under a Public Ban)—is a reference to and a pun on the very famous French song by Georges Brassens, "Les Amoureux des bancs publics" (Lovers on public benches).
3. Fassin writes: "By external borders (*frontières externes*), I mean the limits of the national territory ... [which] juridically separate nationals and foreigners ... By internal boundaries (*frontières internes*), I mean the limits between racialized social categories inherited from a dual history of colonization and immigration: these limits distinguish between individuals and groups based on varying indexes of color, origin, culture and even religion" (Fassin 2010a: 6).

4. Ayşe Parla (this volume) makes a similar point about the Turkish term *soydaş* (racial kin) and the way it embodies what she calls "the paradoxical interplay between border and boundary" (61).
5. Article 26.4 of the Civil Code allows for the public prosecutor to contest, post facto, the naturalization of a nonnational via marriage if the marriage was based on lies or fraud.
6. As Jennifer Cole (2014) points out in an article on Malagasy-French unions, immigration regulations also promote the nuclear family as the normative family.
7. I do not attend here to the effects of this intrusion on the lives of individual subjects, a subject I have discussed elsewhere (Fernando 2014a). Neveu Kringelbach (2013) also details how this process is experienced by couples. In an article on Franco-Malagasy unions and subsequent attempts to bring Malagasy family members to France, Cole explores in ethnographic depth how Malagasy women and their French husbands negotiate intrusions into their domestic and intimate lives, and the toll this kind of intrusion can take. She notes, for instance, that "Men who want to marry Malagasy women resent the obstacles that the French state puts in their path. Often, however, they cannot quite shake the fear that they are perhaps being tricked by their spouses" (Cole 2014: 538). Obviously, this has an impact on the relationship, and French officials' doubts about the viability of a marriage can become a self-fulfilling prophecy.
8. For more on the specifics of these and other integration measures, including their gendered dimension, see Farris (2017).
9. Farris writes of the "deep contradictions" that traverse the gender-equality rhetoric of French integration policy: "on the one hand, non EU-migrant women are strongly encouraged to liberate themselves from the patriarchal cultures supposedly preventing them from knowing their civil rights; on the other hand, they are invited to be good mothers, whereby 'good motherhood' means conforming to strictly sanctioned models of French parenthood and, above all, womanhood" (Farris 2017: 99).
10. Méliane uses slang terms for ethno-racial categories: *rebeus* is back slang for Arabs, and *gaulois* refers to White French. *Blacks* refers to youths of Antillean or sub-Saharan African descent.
11. See also Rhacel Parreñas (this volume), who argues that the Philippines government's (half-hearted) attempts to safeguard Filipina domestic workers going abroad speaks to the protectionist impulses of the modern nation-state when it comes to "its" women. However, as both Parreñas and I underscore, the state is less interested in the actual welfare of these women –Parreñas shows how many of these measures are actually counterproductive to the domestic workers' welfare—and more interested in appearing as a father-figure like protector.

References

ABP (Les Amoureux au Ban Public). 2008. "Peu de meilleur et trop de pire: soupconnés, humiliés, réprimés, des couples mixtes témoignent." La Cimade.

Available at: https://www.lacimade.org/publication/peu-de-meilleur-et-trop-de-pire-soupconnes-humilies-reprimes-des-couples-mixtes-temoignent/ (accessed July 26, 2019).

Amara, Fadela. 2006. *Breaking the Silence: French Women's Voices from the Ghetto*, trans. Helen Chenut. Berkeley: University of California Press.

Balibar, Etienne. 2007. "Uprising in the Banlieues." *Constellations* 14(1): 47–71.

Benabdessadok, Chérifa. 2004. "Ni putes ni soumises: de la marche à l'université d'automne." *Hommes et Migrations* 1245: 64–74.

Cole, Jennifer. 2014. "Working Mis/Understandings: The Tangled Relationship between Kinship, Franco-Malagasy Binational Marriages, and the French State." *Cultural Anthropology* 29(3): 527–51.

Farris, Sara R. 2017. *In the Name of Women's Rights: The Rise of Femonationalism*. Durham, NC: Duke University Press.

Fassin, Didier. 2010a. "Introduction: Frontières extérieures, frontières intérieures." In Didier Fassin (ed.), *Les nouvelles frontières de la société française*, 5–24. Paris: La Découverte.

Fassin, Didier (ed.). 2010b. *Les nouvelles frontières de la société française*. Paris: La Découverte.

Fassin, Didier, and Éric Fassin (eds). 2006. *De la question sociale à la question raciale? Representer la société française*. Paris: La Découverte.

Fassin, Éric. 2010. "National Identities and Transnational Intimacies: Sexual Democracy and the Politics of Immigration in Europe." *Public Culture* 22(3): 507–29.

Fernando, Mayanthi L. 2009. "Exceptional Citizens: Secular Muslim Women and the Politics of Difference in France." *Social Anthropology* 17(4): 379–92.

——— 2013. "Save the Muslim Woman, Save the Republic: Ni Putes Ni Soumises and the Ruse of Neoliberal Sovereignty." *Modern and Contemporary France* 21(2): 147–65.

——— 2014a. "Intimacy Surveilled: Religion, Sex, and Secular Cunning." *Signs* 39(3): 685–708.

——— 2014b. *The Republic Unsettled: Muslim French and the Contradictions of Secularism*. Durham, NC: Duke University Press.

Foucault, Michel. 1991. "Governmentality." In Graham Burchell, Colin Gordon, and Peter Miller (eds), *The Foucault Effect: Studies in Governmentality*, 87–104. Chicago: University of Chicago Press.

Hachimi Alaoui, Myriam. 2012. "L'intégration sous condition: valeurs non négociables et égalité des sexes." *Canadian Journal of Women and the Law* 24(1): 114–34.

Kemp, Anna. 2009. "Marianne d'aujourd'hui? The Figure of the Beurette in Contemporary French Feminist Discourse." *Modern and Contemporary France* 17(1): 19–33.

Méliane, Loubna. 2003. *Vivre libre*. Paris: Oh!

Neveu Kringelbach, Hélène. 2013. "'Mixed Marriage', Citizenship and the Policing of Intimacy in Contemporary France." International Migration Institute, Working Paper No. 77. Available at: https://www.imi-n.org/publications/wp-77-13 (accessed July 26, 2019).

Scott, Joan Wallach. 2018. *Sex and Secularism*. Princeton: Princeton University Press.
Surkis, Judith. 2010. "Hymenal Politics: Marriage, Secularism, and French Sovereignty." *Public Culture* 22(3): 531–56.
Ticktin, Miriam. 2008. "Sexual Violence as the Language of Border Control: Where French Feminists and Anti-Immigrant Rhetoric Meet." *Signs* 33(4): 863–89.
Winter, Bronwyn. 2009. "Marianne Goes Multicultural: *Ni putes ni soumises* and the Republicanisation of Ethnic Minority Women in France." In Vesna Drapac and André Lambelet (eds), *French History and Civilization: Papers from the George Rudé Seminar*, Vol. 2, 228–40. Available at: https://h-france.net/rude/wp-content/uploads/2017/08/vol2_Winter_Final_Version.pdf (accessed July 26, 2019).

PART II

Legal Disbarring

6
An Earlier Ban
Chinese Exclusion and Plenary Power

Mae Ngai

The first two executive orders pronounced by Donald Trump upon assuming office in 2016 concerned immigration and refugee policy, emphasizing the hard nativist lines he took during his campaign: a temporary ban on refugee admissions and all entries from seven majority-Muslim countries (the "Muslim ban"),[1] and an order to aggressively stop the entry and pursue the removal of undocumented immigrations (the "Wall").[2] Over the eighteen months after the orders were issued, implementation was uneven, but seemingly inexorable in the pursuit of its aims. Although legal challenges slowed the Muslim ban from taking full effect until the US Supreme Court upheld it in June, 2018, and Congress has yet to authorize funding for building the border wall, an aggressive campaign to deport undocumented immigrants has swept the country. The president also ordered the end of the Temporary Protected Status program, which shielded 60,000 Haitian unauthorized refugees from deportation; the end to the Deferred Action for Childhood Arrivals (DACA), which protects 750,000 young undocumented immigrants, the so-called DREAMers; threatened to cut federal funding to states and cities that decline to "cooperate" with immigration law enforcement; and announced his desire to end "chain migration," that is, family-sponsored migration, which has long been the principal method of issuing visas for permanent residents (green cards). Perhaps most shocking was the decision in the spring of 2018 to bring criminal charges against asylum seekers and to take more than 2,000 children from their parents, detaining them in cages in separate detention facilities.[3] Throughout 2018 and 2019 the Trump administration continued to prevent asylum seekers from entering the country and from making lawful claims to asylum.

The Trump administration's immigration policies—notably, the Muslim ban and border enforcement, discussed by Farris (this volume)—have important legal and political precedents. They recall the so-called Tribal Twenties (Higham 1988) when racial nativism triumphed when Congress passed the Immigration Act of 1924, which imposed national origin quotas against eastern and southern European immigration and reduced overall immigration to just 15 percent of the annual average before World War I. Policies based on the racialized demonization of Mexicans and Muslims rehearse the historical treatment of Asian Americans, including the Chinese and Asiatic exclusion laws and the internment of Japanese Americans in concentration camps during World War II. On the one hand, these precedents give the president's nativist agenda extraordinary support and power. On the other hand, contemporary responses to Trump's policies, in both popular opinion and in the rulings of lower federal courts, suggest a growing unease over the legal foundation of immigration policy, that is, plenary power.

Chinese Exclusion

Plenary power refers to Congress's plenary, or absolute, authority over certain matters pertaining to the nation's sovereignty. These include the conduct of foreign relations (including ratifying treaties and declaring war); authority over peoples and territories under US sovereign control (Native American tribes; Puerto Rico, Guam, and other island possessions; and military bases such as Guantanamo); and immigration (entry and removal). Constitutional protections do not apply to parties governed under plenary power (Aleinikoff 2002).

Immigration plenary power is rooted in the assertion that the regulation of immigration is a matter of national security. But this was not always the case. Before the American Civil War there was no regulation of immigration by the national government, owing to the slave states' refusal to allow federal control over the movement of property in enslaved persons. In the North during the colonial period and the early republic, towns and states invoked a kind of territoriality to disqualify certain "outsiders" from poor relief, but in the nineteenth century emigration increasingly became viewed as a question of labor and labor mobility (hence the Southern opposition). When the Supreme Court ruled in 1875 that the regulation of immigration was a federal matter, specifically the collection of a head tax (the fee that states imposed on each arriving person as a bond against future indigence), the court classified immigration as a form of "foreign commerce" and immigrants as "articles of commerce," and therefore subject to federal and not local regulation (Bilder 1996; Hirota 2017; Parker 2015).[4]

The Chinese Exclusion Act of 1882 was the first law to exclude a class of aliens from entering the country.[5] After several hundred years of virtually unfettered colonial settlement and immigration, the Chinese Exclusion Act was the first law of categorical exclusion. It was also the first to explicitly name a country or people for exclusion.

Exclusion means not just barring entry from those on the outside. It also underwrites the idea that those already domiciled in the country have no right to be there. Immigration exclusion is therefore a policy that erects both external borders and internal boundaries. In a sense, the anti-Chinese movement first created an internal boundary, with the aim of establishing an external border, which in turn reinforced the internal boundary. Passage of the Chinese Exclusion Act culminated in several decades of nativist agitation in California, which organized around the racist theory that Chinese were a "coolie race," innately servile, incapable of liberal subjecthood and its qualities of political independence and free labor, and hence unassimilable (Hsu 2000; Ngai 2010, 2015; Salyer 1995; Saxton 1976). The power of the coolie trope lay in its association with African slavery in the South; it was racial shorthand for the idea that Chinese were a threat to free (white) labor. In fact the Chinese who came to America were not enslaved or indentured but came as voluntary migrants, first during the California gold rush of 1849. They worked as independent prospectors, as members of share cooperatives and small Chinese companies, and as waged workers for white-owned companies, and least of all on contracts.[6]

The idea that Chinese were unfree "coolies" emerged during the state gubernatorial election campaign of 1852, a central plank in the platform of John Bigler, the governor who was running for reelection. Bigler issued a "special message," which warned that tens of thousands of Chinese, under contracts to work for $3 or $4 a month, were flooding the state and called for laws restricting their immigration. The message was published in the newspapers and printed on leaflets that were distributed throughout the gold mining districts.[7] Bigler would be the first but not the last California politician to ride the Chinese Question to office. The Chinese "coolie question" became a staple in Democratic Party demagoguery in California, surviving the Civil War and sustaining a racist vision of "free labor" well into the twentieth century.

Leaders of San Francisco's Chinese community spoke out against Bigler's message. Yuan Sheng (also known as Norman Assing) wrote a letter to the governor, which was published in the nineteenth-century San Francisco newspaper the *Daily Alta*, in which he announced himself as "a Chinaman, a republican, and a lover of free institutions; [and] much attached to the principles of the Government of the United States."[8] The letter was angry and direct: the "effects of your late message has been thus far to prejudice the public mind against my people, to enable those who wait the opportunity to hunt them down, and rob them of the rewards of their toil." He challenged the logic of Bigler's notion that "by excluding population from this State, you enhance its wealth. I have always considered that population was wealth; particularly a population of producers."

Assing pointedly reminded Bigler of his own immigrant heritage, and America's: "immigration made you what you are—your nation what it is ... I am sure your Excellency cannot, if you would, prevent your being called the descendant of an immigrant, for I am sure you do not boast of being a descendant of the red men," which got to the heart of American historical amnesia. He acknowledged that "you have degraded the negro because of your holding him in involuntary servitude, and because for the sake of union in some of your states such is tolerated." More to the point, Assing wrote, "amongst this class you would endeavor to place us; and no doubt it would be pleasing to some would-be freemen to mark the brand of servitude upon us." He insisted, "we are not the degraded race you would make us. We came amongst you as mechanics or traders, and following every honorable business of life."

Norman Assing used his own case as a naturalized citizen to refute Bigler's claim that no Chinese had ever made the United States his domicile or applied for naturalization. Two other Chinese leaders, Hab Wa and Tong Achick, similarly argued that, "if the privileges of your laws are open to us, some of us will doubtless acquire your habits, your language, your ideas, your feelings, your morals, your forms, and become citizens of Your country; many have already adopted your religion (as) their own; —and we will be good citizens."[9] These men knew the self-fulfilling consequences of marginalization, that immigrants kept separate and apart are far less likely to become integrated into the host society.

It would be thirty years from the time of Bigler's election for the anti-Chinese movement to secure national exclusion legislation in 1882. During these decades Chinese in California came under increasing legal and bodily attack. San Francisco passed municipal ordinances to oppress the Chinese—for example, walking on the sidewalk with a bamboo pole in order to harass Chinese vegetable peddlers; and the "cubic air ordinance," aimed at Chinese tenants rather than the landlords who rented small rooms (Ngai 2010). The Chinese Question became relevant in national politics only after the Civil War and after Northern liberals tired of race politics and turned their back on Reconstruction. The Chinese Question offered a new racial politics that enabled the rebuilding of the Democratic Party without reference to the Negro Question (Saxton 1976).

Exclusion unleashed a wave of lynching, assault, and arson aimed at driving out the Chinese, one even greater than the violence that occurred during the lead-up to the law's passage in 1882 (Lew-Williams 2018; Pfaelzer 2007). Congress also raised the stakes of exclusion. The Scott Act of 1888 declared null and void government-issued return certificates that granted Chinese living in America the right to reenter if they traveled abroad. Chae Chan Ping had left the United States in 1884 for a visit to China, and was aboard a ship with a return certificate when the Scott Act was passed. Immigration agents denied him entry when he landed at San Francisco. Chae Chan Ping then sued the government, arguing that his return certificate had been duly issued. In order to justify the unprecedented nature of Chinese exclusion the US Supreme Court shifted its view of immigration from being a matter of commerce to one concerning the nation's sovereignty. The court stated:

> To preserve its independence, and give security against foreign aggression and encroachment, is the highest duty of every nation, and to attain these ends nearly all other considerations are to be subordinated. It matters not in what form such aggression and encroachment come, whether from the foreign nation acting in its national character, or from vast hordes of its people crowding in upon us ... If, therefore, the government of the United States, through its legislative department, considers the presence of foreigners of a different race in this country, who will not assimilate with us, to be dangerous to its peace and security, their exclusion is not to be stayed because at the time there are no actual hostilities with the nation of which the foreigners are subjects.[10]

The idea that Chinese were agents of a foreign power was, at one level, ironic, in light of the Qing government's ban on emigration through most of the nineteenth century on the one hand, and the history of American colonial settlement by Europeans with royal patents and charters on the other. Of greater consequence was the fundamental assertion of the sovereign right to exclude and expel on grounds that all immigrants are agents, or potential agents, of foreign states. The geopolitical cast given to immigration belied the fact that in the nineteenth century the preponderance of global migration was driven by individual (and family) desires for economic improvement. In cases of political motivation, it was usually to escape tyranny, not to transplant it. Moreover, migrants often identified with regions and dialect groups, not nation-states, which in some cases had not yet formed (Italy and Germany being cases in point). But by making immigration a matter of national security, the Supreme Court gave Congress absolute authority over its regulation and denied that aliens had any presumptive rights in matters of entry and removal. In *Fong Yue Ting v. US* (1893), which upheld summary deportation of Chinese, the Supreme Court extended the right to exclude to the right to expel, asserting that aliens "remain in this country except by the license, permission, and sufferance of Congress."[11]

If the trend began with the Chinese, with whom few Americans had sympathy, the jurisprudence that upheld arbitrary treatment of the Chinese became the normative basis for all immigration law. Justice Brewer dissented in *Fong Yue Ting v. US* (1893) on the grounds that the absolute right to expel denied constitutional rights of due process, presciently asking:

> It is true this statute is directed only against the obnoxious Chinese, but, if the power exists, who shall say it will not be exercised to-morrow against other classes and other people? If the guaranties of these [constitutional] amendments can be thus ignored in order to get rid of this distasteful class, what security have others that a like disregard of its provisions may not be resorted to?

Racialized Alienage and Alien Citizens

By treating immigration control as an incidence of national sovereignty, the Supreme Court carved out a special realm for immigrants where constitutional rights do not apply: rights of equal treatment and due process, the right to legal counsel and a jury of one's peers, the right to be protected from unreasonable search and seizure—even the presumption of innocence (Salyer 1995). This exception pertains only to matters of admission and expulsion—at the border, as it is imagined. It does not apply to immigrants while they are territorially present. The US Constitution protects all persons who are present on US soil, whether they are citizens or noncitizens. These two realms of rights are theoretically distinct, one operating at the border and the other within the nation's borders but, as Linda Bosniak (2008) and Kevin R. Johnson (2000) have argued, they are entangled in myriad ways and in fact not separable. The lack of immigration rights leads to the violation of civil rights. For example, what does it mean for the government to apprehend someone crossing the border without authorization? Does it mean that Border Patrol agents must witness someone at the moment when he or she literally crosses the international boundary line? In 1933 the Immigration Bureau asserted that unlawful border crossing was an act that "continued" until the alien reached the city that was their "final destination," and hence its authority to search and detain without warrant suspected unlawful entrants extended to the entire interior of the country (Ngai 2004). Since the 1940s immigration authorities have defined a 100-mile zone from the boundary line, within which Border Patrol officers may operate with certain extra-constitutional powers (ACLU n.d.).[12] Since the 1970s the courts have upheld the use of racial profiling by immigration agents against persons who appear to be Mexican or Hispanic (Johnson 2000).[13] In 1996 the government instituted a policy of "expedited removal" (no hearing and removal in 24 to 48 hours) for those apprehended within the 100-mile border zone within two weeks of arrival.[14] The Trump administration has declared its intention to extend expedited removal to the entire interior of the United States.[15]

The collapsing of the border into the interior thus produces legal disadvantages for immigrants—theoretically all immigrants but, practically, all people who look like "illegal immigrants," a racial stereotype that over time has applied to mostly non-Europeans, regardless of their actual legal status: Chinese and other Asians; Mexicans and other Latino/as; and persons who appear to be "Middle Eastern, Arab, or Muslim," the last an artful racial-religious stereotype that emerged after 9/11 (Volpp 2002). The operation of immigration law under plenary power allows for racial discriminations, as Justice Frankfurter remarked in a Cold War case, "whether immigration laws have been crude and cruel, whether they may have reflected xenophobia in general or anti-Semitism or anti-Catholicism, the responsibility belongs to Congress."[16] Communities of color are selectively targeted for surveillance, harassment, and deportation, often tearing long-time immigrants from their families, jobs, and property. And owing to plenary power, including laws passed in 1996 for "mandatory" and "expedited" removals, immigrants have few if any rights of due process in deportation proceedings.

Immigration law, with its extra-constitutional means of enforcement, contributes fundamentally to the racialization of non-European groups. Plenary power, with its power to discriminate, both results from and reproduces the racial formations of nonwhites. One could say that immigration law is a basic mode of racial management for non-native-born nonwhite groups: just as slavery, Jim Crow segregation, and post-civil-rights mass incarceration have structured the racial subordination of African Americans, immigration law structures racism against Asians, Latino/as, and Muslims.

The racialization of foreignness creates internal boundaries of difference that exceed immigration matters. It produces a category that I have called the "alien citizen," that is, a person who is an American citizen—whether by virtue of his or her birth in the United States or by naturalization—but whose citizenship is suspect, if not denied, on account of the racialized identity of his or her immigrant ancestry (Ngai 2007). In this construction, the foreignness of non-European peoples is deemed unalterable, making nationality a kind of racial trait. Alienage, then, becomes a permanent condition, passed from generation to generation, adhering even to the native-born citizen. Qualifiers like "accidental" citizen, "presumed" citizen, or even "terrorist" citizen, have been used in political and legal arguments to denigrate, compromise, and nullify the US citizenship of "unassimilable" Chinese, "enemy-race" Japanese, Mexican "illegal aliens," and Muslim "terrorists."[17] The social currency of alien citizenship derives from the idea that non-European peoples are racially—or, in modern expression, culturally—backward, that they are unable or unwilling to assimilate, and that they are unfit for liberal citizenship. Racism thus creates a problem of misrecognition for citizens of Asian or Latino descent and those of Muslim faith.

Alien citizenship is more than a racial metaphor. As a legal matter, alien citizenship involves the nullification of the rights of citizenship—from the right to be territorially present to the range of civil rights and liberties—without the formal revocation of citizenship status. The repatriation (territorial removal) of 400,000 ethnic Mexicans during the Great Depression, half of them US citizens (Hoffman 1974; Balderrama & Rodriguez 1995), and the internment of 120,000 people of Japanese descent during World War II, two-thirds of them US citizens (Ngai 2004; Weglyn 1976), may be considered instances of official alien citizenship. In both cases, alien citizenship derived directly from the legal exclusion of the citizens' immigrant forebears from the normative path of immigration and naturalization (that is, legal entry to settlement to citizenship), whether by statutory exclusion from naturalization or by undocumented status.

The concept of alien citizenship is, of course, an oxymoron. Asian Americans' and Mexican Americans' struggles against racial exclusion and subordination have always included efforts to secure full rights of citizenship, which is to say, to eliminate the "alien" from "alien citizen." But, from the other direction, there also have been efforts to resolve the contradiction by formally denying territorial birthright citizenship to certain groups—that is, to eliminate the "citizen" from the "alien citizen," to render her wholly alien. These efforts are diverse but invariably involve challenges to the Citizenship Clause of the Fourteenth Amendment, which provides that, "All persons born or naturalized in the United States, and subject to the jurisdiction thereof, are citizens of the United States and of the State wherein they reside."

Immigration Policy under Trump: Wither Plenary Power?

Notwithstanding Trump's loyal base of ardent nationalists, public opposition to his administration's immigration policy is widespread and strong. Polling data as of June 2018 show that a majority of people continue to oppose building the wall (58 percent) and the Muslim ban (52 percent), and support the legalization of undocumented persons (70 percent). The data are generally consistent over time and across polling organizations (Jones 2016; Telhami 2016).[18] On the ground, moreover, there is active resistance to the nativist agenda, as indexed by mass demonstrations, the mobilization of local governments and institutions of civil society (for example, universities) to provide resources and sanctuary for immigrants, and community organizing to defend and protect immigrants ("know your rights" and "rapid response" training).

Notably, during the first year of Trump's immigration orders, federal judges issued temporary restraining orders and temporary injunctions against the Muslim ban, until the Supreme Court upheld it in June 2018.[19] Meanwhile, federal judges in San Francisco, Chicago, and Philadelphia blocked the administration from punishing so-called sanctuary cities by withholding federal funds if they did not cooperate with immigration enforcement.[20]

The latter case is grounded in the anti-commandeering principle of the Tenth Amendment, which states that the federal government cannot compel states to enforce federal laws. The Supreme Court's conservative justices may not be willing to jettison states' rights in this case. However, the success of legal challenges to the Muslim bans in federal district courts and circuit courts of appeal are somewhat surprising in light of the entrenched doctrine of immigration plenary power. In fact, the administration was right in its claim that it holds broad executive authority over immigration matters. One might have expected that the courts would uphold the Muslim ban on grounds that the president acted in the interest of national security, as he averred, and as provided for by section 212(f) of the Immigration and Nationality Act, which gives the president authority to suspend entry of any alien or class of aliens when considered to be "detrimental to the interests of the United States." Yet circuit courts of appeal for the Fourth and Ninth circuits found Trump's animus against Muslims so manifest and odious that it agreed that the exclusion order is probably a violation of the establishment and religious freedom clauses of the First Amendment. The Ninth Circuit ruled against the travel ban on similar grounds, as well as on the narrower statutory grounds that it violated the nondiscrimination provision of the Immigration and Nationality Act and that the president had not proved that the entry of foreign nationals from the targeted seven countries would be detrimental to the interests of the United States.[21] The Supreme Court's upholding of the ban was a narrow ruling, in which the five-to-four majority willfully ignored evidence of anti-Muslim animus and suggested that, had there been religious discrimination, the ban would in fact have failed.

There have been far fewer legal challenges to the administration's aggressive removal policies, many of which would seem to violate due process, especially the planned extension of expedited removal to the entire interior of the country. The premise that expedited removal applies to persons within two weeks of unauthorized entry runs into considerable complication in most of the "interior," including in cities, where a majority of undocumented immigrants live and have resided for much longer periods of time. An estimated two-thirds of the 11 million undocumented immigrants in the United States have been living in the country for more than ten years (Krogstad et al. 2017).

Although the interior enforcement of expedited removal has not yet been implemented at the time of writing, the Department of Homeland Security has aggressively pursued a broad removal program, prompting immigration agents to celebrate the removal of their "shackles." In March 2017, the secretary of homeland security announced, pursuant to the executive order, elimination of all enforcement "priorities," in effect making every undocumented person an equal priority for deportation, regardless of circumstance and despite the fact that the government does not have the wherewithal to actually attempt removal of the 11 million undocumented people living in the United States. Under the Obama administration the number of deportations rose considerably, but the administration set priorities that emphasized border enforcement over interior enforcement and deportation of persons with criminal records over noncriminals. Deportations from the interior between January and September 2017 increased dramatically by 37 percent compared to the same time period in 2016. Immigration and Customs Enforcement officers monitor local courthouses in order to apprehend people who appear as plaintiffs and witnesses. Immigrants with standing orders of deportation who have been allowed to remain in the country (some for many years) because they are stable working members of the community and pose no threat to society as long as they "checked in" once a year are now routinely removed (Pierce & Seeley 2017).

Border Patrol officers are denying Mexican and Central American asylum seekers interviews and summarily returning them to whence they came, in violation of US policy and international convention. That policy became even more cruel (and likewise unlawful under US and international law) in the spring of 2018 when the Department of Justice decided to bring criminal charges against asylum seekers and to separate children (some less than a year old) from their parents (Hegarty 2018; HRF 2017). Amidst widespread outrage, a federal judge ordered the Trump administration to return the children taken at the border to their parents within thirty days (fourteen days for children under the age of five).[22]

The actions of the administration against Muslim immigrants, undocumented immigrants, and asylum seekers have created tremendous fear and suffering and are broadly opposed by the public. Yet plenary power would appear to make Trump's deportation policies largely impervious to judicial interference. Congress repealed the Chinese exclusion laws in 1943 but the principles of national security and plenary power continue to undergird American immigration law. It is highly unusual for the federal courts, especially the Supreme Court, to set aside precedent in response to contemporary moral and political sensibilities. The overturning of segregation and the racist philosophy of "separate but equal" by the Supreme

Court in *Brown v. Board of Education* (1954) is a rare case. Rulings in the federal courts against the Muslim ban (at least before the Supreme Court upheld it) suggest that it may be becoming more difficult to call "national security" into service to support racial and religious animus. To be sure, this is an optimistic view. The more pessimistic reading of our times is one of an authoritarian regime that disregards even its own laws and courts when they do not suit its agenda of racial nativism.

Notes

1. Executive Order No. 13769, January 27, 2017 (https://www.whitehouse.gov/presidential-actions/executive-order-protecting-nation-foreign-terrorist-entry-united-states/, accessed August 3, 2019), banned all travel from seven countries (Iran, Iraq, Libya, Somalia, Sudan, Syria, and Yemen) and all refugee entries for 120 days, and other measures. Executive Order No. 13780, March 6, 2017 (https://www.whitehouse.gov/presidential-actions/executive-order-protecting-nation-foreign-terrorist-entry-united-states-2/, accessed August 3, 2019) removed Iraq from the list, delayed the implementation date, and exempted certain persons who were previously authorized to travel to the United States. Presidential Proclamation No. 9645, September 24, 2017 (https://www.whitehouse.gov/presidential-actions/presidential-proclamation-enhancing-vetting-capabilities-processes-detecting-attempted-entry-united-states-terrorists-public-safety-threats/, accessed August 3, 2019) designated seven countries (Chad, Libya, Syria, Yemen, Somalia, North Korea, and Venezuela) for partial or full restriction on entry to the United States until such time that the country in question provides "adequate information" on their citizens who apply for US visas. Implementation of the travel bans were enjoined by federal courts until the US Supreme Court ruled on December 5, 2017, that they could be implemented immediately, pending the court's review of lower court rulings against the bans.
2. Executive Order No. 13767, January 25, 2017 (https://www.whitehouse.gov/presidential-actions/executive-order-border-security-immigration-enforcement-improvements/, accessed August 3, 2019) ordered the planning, funding, and building of a southern border wall; expanding detention facilities; expanding expedited removal programs; expanding the Border Patrol force; and encouraged federal–state cooperation agreements among other measures.
3. For a summary of the Trump administration's first year of immigration initiatives, see Shear and Davis (2017).
4. *Chy Lung v. Freeman*, 92 US 75 (1875); *Henderson v. Mayor of New York*, 92 US 259 (1875).
5. The initial act called for a ten-year suspension of Chinese laborers; it was renewed in 1892 for another ten years, renewed indefinitely in 1902, and repealed in 1943. Chinese exclusion extended to all Asians by the Immigration Act of 1917 (creating a "barred Asiatic zone") and the Immigration and Nationality Act of 1924 (excluding all persons "ineligible to citizenship," a reference

to all Asians as ruled by the US Supreme Court in Ozawa v. US, 260 US 178 [1922] and US v. Thind, 261 US 204 [1923]).
6. A small number of Chinese came on contracts in the first years of the gold rush, but these ventures, usually backed by European investors in China, were quickly abandoned because contracts were not enforceable. The same was the case among gold-seekers of other nationalities (Chileans, Mexicans, white Americans), who also brought workers under contract. Irrespective of nationality, contracted workers simply walked away to find their own diggings (Navarro 2000; Ngai 2015).
7. See John Bigler, "Special Message from the Governor," *Journal of Third Session of Legislature of the State of California* 78 (January 1852).
8. Assing (1852). All quotes in this and the next paragraph are from this source.
9. Hab Wa and Tong K. Achick, "Letter of the Chinamen to His Excellency, Gov. Bigler," in *An Analysis of the Chinese Question: Consisting of a Special Message of the Governor, and, in reply thereto, Two Letters of the Chinamen and a Memorial of the Citizens of San Francisco* (San Francisco, 1852).
10. Chae Chan Ping v. US ("Chinese Exclusion Case"), 130 US 581 (1889).
11. Fong Yue Ting v. US, 149 US 698 (1893).
12. Amendments to the Immigration and Nationality Act, HR 386, 79th Congress (1946); Dept of Justice regulations issued 1953, now codified as 8 USC § 1357(a)(3).
13. US v. Brignoni-Ponce, 422 US 873 (1975). The court ruled that Mexican appearance alone did not justify stopping someone, but had to be combined with other factors, which were defined as loosely as the appearance of a car.
14. Illegal Immigration Reform and Immigrant Responsibility Act (1996).
15. Executive Order No. 13767. The 100-mile zone does not apply just to the southern border but to all borders; hence New York, Los Angeles, and other major cities lie within it.
16. Harisiades v. Shaughnessy, 342 US 580 (1952).
17. See e.g. United States v. Wong Kim Ark, 169 US 649, 731 (1898) (Harlan, J., dissenting); Hamdi v. Rumsfeld, 542 US 507, 554 (2004) (Scalia, J., dissenting); Padilla v. Rumsfeld, 352 F.3d 695, 728 (2d Cir. 2003) (Wesley, J., concurring in part, dissenting in part).
18. See also the figures compiled by Polling Report (available at: http://www.pollingreport.com/immigration.htm, accessed October 10, 2019).
19. Trump v. Hawaii, 138 S. Ct. 542 (2017).
20. City and County of San Francisco v. Trump, No. 3:17-cv-00485, US District Court for the Northern District of California Case (2018); City and County of San Francisco v. Sessions, No. 3:17-cv-04642, US District Court for the Northern District of California (2018); City of Chicago v. Sessions, No. 17-2991, CA 7th (2018); City of Philadelphia v. Sessions, 280 F. Supp. 3rd 579 (2017).
21. Hawaii v. Trump, No. 17-15589 (9th Cir. 2017); International Refugee Assistance Project v. Trump, 857 F.3d 554 (4th Cir. 2017).
22. Ms. L. et al. v. ICE, Order granting plaintiffs' motion for class-wide preliminary injunction, US District Court, Southern District of California (June 27, 2018).

References

ACLU (American Civil Liberties Union). n.d. "The Constitution in the 100-mile Border Zone." Available at: https://www.aclu.org/other/constitution-100-mile-border-zone (accessed July 29, 2019).

Aleinikoff, T. Alexander. 2002. *Semblances of Sovereignty: The Constitution, the State, and American Citizenship.* Cambridge, MA: Harvard University Press.

Assing, Norman. 1852. "To His Excellency Gov. Bigler," *Daily Alta California,* May 5, 1852, p. 4.

Balderrama, Francisco E., and Raymond Rodriguez. 1995. *Decade of Betrayal: Mexican Repatriation in the 1930s.* Albuquerque: University of New Mexico Press.

Bilder, Mary Sarah. 1996. "The Struggle over Immigration: Indentured Servants, Slaves, and Articles of Commerce." *Missouri Law Review* 61(4): 743–824.

Bosniak, Linda. 2008. *The Citizen and the Alien: Dilemmas of Contemporary Membership.* Princeton: Princeton University Press.

Hegarty, Aaron. 2018. "Timeline: Immigrant Children Separated from Families at the Border." *USA Today,* June 27. Available at: https://www.usatoday.com/story/news/2018/06/27/immigrant-children-family-separation-border-timeline/734014002/ (accessed July 29, 2019).

Higham, John. 1988 [1955]. *Strangers in the Land: Patterns of American Nativism, 1860–1925.* New Brunswick, NJ: Rutgers University Press.

Hirota, Hidetaka. 2017. *Expelling the Poor: Atlantic Seaboard States and the Origins of American Immigration Policy.* New York: Oxford University Press.

Hoffman, Abraham. 1974. *Unwanted Mexican Americans in the Great Depression: Repatriation Pressures 1929–39.* Tucson: University of Arizona Press.

HRF (Human Rights First). 2017. "Violations at the Border: El Paso Sector." Available at: http://www.humanrightsfirst.org/sites/default/files/hrf-violations-at-el-paso-border-rep.pdf (accessed July 29, 2019).

Hsu, Madeline. 2000. *Dreaming of Gold, Dreaming of Home.* Stanford: Stanford University Press.

Johnson, Kevin R. 2000. "The Case Against Racial Profiling in Immigration Enforcement." *Washington University Law Review* 78(3): 675–736.

Jones, Bradley. 2016. "Americans Views of Immigrants Marked by Widening Partisan, Generational Divides." Pew Research Center. Available at: http://www.pewresearch.org/fact-tank/2016/04/15/americans-views-of-immigrants-marked-by-widening-partisan-generational-divides/ (accessed July 29, 2019).

Krogstad, Jens Manuel, Jeffrey Passel, and D'Vera Cohn. 2017. "Five Facts about Illegal Immigration in the US." Pew Research Center. Available at: http://www.pewresearch.org/fact-tank/2017/04/27/5-facts-about-illegal-immigration-in-the-u-s/ (accessed July 29, 2019).

Lew-Williams, Beth. 2018. *The Chinese Must Go: Violence, Exclusion and the Making of Alien America.* Cambridge, MA: Harvard University Press.

Navarro, Rámon Gil. 2000. *The Gold Rush Diary of Ramón Gil Navarro,* ed. and trans. María del Carmen Ferreyra and David S. Reher. Lincoln: University of Nebraska Press.

Ngai, Mae. 2004. *Impossible Subjects: Illegal Aliens and the Making of Modern America*. Princeton: Princeton University Press.
—— 2007. "Birthright Citizenship and the Alien Citizen." *Fordham Law Review* 75(5): 2521–30.
—— 2010. *The Lucky Ones: One Family and the Extraordinary Invention of Chinese America*. Boston: Houghton Mifflin Harcourt.
—— 2015. "Chinese Gold Miners and the 'Chinese Question' in Nineteenth-Century California and Victoria." *Journal of American History* 101(4): 1082–1105.
Parker, Kunal. 2015. *Making Foreigners: Immigration and Citizenship Law in America, 1600–2000*. New York: Cambridge University Press.
Pfaelzer, Jean. 2007. *Driven Out: The Forgotten War Against Chinese Americans*. Berkeley: University of California Press.
Pierce, Sarah, and Andrew Seeley. 2017. "Immigration under Trump: A Review of Policy Shifts in the Year since Election." Migration Policy Institute, Policy Brief. Available at: https://www.migrationpolicy.org/research/immigration-under-trump-review-policy-shifts (accessed July 29, 2019).
Salyer, Lucy. 1995. *Laws Harsh as Tigers: Chinese Immigrants and the Shaping of Modern Immigration Law*. Chapel Hill: University of North Carolina Press.
Shear, Michael D., and Julie Hirschfeld Davis. 2017. "Stoking Fears, Trump Defied Bureaucracy to Advance Immigration Agenda," *New York Times*, December 23. Available at: https://www.nytimes.com/2017/12/23/us/politics/trump-immigration.html (accessed July 29, 2019).
Saxton, Alexander. 1976. *The Indispensable Enemy*. Berkeley: University of California Press.
Telhami, Shibley. 2016. "American Attitudes towards Muslims and Islam." Brookings Institute. Available at: https://www.brookings.edu/research/american-attitudes-toward-muslims-and-islam/ (accessed July 29, 2019).
Volpp, Leti. 2002. "The Citizen and the Terrorist." *UCLA Law Review* 49: 1575–1600.
Weglyn, Michi. 1976. *Years of Infamy: The Untold Story of America's Concentration Camps*. New York: William Morrow.

7
Manners of Exclusion
From the Asiatic Barred Zone to the Muslim Ban

Sherally Munshi

From the moment President Donald Trump signed it into law, on January 27, 2017, "the Muslim ban" became the focus of sustained outrage.[1] Almost immediately, tens of thousands of Americans gathered at airports across the country to protest the order and to embrace travelers. Lawyers were quick to file challenges and, within a day, obtained court orders suspending implementation of the ban. Nobel laureates, university presidents, tech company executives, former secretaries of state all condemned the Muslim ban. Even former Vice President Dick Cheney declared that the ban "goes against everything we stand for" (quoted in Moyer 2015).

Earlier that same week, the president signed another executive order, directing his administration to unleash the full force of the federal government on finding, arresting, and deporting undocumented immigrants living in the United States.[2] The order called for intensified interior enforcement, beginning with the hiring of some 10,000 immigration officials—a deportation force—to hunt undocumented persons. The order empowered local and state police officers to enforce immigration policies. According to a memorandum released by the Department of Homeland Security, Immigration and Customs Enforcement should make no distinction between "classes or categories of removable aliens ... All of those in violation of the immigration laws may be subject to immigration arrest, detention, and [deportation]" (DHS 2017). That order, though it exposes tens of millions of undocumented immigrants and visa holders to confinement and expulsion, generated far less outrage—no massive protests, few editorials.

What accounts for the differing response? Why does the one compel universal condemnation while the other is met with relative complacence? Why does the Muslim ban seem to betray "everything we stand for" but not an immigrant purge? This chapter seeks to answer these questions by recalling earlier controversies surrounding the exclusion of Asian immigrants. The Muslim ban, as critics have pointed out, recalls a crude nativism reminiscent of the Chinese Exclusion Act of 1882. As such, it represents a form of racist exclusion that, at least since the civil rights era, has been almost universally condemned. But this focus on expressive racism and official discrimination obscures the continuing legacies of Chinese exclusion, including, as Mae Ngai (this volume) argues, the establishment of the plenary power doctrine, which allows Congress almost absolute authority to exclude or deport immigrants for any reason. Moreover, while racist rhetoric has disappeared from the official language of law, the racial design of our exclusionary immigration regime has become almost entirely naturalized—so naturalized that those who decry the Muslim ban seem to tolerate what might otherwise be condemned as an intolerable human purge. In the United States, the cultural nativism that gave rise to Asian exclusion in the late nineteenth century has been strenuously disavowed in public discourse. But it left in place an architecture of nativism—legal structures and a rationale for excluding others—which remain a regular, if unremarkable, feature of our contemporary landscape.

The recent attempt to enact a Muslim ban is particularly resonant with attempts to pass a "Hindu" ban a century ago. Between 1910 and 1917, congressmen in the United States sought to pass a "Hindu exclusion" bill, loosely modeled after the Chinese Exclusion acts. Though the Supreme Court recognized in the "Chinese Exclusion Cases" that Congress had broad authority to restrict immigration—"however it may see fit"—congressmen seeking to pass a Hindu exclusion bill found themselves maneuvering within a changed political landscape. For a number of reasons they were frustrated in their efforts to pass such a crudely racist restriction. Eventually, exclusionists succeeded in reformulating their Hindu ban by replacing avowedly "offensive" vocabularies of race with more elegant, apparently race-neutral designs of geographic exclusion. In 1917, with overwhelming support, Congress passed a law barring immigration from an invented "Asiatic Barred Zone," dividing the human community not in terms of "race" but in terms of their place of origin and, later, nationality (Munshi 2016a).

February 2017 marked the centenary of the passage of the Asiatic Barred Zone Act. For the entire month, proponents of the Muslim ban scrambled to recast their own offensive legislation in other terms, insisting that the

Muslim ban was *not* a Muslim ban. As the president explained: "I'm now looking at territories. People were so upset when I used the word Muslim. Oh, you can't use the word Muslim. And I'm okay with that, because I'm talking territory instead of Muslim" (quoted in Johnson 2016). Federal judges and lawyers of the American Civil Liberties Union, among other legal advocates, have seized upon such statements as "smoking guns," evidencing impermissibly discriminatory intent (Cole 2017). But what is telling about the president's statements is not that they reveal a (barely disguised) discriminatory purpose, but that they disclose the ways in which "territory" and nationality continue to provide a legitimate basis for plainly discriminatory immigration policies.

By exploring the resonances between immigration restrictions past and present, my point is not to suggest merely that the past prefigures the present. Instead, I mean to foreground the ways in which collective memory, or committed amnesia, shapes contemporary immigration debates, informs a shared understanding of "what we stand for," and blinds us to forms of racial exclusivity, even cruelty, to which we remain inured.

"The Traditions of Empire ... Make No Distinction": Reformulating Race

In 1907, when thousands of Canadians gathered at the port of Vancouver to protest against the arrival of a few hundred Indian laborers, there was no clear precedent for excluding them. Until the turn of the twentieth century, there were relatively few restrictions on migration to the New World. Early laws regulating immigration to Canada were primarily concerned with facilitating migration, for instance, by guaranteeing safe passage to British settlers.[3] The British imperial system was sustained by the voluntary migration of colonial settlers as well as the involuntary migration of colonized subjects. By the turn of the twentieth century, more than 2 million British Indians had been transferred to colonies around the world as involuntary migrants. But it was the voluntary migration of a few thousand British Indians to the white-settler dominions—South Africa, Australia, and Canada—that precipitated a crisis within the British Empire, giving rise to new forms of migration control and new articulations of national identity (Mongia 2005).

Indian immigration to the white-settler dominions thus exposed a racial asymmetry within the British imperial system. By the late nineteenth century, British subjects living in the white-settler dominions had been granted rights to self-government. Indians, denied the same rights, were instead guaranteed "equal and impartial protection" within the British Empire under the Government of India Act of 1858. Settler independence and imperial equality had become incommensurable: the white-settler dominions asserted that self-government consisted in the right to exclude unwanted foreigners, Indians in particular; Indians argued that, as British subjects entitled to equal protection, they were guaranteed the same rights to travel within the empire as other imperial subjects (Munshi 2016a). As one observer wrote, Indian immigration to Canada presented the imperial government with a test: "There will either be one standard, or two, within the Empire of British subjects, interests, and privileges. If the latter, then it must be based on race privileges or race superiority" (quoted in Jensen 1988: 128).

To manage the crisis, the imperial government encouraged exclusionists in the white-settler dominions to adopt policies that carefully disguised discriminatory treatment. For instance, in 1896, before a gathering of colonial officials from the white-settler dominions, Joseph Chamberlain, secretary of state in the Colonial Office, reminded those assembled of the "traditions of the Empire, which make no distinction in favor of, or against, race or colour" (quoted in Lake & Reynolds 2008: 132). Expressing sympathy toward white exclusionists on the one hand, while emphasizing the importance of India to the British Empire on the other, Chamberlain cautioned against the drafting of overtly discriminatory legislation, which was bound to enrage Indians, particularly those who had already begun to agitate for independence. He continued:

> It's not because a man is of a different color from ourselves that he is necessarily an undesirable immigrant, but it is because he is dirty, or he is immoral, or he is a pauper, or has some other objection which can be defined in an Act of Parliament, and by which exclusion can be managed with regard to all those whom you really desire to exclude … I hope therefore [that] it may be possible for us to arrange a form of words which will avoid hurting the feelings of Her Majesty's subjects. (quoted in ibid.: 132)

The more artful form of exclusion recommended by Chamberlain on that occasion was the literacy test recently adopted by the colony of Natal. The prime minister of Natal, Henry Escombe, had modeled his literacy test after the United States' Immigration Restriction Act of 1897, which had been designed to restrict immigration from Southern and Eastern Europe. The American law required that new arrivals be able to read or write in their own language, but the Natal law, Escombe explained, "goes further." "To see the requirements of Natal in connection with India," immigrants would be required to demonstrate proficiency in a European language. The primary virtue of the literacy test was that it avoided any reference to race; as officials explained, it was not "open to objection that it persecuted persons of a particular color" (Lake & Reynolds 2008: 132). Though a similar literacy test had been vetoed in the United States by President Grover Cleveland, who described it as a "radical departure" from existing immigration policy, the "Natal Compromise" was seen as a model for emulation across the British Empire—a compromise between the imperial principle of equal treatment on the one hand, and emerging white nationalism on the other.[4] Within a few years, in one of its first acts of legislation as a new Commonwealth, Australia adopted a similar literacy test.

Notwithstanding the self-satisfaction of colonial governors, Indian subjects across the British Empire recognized that variations of the literacy test were intended to exclude Indians. Mohandas Gandhi, even after a decade challenging anti-Indian laws in South Africa, maintained his faith in the British promise of equal protection. But he did not fail to recognize or to point out to Prime Minister Chamberlain that "the Natal Act was passed with the deliberate intention of applying it almost exclusively to Indians" (quoted in Lake & Reynolds 2008: 132). Gandhi and others, increasingly frustrated with the British government's dissembling, began agitating not for equality but independence.

By the time the arrival of a few Indian passengers in Vancouver began drawing thousands of white protestors, declaring "Canada for Canadians," British imperial officials, sympathetic to their settler counterparts, recognized the desirability of restricting Indian immigrants. But they worried that a literacy test like the one adopted in Natal would no longer be tolerated, given the way such discriminatory policies had enraged Indian subjects across continents, galvanizing the increasingly transnational movement for Indian independence. Canadian officials then began scrambling to find a legal solution—again, one that would effectively bar Indians but without shattering the illusion of nondiscrimination. Canadian officials rehearsed a variety of rationales—including "humanitarian" concern for Indians' climactic incompatibility—before arriving at a remarkably elegant solution (Mongia 2005).

In 1908, the Canadian government passed an order-in-council limiting travel to those who "come from the country of their birth or citizenship by a continuous journey and or through tickets purchased before leaving their country of birth or nationality."[5] The "continuous journey" provision, as it came to be known, did not appear to single out any particular group for exclusion, but in practice barred everyone traveling from India. At the time, there was no way to travel continuously from India to Canada; the only routes offered by shipping companies included stops in Japan or Hawaii. The particular brilliance of the ordinance was not only that it barred Indians without naming them, but that it also barred the small number of especially despised "remigrants," Indian laborers who had completed their term of indenture in other parts of the British Empire, from entering Canada. In the following year, only a handful of Indian immigrants entered the country—all of these, returning residents (Mongia 2005; Sohi 2014).

"Without Naming Anyone": Racial Exclusion by Design

In the United States, as in other parts of the white-settler world, it was the arrival of Asian immigrants that precipitated new forms of migration control and new articulations of national identity (McKeown 2011). But unlike their counterparts in Australia and Canada, exclusionists in the United States were less constrained by guarantees of equal protection or other universalist pretensions.

In 1882, when US congressmen deliberated the exclusion of Chinese immigrants, they were relatively unembarrassed about stating their reasons. For instance, Senator James Farley of California, who introduced the bill, explained to his colleagues that Chinese immigrants belong to a "degraded and inferior race."[6] Others referred to Chinese immigrants as "rats" and "swine," warning that the soulless, "machine-like" manner in which they went about their work threatened the welfare of working white Americans. (Lee 2015: 89). When a lone senator objected to the proposed ban, describing it as a form of the "old race prejudice" that more enlightened men had consigned to the past, Senator Farley ridiculed him for his bookish propriety—or, in contemporary parlance, political correctness:

> I notice that the honorable Senator ... spoke of this race as not an inferior race; and he quoted from Sumner and Humboldt to show that

we ought not to recognize [races as inferior] ... [That] may be all right in theory; but in practice nobody pretends that is true.[7]

After only two months of deliberation, over the objection of only one senator, the United States passed the Chinese Exclusion Act of 1882, the first federal law to restrict immigration primarily on the basis of racial identity. But, as Ngai (this volume) demonstrates, perhaps the more lasting legacy of Chinese exclusion is to be found not in the legislation itself but in the judicial decisions upholding their legitimacy. In the "Chinese Exclusion Cases," the Supreme Court announced for the first time that Congress had an "absolute and unqualified" right to exclude and deport foreigners, "however it may see fit."[8] This is what is referred to as the plenary power doctrine. Moreover, the court went on to explain, the power to exclude foreigners from national territory was itself constitutive of territorial sovereignty and essential to demographic "self-preservation."[9] Thus, as in other white-settler contexts, the arrival of Asian immigrants led not only to the proliferation of immigration controls but to new articulations of territorial sovereignty and national identity—an imperiled homeland and American people, which the federal government would enlarge itself to protect.[10] Though the expressive nativism that animated the passage of the Chinese Exclusion acts has been largely banished from US public discourse—until recently, at least—the legal architecture it established remains the foundation of contemporary immigration law and policy.

Notwithstanding the broad legal authority of Congress to restrict new immigration, only a few decades after the passage of the Chinese Exclusion Act, congressmen seeking to exclude "Hindus" from the United States were frustrated by a changing, more restrictive set of political and rhetorical norms. Between 1910 and 1917, congressmen from California introduced several versions of a Hindu exclusion bill, but for a number of reasons, the passage of another explicitly racial bar to immigration would prove difficult.

Hindu exclusion was complicated by the racial and legal status of Indian immigrants. While Chinese and Japanese immigrants, in the minds of many Americans, belonged to "a race so different from our own," Indian immigrants, many were prepared to accept, belonged to the same racial family as Europeans. In the words of one exclusionist, the "tide of turbans" presented a "new and anxious question": if not on grounds of racial difference, then how would Americans exclude "our brothers of the East?"[11] (Scheffauer 1910: 616).

Moreover, as subjects of the British Empire, under existing treaties, Indians were guaranteed the same rights of entry to the United States as other British subjects. Having studied the campaigns to exclude Indian immigrants from Canada and Australia, exclusionists in the United States hoped that the British government would cooperate in restricting the emigration of British Indians. To the contrary, precisely because the restriction of Indian migration had so outraged Indians on four continents, effectively globalizing the movement for Indian independence, the British government was reluctant to implicate itself further in discrimination against Indians. Thus, as within the British imperial system, exclusionists in the United States found themselves constrained to formulate legislation that avoided any reference to racial difference or hierarchy, or otherwise invited international controversy (Jensen 1988; Mongia 2005; Munshi 2016b).

Though a few congressmen, primarily from the western states, were determined to ban Hindus, most others worried that an explicitly racial bar would generate diplomatic tension—not only with Britain but Japan. By the early twentieth century, Japan had begun to prove itself to be a formidable military and industrial power, threatening Anglo-American hegemony in the Pacific on the one hand, and energizing anti-colonial movements throughout Asia and Africa on the other. As Japan grew in both power and prestige, it demanded recognition as an equal among Western (imperial) nations, and began to challenge anti-Asian policies in the United States and elsewhere. In 1906, for instance, when San Francisco adopted a regulation requiring Asian children to attend separate, segregated schools, the Japanese government appealed to the president of the United States to block its enforcement. As more circumspect members of Congress recognized, immigration policies based on racialized distinctions were becoming harder to defend within a changing world, as diverse forces challenged the moral legitimacy of Western imperialism and white supremacy (Munshi 2016a).

In 1910, a congressional commission established to investigate the patterns and effects of "new immigration" to the United States concluded that new immigrants from Southern and Eastern Europe were inferior to earlier immigrants from Northern Europe. And it found that Hindus were "universally regarded as the least desirable race of immigrants thus far admitted to the United States."[12] To restrict new immigration, the commission recommended adopting a literacy test, though such a test had already been vetoed twice before. Congressman John Raker of California, the ardent force behind the long campaign to exclude Hindus, recognized the proposed literacy test to be a delaying tactic. He reminded his colleagues that "the real object and intent and promise was that there should be real exclusion of Asiatic laborers. This bill is not within the terms of that promise."[13] Another of his colleagues objected that the proposed test was not "broad enough to exclude Japanese, Hindus, and other Asiatic laborers," admonishing his colleagues for failing to recognize that "the Hindu and the Japanese [are the] greatest problem of the greatest plague we have in the west."[14]

Unconcerned about giving offense, Congressman Raker, among others, insisted on excluding "Hindus by name." More than one exclusionist insisted that Congress should "strike ... at the race problem as a race problem."[15] Some seemed to suggest that there was something dishonorable or unmanly about avoiding racial expression, arguing that Congress should "declare in plain language our purpose and intent ... We do not desire Mongolian immigration ... No one can be offended if we say it plainly rather than hide behind court decisions."[16]

It was another bill, introduced by Congressman Denver S. Church, that eventually gained enough support to pass into law in 1917. The Church bill would restrict Indian immigration not on the basis of identity—defined either in terms of race or nationality—but on the basis of geographic origin. The great advantage of the Church bill was that it would effectively exclude "Hindus" but without naming them. One congressman explained that the word "Hindu" disappeared from the legislation because the "Senate said, 'We do not like that wording . . . excluding Hindus and other persons. We are going to put the matter in another form which will not be offensive to anybody.'"[17]

While the Immigration Act of 1917, sometimes referred to as the Asiatic Barred Zone Act, did not exclude "Hindus" by name, another congressman assured his colleagues, "of course, the great body of the population from which that formidable immigration is coming is in British India." He continued:

> Objection was made to that form of words by the State Department. They told the committee that that form of words would be extremely offensive to Japan ... Therefore instead of describing the excluded persons as "Hindus," the committee took the same people within geographic lines and excluded them ... The only difference is that under this, I freely admit, clumsy method of excluding what we seek to exclude,

we excluded Asiatic immigration from other places, it is [desirable] to exclude. The purpose of this [bill] is to exclude the people we started out to exclude, without offending somebody else.[18]

Before the Asiatic Barred Zone Act was passed into law, a number of congressmen expressed frustration with the final form of exclusion, identifying the many ways in which cartographic boundaries failed to correspond to "moral" or racial boundaries. For instance, Senator James Reed of Wyoming complained:

> [Congress] undertook for the first time to exclude people from entering this country by lines of latitude and longitude, not by races, not by intellectual qualification, not by moral attributes, but by arbitrary lines … If we want to exclude the Mongolian, let us exclude him … You do not follow the lines that mark the division of races. You follow the parallels and meridians drawn on the map of the surface of the earth, utterly disregarding the lines of countries or the lines of races … The trouble is that instead of drawing this bill to exclude men because of character and blood, or even by countries, you exclude them in accordance with parallels of latitude and degrees of longitude.[19]

Representative Raker, perhaps the most tenacious opponent of Indian immigration, sought to placate his fellow congressmen by pointing out the relative advantage of the act. While it was always his purpose to exclude "Hindus … by name," he found that, given international circumstances, by recasting exclusion in geographic terms, by "glossing it over, making it smooth so that it may be swallowed without naming anyone," Congress had taken "another ground that will make it stronger … and we ought to make our laws sufficiently strong so as to prohibit and exclude all Asiatic laborers now so that there will be no question in the future."[20] It is the congressman's confidence—that exclusionary policies might be devised so that "there will be no question in the future"—that should goad us in the present (Munshi 2016a).

Racism and Rhetorical Discipline

The practice of excluding "Hindus" not "by name" but by latitude and longitude anticipates what contemporary scholars have identified as the new racism of our contemporary world order (Balibar 1991; Bonilla-Silva

2017; Goldberg 2015). The antiracist movements of the twentieth century brought an end to formal empire in Asia and Africa and extended civil rights to racial minorities in the United States and other white-settler countries. They did not, however, bring an end to racism or racial order. The humiliations visited upon Indian subjects traveling to the white-settler world played an important role in galvanizing the movement for national independence. But for Indians, national independence did not usher in a new era of equality between former colonizers and the formerly colonized. When peoples of the colonized world finally gained their independence—in the limited form of territorial sovereignty—they did not gain the right to free movement long enjoyed by the citizens of former colonizing countries. In the postcolonial era, abstract equality among sovereign nations, consisting in the mutual right to territorial exclusion, would in practice limit only the mobility of the formerly colonized. The emerging system of nation-states would preserve the asymmetries that had defined formal imperialism. Similarly, the civil rights movement in the United States did not end racial inequality. Instead, racial inequality would flourish under a "color-blind" legal regime that outlawed intentional and expressive racism but not structural inequality (Gotanda 1991).

Eduardo Bonilla-Silva (2017), writing about the persistence of racial inequality in the United States, observes that the race-consciousness of the civil rights era eventually gave way to a new racial regime, within which racial arrangements are reproduced without explicit reference to race. What he identifies as the "color-blind racism" of the post-civil rights era is characterized by rhetorical discipline of avoidance. Racial inequality has been maintained in part by a refusal to redress the effects of past unequal treatment, in part through the unequal enforcement of apparently race-neutral laws, and in part through covert practices. He uses the term "racism without racists" to describe the contemporary racial regime in the United States, emphasizing the way in which the beneficiaries of racial arrangements are able to deny responsibility for the perpetuation of those arrangements. Color-blindness, or the principle of race neutrality, is often asserted by conservatives to undermine race-conscious policies, like affirmative action, intended to redress historic racism. The ideal of color-blindness is also often embraced by liberals as the progressive hope that phenotypic markers of difference will lose their meaning over time so that, one day, all Americans might recognize in one another their essential equality as human beings. But this liberal vision shares with more cynical assertions of color-blindness a narrowed, ahistorical understanding of racism. "Color" appears as the residual artifact of a racism confined to the past, an obstacle to the eventual realization of a post-racial future. If we cannot exactly blind ourselves to color, as a mode of racial remediation, color-blindness recommends that we mute our response to it. "Racism," then, becomes a matter of rude observation, and the term "racist" is reserved for those who insist on name-calling. A contemporary dictionary definition of "racist" is illustrative: "a person who shows or feels discrimination or prejudice against people of other races, or who believes that a particular race is superior to another."[21] The term is reserved, in other words, for those deplorable few who express or harbor particularly well-formed racist ideas, rather than the overwhelming majority of Americans who hold an unexamined investment—ideological as well as material—in structures of differentiation that cast persons from the sphere of belonging.

"I Refuse to Be Politically Correct": Rhetorical Defiance

In 2016, Donald Trump strode into office in stunning defiance of contemporary norms governing racial rhetoric—or what he and his supporters routinely denounce as "political correctness." In a speech announcing his candidacy, Trump claimed that undocumented immigrants from Mexico were "bringing drugs. They're bringing crime. They're rapists" (quoted in Philips 2017). He promised to build a wall to prevent any more from coming. He called for a "total and complete shutdown of Muslim" immigration and vowed to prevent Syrian refugees from entering the country. Long before announcing his run for president, Trump began to consolidate a political base by delegitimizing his predecessor, Barack Obama, by insisting that the United States' first black president was not an American citizen. In a remarkably insightful essay on the rise of white nationalism, Adam Serwer (2017) observes that Trump's "great political insight" was his recognition that the election of a black president "inflicted a powerful psychological wound upon many white Americans." Their suffering found new, nearly respectable expression in Trump's "birther" conspiracy. If it was no longer respectable to disavow the first black president because he was black, "birtherism" allowed white racists to reject Obama because he was disqualified, foreign-born, Muslim. Birtherism gave cover to an old, festering antiblack animus and dressed it up in new terms of immigrant illegality and Muslim ungovernability. As Serwer suggests, birtherism synthesized a resentment toward blacks, immigrants, and Muslims that had been simmering in suppressed silence for more than a decade.

Though much of the country was alarmed by Trump's open expression of hatred and bigotry, many of his supporters elected him because of—not in spite of—his rhetorical transgressions. Throughout his campaign, Trump said and did things that seasoned observers believed would destroy his viability as a candidate. He encouraged violence against racial minorities at his rallies; he mocked a disabled person; he hesitated to distance himself from a Ku Klux Klan member; he insulted war veterans; he boasted about assaulting women. When confronted about his rhetoric, the candidate deflected by saying—to great applause during the first Republican debate—"I don't frankly have time for total political correctness … This country doesn't have time either" (quoted in Weigel 2016).

Almost immediately, Trump's defiance of "political correctness" would become the centerpiece of his campaign, the irrepressible force behind his rising populist appeal. For his supporters, "political correctness" seemed to conjure a variety of injuries—an assault on free speech, a shaming of the expressive culture of white Americans, a resentment toward formerly subordinate communities now asserting their collective power by reshaping the norms of public discourse. By freeing himself of the strictures of political correctness, Trump, according to his supporters, can say what ordinary Americans think and feel but have been made ashamed to say. Trump's volubility assures his supporters that their unspoken feelings are nothing to be ashamed of. Even when supporters claim to disapprove of the content of his message, they express approval of his style of delivery—his refusal to discipline his rhetoric.

Throughout his campaign, Trump brandished his defiance of political correctness as though it were his primary qualification for the presidency. He argued that his critics and opponents were weakened by their faith in political correctness. Referring to threats that criminals, immigrants, and terrorists posed to white Americans, Trump routinely asserted that political elites were not just failing to confront the nation's problems, they wouldn't even let anyone else talk about them (Weigel 2016). "The special interests, the arrogant media, and the political insiders don't want me to talk about the crime that is happening in our country … They want me to just go along with the same failed policies that have caused so much suffering" (quoted in ibid.). He accused Barack Obama and Hillary Clinton of "putting political correctness above common sense, above your safety" (quoted in ibid.). Freed of the constraints of political correctness, the candidate could not only speak more clearly, he could see and think more clearly.

Trump's refusal to discipline his rhetoric was particularly pronounced in his insistence that Muslim immigration exposes Americans to the threat of "radical Islamic terror." Trump claimed that Obama and Clinton avoided using the phrase "radical Islamic terrorism" not only because they were cowardly and dishonest, but because their anti-racism had clouded their judgment. His predecessors were in "denial" of the real threat that "radical Islam" posed to the West. As a candidate, Trump asserted that Clinton "had no clue what radical Islam is ... [W]hen it comes to Islamic terrorism, ignorance is not bliss—it's deadly" (quoted in Saletan 2017). In fact, the Obama administration avoided the phrase "radical Islam" both because it misstates the relationship between Islam and terrorism and because it confirms to the already radicalized few that America hates Islam (Stengel 2017). "These are radical Islamic terrorists," Trump has insisted over and over, nonetheless. "To solve a problem, you have to be able to state what the problem is, or at least say the name" (quoted in ibid.). Days after a Muslim couple carried out a mass shooting in San Bernardino, California, Trump's campaign released a statement calling for a "total and complete shutdown of Muslims entering the country" (quoted in Beauchamp 2017). After a mass shooting in Orlando, six months later, Trump congratulated himself for "being right on radical Islamic terrorism," called for federal surveillance of "the mosques," and reiterated, "I refuse to be politically correct" (quoted in ibid.).

"The Right Way to Do It Legally": From Muslim to Nationality

In late January of 2017, only seven days after taking the oath of office, President Donald Trump signed Executive Order 13769, immediately suspending the entry of foreign nationals traveling from seven Muslim-majority countries—Iran, Iraq, Libya, Somalia, Sudan, Syria, and Yemen. The stated purpose of the order was to "protect the American people from terrorist attacks by foreign nationals." To achieve that purpose, the order explained, the federal government would review its visa-issuance process to ensure that those admitted to the country "do not bear hostile attitudes toward it and its founding principles." Moreover, the process should exclude individuals engaged "in acts of bigotry and hatred," including "violence against women," or the "persecution of those who practice religions different from their own."[22] In a form of reversal, characteristic of the new racism, the Trump administration's executive order denies its own bigotry and religious discrimination while projecting it onto the targets of its bigotry and discrimination. At the same time, the order allows Trump and his supporters to proclaim that they actually care about persecuted minorities and women—more than liberal elites whose political correctness prevents them from calling out bigotry and sexism among Muslims.

Though the provisions barring Muslim immigrants received most attention, the executive order also restricted the admission of refugees, generally considered detrimental to national interests. The order suspended new refugee admissions from Syria, established a temporary suspension on all other refugee admissions, and reduced the number of refugees admitted in any year by more than half. The order also directed officials to prioritize claims of religious persecution made by individuals belonging to a minority religion.[23] As the president explained to a Christian news organization, the order would give preference to Christian refugees, adding, erroneously, "do you know if you were a Christian in Syria, it was impossible, at least very tough, to get into the United States? If you were a Muslim you could come in, but if you were a Christian, it was impossible" (quoted in Kessler 2017).

The following morning, stories began to circulate of family members detained at airports; students refused permission to board a plane; long-suffering refugees sent back to refugee camps. The order was widely condemned by political organizations, religious authorities, businesses, and universities. Critics responded by linking the executive order to the president's campaign rhetoric, betraying surprise, not only that the president would do what he said he would do, but that he *could do* what he said he would do. The incredulity and alarm that Trump's rhetoric aroused in opponents throughout the campaign, it seems, had been tempered by their faith in American institutions—the American legal system, in particular. Numerous reports and editorials assured readers that the president could not *really* ban Muslims; a Muslim ban would likely be found unconstitutional (Cole 2016; Mebler 2015). Though the executive order did not explicitly reference Muslims, critics of the ban argued that the executive order was plainly a thinly veiled version of the Muslim ban that he had promised. Just before signing the executive order, the president read the official title of the order, "Protecting the Nation from Foreign Terrorist Entry into the United States," and added, "We all know what that means."[24]

Even as the president signaled to his supporters that he had fulfilled his campaign promise, in response to public protests, media backlash, and legal challenges, Trump and his advisors began to deny that the executive order was a Muslim ban. The day after the order was signed, Trump's attorney Rudolph Giuliani appeared on Fox News and was asked, "How did the president decide the seven countries?" With stunning self-satisfaction, he answered:

> OK, I'll tell you the whole history of it. So when [the president] first announced it, he said "Muslim ban." He called me up. He said, "Put a commission together. Show me the right way to do it legally." I put a commission together ... a whole group of ... very expert lawyers on this, and what we did was, we focused on—instead of religion—danger, the areas of the world that create danger for us, which is a factual basis, not a religious basis. Perfectly legal, perfectly sensible. (quoted in Eleftheriou-Smity 2017)

In a more carefully-worded statement, issued a few days later, Giuliani "clarified": "I have not served on any Trump administration commission 'relating to the so-called Muslim Ban Executive Orders.'" (quoted in Beavers 2017).

Dozens of lawsuits were filed against the order, resulting in a series of injunctions blocking its implementation. These were focused primarily on the claims of individuals with established ties to the United States. Days after the order was issued, a federal judge in New York blocked the deportation of individuals traveling with valid visas, approved refugee status, or who were otherwise "legally authorized to enter the United States."[25] A judge in Virginia meanwhile issued a restraining order to block the removal of green card holders at Dulles International airport,[26] and a judge in the state of Washington issued a nationwide injunction, preventing the federal government from enforcing the order.[27] The Ninth Circuit upheld the injunction, rejecting the government's appeals.[28]

On March 6, 2017, out of public view, the president signed a second executive order, revoking and replacing the first. The second executive order, unlike its predecessor, included a long discussion explaining *why* travel from certain countries, and not others, should be banned. The visa application process in the banned countries warranted "additional scrutiny" the order explained, "because the conditions in these countries present heightened threats." The second order excluded Iraq from the original list of Muslim-majority countries, recognizing Iraq to be a "special case," given the "close cooperative relationship between the United States and the democratically elected Iraqi government" and "the significant presence of United States forces in Iraq." The revised order explicitly denied that the ban was "motivated by animus toward any religion." Refugee admissions from Syria would be barred for a period of 120 days, rather than indefinitely, as originally ordered.[29]

Finally, the second executive order narrowed the scope of the original ban. The second order would continue to bar new immigrants from the designated countries, but it would allow entry of certain individuals with established ties to the United States: lawful permanent residents, dual citizens traveling under a passport issued by a non-designated country, and individuals who had already been granted asylum or refugee status. The revised order also included a provision that would allow consular officials to issue waivers on a case-by-case basis, for instance, to foreign nationals previously admitted for work or study.[30] Judging by public and judicial response, perhaps the most problematic feature of the original travel ban was that it affected individuals with established ties or existing claims to maintaining their "presence" in the United States—to invoke the analysis of Linda Bosniak (this volume)—prompting a powerful and sympathetic challenge from corporate employers, universities, and family members. Like its predecessor, the revised Muslim ban would continue to affect the nearly 200 million people living in some of the poorest and most violent parts of the world. But by excluding corporate employees, students, and relatives from the scope of the ban, the second order managed to avoid the disruption and public outrage generated by the first.

Lawyers, once again, filed lawsuits. And courts, once again, issued a series of preliminary injunctions, blocking enforcement of the order's provisions.[31] The injunctions were upheld by the Fourth Circuit Court of Appeals, which found that the second executive order probably violates constitutional protections against religious discrimination,[32] and by the Ninth Circuit Court of Appeals, which found that the order violated two provisions of the Immigration and Nationality Act (INA) of 1965—one defining the president's authority to suspend the entry of certain immigrants when their entry would be "detrimental to the interests of the United States," and another prohibiting discrimination on the basis of "nationality."[33]

On September 24, 2017, a few weeks before the government was scheduled to defend the second executive order before the Supreme Court,

President Trump revoked it and signed a third version of his travel ban.[34] The third executive order restricted immigration from six Muslim-majority countries—Chad, Iran, Libya, Somalia, Syria, and Yemen—and added two non-Muslim-majority countries to the list—North Korea and Venezuela. The third order also differed from its predecessor in that it did not ban everyone traveling from one of the designated countries; instead, it imposed different visa restrictions on each of the designated countries. The restriction on travel from Venezuela would affect a few government officials and their families; the restriction on travel from North Korea would affect almost no one, as North Korea itself restricts emigration. Thus nearly everyone affected by the order is a citizen of the six remaining Muslim-majority countries. The Trump administration argued that the executive order could not be called a "Muslim" ban, because it did not ban *only* Muslims, nor did it ban *all* Muslims.

Within a few days, judges in Hawaii and Maryland issued injunctions blocking implementation of the third iteration of the ban.[35] The Ninth Circuit Court of Appeals, focusing on executive overreach rather than the discriminatory character of the ban, upheld the injunction and conveyed its disapproval of the president's attempt to regulate immigration independently of congressional restraint or judicial review: "The Executive cannot without the assent of Congress supplant its statutory scheme [for immigration] with one stroke of a presidential pen."[36] The president's authority to enact a Muslim ban, the court explained, had been clearly limited by acts of Congress. The court did not explain, as it could have, that Congress itself retains broad authority to enact a Muslim ban. The Fourth Circuit Court of Appeals upheld the lower court injunction, finding that the president's executive order was plainly motivated by religious animus and in violation of the First Amendment of the US Constitution, which protects religious freedom.

In June of 2018, the Supreme Court of the United States upheld the Muslim ban, finding that it violated neither federal immigration law nor the Constitution. Chief Justice Roberts, writing for a narrow majority, found that Trump's executive order was "squarely within the scope of Presidential authority" delegated under the Immigration and Nationality Act. Roberts argued that the INA grants the president sweeping authority, adding that the law "exude[s] deference" to the executive branch.[37] All that the INA requires of the president, Roberts explained, is that he "find" that the entry of excluded immigrants would harm national interest. "The President has undoubtedly fulfilled that requirement here," he concluded, dismissing questions about the persuasiveness of the president's "findings."[38] Remarkably, the majority found that the nondiscrimination provisions of the INA do not constrain the president in his exercise of authority. In other words, as long as the president points to some national interest, he is free to discriminate on the basis of nationality—or anything else.

Finally, the Supreme Court found no unconstitutional discrimination. "The text says nothing about religion."[39] The court's majority was evidently satisfied that the final iteration of the Muslim ban was "neutral on its face."[40] The plaintiffs had argued that Trump's campaign promise and anti-Muslim rhetoric should inform the court's reading of the executive order, but the majority disagreed. Acknowledging the president's insistent rhetoric, Roberts maintained that "the issue ... is not whether to denounce the President's statements." Instead, the president is owed deference in his handling of national security, and because he has offered "a legitimate grounding in national security concerns, quite apart from any religious hostility, we must accept that independent justification."[41]

Conclusion

The main problem with the Muslim ban, according to its most voluble critics, is not that it harms vulnerable people or that it perpetuates inequalities rooted in European colonialism or American imperialism. Instead, the main problem is that it appears as a form of barely concealed racism reminiscent of slavery or Japanese internment, as Judge James Wynn conveyed in his Fourth Circuit opinion:

> Invidious discrimination that is shrouded in layers of legality is no less an insult to our Constitution than naked invidious discrimination. We have matured from the lessons learned by past experiences documented, for example, in *Dred Scott* and *Korematsu*. But we again encounter the affront of invidious discrimination—this time layered under the guise of a President's claim of unfettered ... authority to control immigration and his proclamation that national security requires his exercise of authority to deny entry to a class of aliens defined solely by their nation of origin. Laid bare, this Executive Order is no more than what the President promised before and after his election: naked invidious discrimination against Muslims.[42]

The problem with the Muslim ban, in other words, is not that it is "an insult" to Muslims, but that it is insult to "our Constitution." It is an "affront" not to others but to the United States' self-image. The wrong identified over and over is the "naked" display of the old racial animus, a breach of the new racial etiquette. But by focusing outrage at the spectacle of racism, legal advocates—who have played an outsized role in shaping public debates about the Muslim ban—obscure the ways in which nativism and nationality discrimination pervades the legal immigration system.

In numerous opinions, lower court judges offered a meticulous review of Trump's rhetoric during the campaign and as president, strenuously connecting the executive order to expressions of racial animus. While the Supreme Court limited its analysis to the text of the executive orders, Judge Wynn refused, arguing that the "world is not made brand new every morning, nor are we able to awake without the vivid memory of these statements. We cannot shut our eyes to such evidence when it stares us in the face."[43] Nor were judges satisfied by the administration's assertions that the executive orders were justified by national security. In the words of Judge Roger Gregory, chief judge of the Fourth Circuit, the text recites "vague words of national security, but in context drips with religious intolerance, animus, and discrimination."[44] Again, the apparent harm is that the harm itself is too apparent: the administration's shabby attempts at masking not just its discriminatory motives but also the government's extraordinary power over immigration policy undermines the perceived integrity of US immigration laws, and the supposed impartiality of law itself. The harm, in other words, is not the harm dealt to individuals affected by the ban, but the shattering of appearances, of our most guarded national illusions.

This preoccupation with appearances is betrayed, for instance, by media coverage that turned swiftly from a sympathetic focus on travelers affected by the ban—long-suffering refugees, long-separated relatives, translators exiled for their collaboration with American operatives—to a sneering assessment of the new administration's incompetence and ensuing "chaos." According to many commentators, it seemed that the new administration's amateurism was its primary shortcoming rather than its calculated meanness. The media seemed almost nostalgic for the well-mannered, if stealthily brutal, enforcement policies of the Obama era. President Obama delivered soaring speeches about his hope for young DREAMers while steadily deporting 3.1 million immigrants—one million more than were deported during the entire the twentieth century (Binyam 2017).

For many, the essential problem with the Muslim ban was that it manifest a form of discrimination that was supposed to have been abolished during the civil rights era. One immigration scholar anticipated that the plenary power doctrine was a relic of the Jim Crow era of official discrimination, plainly superseded by cases like *Brown v. Board of Education* (1954) and sure to be struck down by the Supreme Court (Cox 2017). Another editorial writer insisted: "the order is illegal. More than 50 years ago, Congress outlawed such discrimination against immigrants on the basis of national origin" (Bier 2017). Comparing the Muslim ban to Asian exclusion a century before, one writer explained that with the Immigration Act of 1965, Congress intended to correct "a long and shameful history" of barring immigrants on the basis of origin:

> Starting in the late nineteenth century, laws excluded all Chinese, almost all Japanese, then all Asians in the so-called Asiatic Barred Zone … Mr. Trump appears to want to reinstate a new type of Asiatic Barred Zone by executive order, but there is just one problem: The Immigration and Nationality Act of 1965 banned all discrimination against immigrants on the basis of national origin, replacing the old prejudicial system and giving each country an equal shot. (ibid.)

The writers' claims about the civil rights era are wishful, but at odds with history. Like other civil rights legislation of the 1960s, the Immigration Act of 1965 brought an end to the most conspicuous forms of racial and ethnic discrimination. Immediately after its passage, various organizations congratulated President Lyndon Johnson for "finally establishing an immigration policy consistent with our national philosophy that all men are entitled to equal opportunity regardless of race or place of birth" (Ngai 2005: 260). But the current immigration regime, even as it has grown more flexible and complex, can hardly be described as indifferent to an immigrant's place of birth. On the contrary, perhaps no biographical fact—not sex, gender, wealth, or education—plays a greater role in determining whether an individual is able to legally migrate to the United States than his or her nationality or country of origin.

The Immigration Act replaced the racial bar and discriminatory national origins quota with a uniform "per-country" limit, marking a general shift toward a policy of equal treatment of all nationalities. In practice, however, the limited guarantee of formal equality tends to amplify existing material inequalities. Though each country is subject to the same numerical limit, this limit affects immigrants from different countries differently, rendering immigrants from certain countries—especially those that are poor, unstable, and densely populated—far less mobile than individuals from certain other countries—those that are rich and tranquil. The per-country limit is the reason why the brother or sister of an American citizen hoping to emigrate from the Philippines can expect to wait 23 years to obtain a visa, while a similarly situated individual from Sweden can expect to wait no time at all.

Almost by definition, the per-country limit discriminates against individuals from high-sending countries, countries from which high numbers of people are eager to leave—because these countries are poor, dangerous, or repressive. Some of the highest-sending countries, like the Philippines, Mexico, El Salvador, and Haiti, have long histories of entanglement with the United States. The Philippines was once an American possession; what is now the United States was once Mexico; and the United States has a long history of intervention in El Salvador, Haiti, and other parts of the southern hemisphere. El Salvador and Iceland are subject to the same limits, though El Salvador (owing to a series of disastrous US policies) ranks among the most murderous places on the planet, Iceland among the most tranquil. Others, like India and China, happen to be among the most populated countries in the world. India has more than 200 times the population of Denmark, but is subject to the same limit. India is home to more of the world's poor than any other country; Denmark, home to more of its most affluent. Though it avoids drawing explicit distinctions among nationalities, as every Third World immigrant knows, US immigration law remains enormously sensitive to nationality or place of birth.

While the law is often celebrated for establishing a race-neutral immigration scheme, it also established newer, increasingly refined mechanisms for distinguishing between desirable and undesirable immigrants. And, while the Immigration Act of 1965 has been broadly heralded as one of the great achievements of the civil rights era, it has had an especially disastrous impact on immigration to the United States from Mexico, immediately transforming long-established patterns of cyclical migration into the contemporary crisis of "illegal" migration that has become the primary target of Trump and his supporters' resentment (Andreas 2009; Massey et al. 2002; Ngai 2005). In their tireless performance of unveiling the "naked" animus that so plainly animates the Muslim ban, the ban's critics leave unexamined the essentially discriminatory design of the legal immigration system as a whole. Moreover, they promote the illusion that our current immigration architecture is race- and nationality-neutral. And they obscure what remains offensive about US immigration law.

Acknowledgements

I am grateful to Hawa Allan, Tugba Basaran, Didier Fassin, Betsy Kuhn, Andrew Lang, Allegra McLeod, Mae Ngai, Hibbah Siddiqui, and Sonali Thakkar for their thoughtful feedback. All errors are my own.

Notes

1. Executive Order No. 13769, January 27, 2017 (https://www.whitehouse.gov/presidential-actions/executive-order-protecting-nation-foreign-terrorist-entry-united-states/, accessed August 3, 2019).
2. Executive Order No. 13768, January 25, 2017 (https://www.whitehouse.gov/presidential-actions/executive-order-enhancing-public-safety-interior-united-states/, accessed August 3, 2019).
3. E.g. the United Kingdom's Passenger Vessels Act of 1803.
4. President Grover Cleveland, "Veto Message Regarding Immigration Legislation," March 2, 1897 (transcript available at: https://millercenter.org/the-presidency/presidential-speeches/march-2-1897-veto-message-regarding-immigration-legislation, accessed July 29, 2019).
5. Act to Emend the Immigration Act, S.C. 1908, c33 (Canada).
6. 13 Cong. Rec. (*Congressional Record*) 1487 (1882).
7. 13 Cong. Rec. 1645 (1882).
8. Fong Yue Ting v. United States,149 US 698 (1898), pp. 705–7.
9. Fong Yue Ting v. United States, p.705.
10. See Chae Chan Ping v. United States, 130 US 581 (1889), p. 604.
11. Herman Scheffauer, "The Tide of Turbans," *The Forum* 43 (1910), pp. 616–18.
12. US Immigration (Dillingham) Commission, S. Doc. 61-633 (1911).
13. 49 Cong. Rec. 2292 (1913).
14. 49 Cong. Rec. 2292 (1913).
15. 52 Cong. Rec. 349 (1914).
16. 51 Cong. Rec. 2824–2825 (1914).
17. 54 Cong. Rec. 1291 (1917).
18. 54 Cong. Rec. 205 (1916).
19. 54 Cong. Rec. 2619 (1917).
20. 54 Cong. Rec. 1492–1493 (1917).
21. *Oxford English Dictionary*, s.v. "racism" (htpps://www.oed.com/view/entry/157097, accessed August 19, 2019).
22. Executive Order No. 13769, secs. 1–2.
23. Executive Order No. 13769, sec. 5.
24. International Refugee Assistance Project v. Trump, 857 F.3d 554 (4th Cir. 2017), pp. 576–7.
25. Darweesh v. Trump, No. 1:17-cv-00480 (E. D. N.Y. 2017).

26. Aziz v. Trump, No. 1:17-cv-00116 (E. D. Va. 2017).
27. State of Washington v. Trump, No. C17-0141-JLR, 2017 WL 462040 (W. D. 2017).
28. Trump v. Washington, 847 F. 3d 1151 (2017).
29. Executive Order No. 13780, March 6, 2017 (https://www.whitehouse.gov/presidential-actions/executive-order-protecting-nation-foreign-terrorist-entry-united-states-2/, accessed August 3, 2019).
30. Executive Order No. 13780.
31. E.g. International Refugee Assistance Project v. Trump No. TDC-17-0361 (D. Md. 2017); Hawaii v. Trump, No. 17-00050 DKS-KSC (D. Haw. 2017); State of Washington v. Trump, No. C17-0141JLR (W. D. Wa. 2017).
32. International Refugee Assistance Project v. Trump, No. 17:1351 (4th Cir. 2017).
33. Hawaii v. Trump, No. 17-15589 (9th Cir. 2017).
34. Proclamation No. 9645, September 24, 2017 (https://www.whitehouse.gov/presidential-actions/presidential-proclamation-enhancing-vetting-capabilities-processes-detecting-attempted-entry-united-states-terrorists-public-safety-threats/, accessed August 3, 2019).
35. International Refugee Assistance Project v. Trump, Case 8:17-cv-00361-TDC (D. Md. 2019); Hawaii v. Trump, No. 17-00050 DKW-KSC (D. Haw. 2019).
36. Hawaii v. Trump, 878 F.3d 662 (9th Cir. 2018), p. 687.
37. Trump v. Hawaii, 585 US 17-965 (2018), p. 10.
38. Trump v. Hawaii, 585 US 17-965, p.11.
39. Trump v. Hawaii, 585 US 17-965, p. 34.
40. Trump v. Hawaii, 585 US 17-965, p.29.
41. Trump v. Hawaii, 585 US 17-965, p.34.
42. International Refugee Assistance Project v. Trump, 857 F.3d 554 (4th Cir. 2017), p. 612.
43. International Refugee Assistance Project v. Trump, 857 F.3d 554, p. 599.
44. International Refugee Assistance Project v. Trump, 857 F.3d 554, p. 572.

References

Andreas, Peter. 2009. *Border Games: Policing the US–Mexico Divide*. Ithaca, NY: Cornell University Press.
Balibar, Etienne. 1991. "Is There a Neo-Racism?" In Etienne Balibar and Immanuel Wallerstein (eds), *Race, Nation, Class: Ambiguous Identities*, 17–28. New York: Verso.
Beavers, Olivia. 2017. "Giuliani Walks Back Claims of Involvement in Trump's Travel Ban," *The Hill*, May 23. Available at https://thehill.com/homenews/administration/334869-giuliani-walks-back-claims-of-involvement-in-trumps-travel-ban (accessed August 22, 2019).
Beauchamp, Zach. 2017. "Trump Loves Saying 'Radical Islamic Terrorism.' He Has a Tough Time with 'White Supremacy.'" *Vox*, August 14. Available at: https://www.vox.com/world/2017/8/14/16143634/trump-charlottesville-white-supremacy-terrorism-islamism (accessed August 22, 2019).

Bier, David. 2017. "Trump's Immigration Ban is Illegal." *New York Times*, January 27. Available at: https://nyti.ms/2kcULPH (accessed July 29, 2019).

Binyam, Maya. 2017. "Spell-Check Nation." *New Inquiry*, May 10. Available at: https://thenewinquiry.com/spell-check-nation/ (accessed July 29, 2019).

Bonilla-Silva, Eduardo. 2017. *Racism Without Racists: Color-Blind Racism and the Persistence of Racial Inequality in America*, 5th ed. Lanham, MD: Rowman and Littlefield.

Cole, David. 2016. "Why Trump's Proposed Targeting of Muslims Would Be Unconstitutional." *Just Security*, November 21. Available at: https://www.justsecurity.org/34682/trumps-proposed-targeting-muslims-unconstitutional/#more-34682 (accessed July 29, 2019).

—— 2017. "We'll See You in Court: Why Trump's Executive Order on Refugees Violates the Establishment Clause." *Just Security*, January 28. Available at: https://www.justsecurity.org/36936/well-court-trumps-executive-order-refugees-violates-establishment-clause/ (accessed July 29, 2019).

Cox, Adam. 2017. "Why a Muslim Ban is Likely to be Held Unconstitutional: The Myth of Unconstrained Immigration Power." *Just Security*, January 30. Available at: https://www.justsecurity.org/36988/muslim-ban-held-unconstitutional-myth-unconstrained-immigration-power/ (accessed July 29, 2019).

DHS (Department of Homeland Security). 2017. "Q&A: DHS Implementation of the Executive Order on Enhancing Public Safety in the Interior." Department of Homeland Security, February 21. Available at: https://www.dhs.gov/news/2017/02/21/qa-dhs-implementation-executive-order-enhancing-public-safety-interior-united-states (accessed July 29, 2019).

Eleftheriou-Smity, Loulla-Mae. 2017. "Donald Trump Asked Rudy Giuliani How to 'Legally' Create 'Muslim Ban,' Claims Former New York Mayor." *Independent*, January 30. Available at https://www.independent.co.uk/news/world/americas/donald-trump-muslim-ban-rudy-giuliani-how-legally-create-islam-us-immigration-entry-visa-new-york-a7552751.html (accessed August 22, 2019).

Goldberg, David. 2015. *Are We All Postracial Yet?* Cambridge: Polity Press.

Gotanda, Neil. 1991. "A Critique of 'Our Constitution is Colorblind.'" *Stanford Law Review* 44(1): 1–68.

Jensen, Joan M. 1988. *Passage from India: Asian Indian Immigrants in North America*. New Haven: Yale University Press.

Johnson, Jenna. 2016. "Donald Trump Is Expanding His Muslim Ban, Not Rolling It Back." *Washington Post*, July 24. Available at https://www.washingtonpost.com/news/post-politics/wp/2016/07/24/donald-trump-is-expanding-his-muslim-ban-not-rolling-it-back/ (accessed August 22, 2019).

Kessler, Glen. 2017. "Trump's Claim that It Is 'Very Tough' for Christian Syrians to Get to the United States," *Washington Post*, January 28. Available at https://www.washingtonpost.com/news/fact-checker/wp/2017/01/28/trumps-claim-that-it-is-very-tough-for-christian-syrians-to-get-to-the-united-states/ (accessed August 22, 2019).

Lake, Marilyn, and Henry Reynolds. 2008. *Drawing the Global Colour Line: White Men's Countries and the International Challenge of Racial Equality*. Cambridge: Cambridge University Press.

Lee, Erika. 2015. *The Making of Asian America*. New York: Simon and Schuster.

Massey, Douglas S., Jorge Durand, and Nolan J. Malone. 2002. *Beyond Smoke and Mirrors: Mexican Immigration in an Era of Economic Integration.* New York: Russell Sage Foundation.

Mebler, Ari. 2015. "Law Experts Weigh Donald Trump's Plan to Ban Muslims From US." *NBC News*, December 8. Available at: https://www.nbcnews.com/politics/2016-election/law-experts-weigh-donald-trumps-plan-ban-muslims-n476041 (accessed July 29, 2019).

McKeown, Adam M. 2011. *Melancholy Order: Asian Migration and the Globalization of Borders.* New York: Columbia University Press.

Mongia, Radhika. 2005. "Race, Nationality, Mobility: A History of the Passport." *Public Culture* 11(3): 527–55.

Moyer, Justin. 2015. "Dick Cheney Slams Trump's Muslim Entry Ban." *Washington Post*, December 8. Available at https://www.washingtonpost.com/news/morning-mix/wp/2015/12/08/dick-cheney-slams-trumps-muslim-entry-ban-and-suggests-u-s-re-invade-middle-east/ (accessed August 22, 2019).

Munshi, Sherally. 2016a. "Race, Geography, and Mobility." *Georgetown Immigration Law Journal* 30(2): 245–86.

——— 2016b. "Immigration, Imperialism, and the Legacies of Indian Exclusion." *Yale Journal of Law and the Humanities* 28(1): 51–104.

Ngai, Mae. 2005. *Impossible Subjects: Illegal Aliens and the Making of Modern America.* Princeton: Princeton University Press.

Philips, Amber. 2017. " 'They're Rapists.' President Trump's Campaign Launch Speech Two Years Later, Annotated." *Washington Post*, June 16. Available at https://www.washingtonpost.com/news/the-fix/wp/2017/06/16/theyre-rapists-presidents-trump-campaign-launch-speech-two-years-later-annotated/ (accessed August 22, 2019).

Saletan, William. 2017. "Trump Finally Understands Something." *Slate*, May 25. Available at: https://slate.com/news-and-politics/2017/05/why-trump-stopped-saying-radical-islamic-terrorism.html (accessed July 29, 2019).

Scheffauer, Herman, 1910. "The Tide of Turbans," *The Forum* 43: 616–18.

Serwer, Adam. 2017. "The Nationalist's Delusion." *Atlantic*, November 20. Available at: https://www.theatlantic.com/politics/archive/2017/11/the-nationalists-delusion/546356/ (accessed July 29, 2019).

Sohi, Seema. 2014. *Echoes of Mutiny: Race, Surveillance and Indian Anticolonialism in North America.* Oxford: Oxford University Press.

Stengel, Richard. 2017. "Why Saying 'Radical Islamic Terror' Isn't Enough." *New York Times*, February 13. Available at: https://nyti.ms/2l6mu56 (accessed July 29, 2019).

Tessler, Michael. 2016. *Post-Racial or Most-Racial? Race and Politics in the Obama Era.* Chicago: University of Chicago Press.

Weigel, Moira. 2016. "Political Correctness: How the Right Invented a Phantom Enemy." *Guardian*, November 30. Available at: https://www.theguardian.com/us-news/2016/nov/30/political-correctness-how-the-right-invented-phantom-enemy-donald-trump (accessed July 29, 2019).

8
Brave New Worlds
The Racial Regimes of the Americas
Michael Hanchard

The Americas in its totality provides an opportunity to examine how borders and boundaries have been constituted out of dynamic relationships involving governments and institutions, territories, populations, and ideologies. Latin America in particular was the first region of the world to have multiple independent nation-states emerge from colonial sites created and managed by European imperial powers. Since the majority of Spanish colonies had become independent by the third decade of the nineteenth century, this period of new nation-state formation occurred nearly four generations before the collapse of the Ottoman and Hapsburg empires and well over 130 years before the proliferation of clusters of newly independent nation-states after World War II in Africa and Asia.

Population diversity—namely, the assemblage of indigenous, African, Asian and European peoples inhabiting common territory, first in colonies and subsequently nation-states—generated what could be characterized as the epistemological and ontological quandaries that human variation posed for makers of nation-states. To pose the epistemological and ontological questions in practical terms, state-makers throughout the New World struggled with three interrelated tasks related to the naming and valuation of divergent populations. First, there was the question of so-called descent, the origins of populations. The second quandary concerned the presumed correlation between a person's or group's origins or descent and their role in new societies. The third problem was in the correlation between identification and political community: should the enslaved, women, indigenous people, the poor and illiterate, who in most cases were identified as unsuitable for citizenship, be formally and forcibly excluded from participation in the polity? If so, on what grounds would the indigenous, the enslaved and their descendants, peasants, the poor and illiterate, be excluded from political participation in a republican society and polity?

The American Revolution in the eighteenth century, and the Haitian and republican revolutions of South America in the early nineteenth century, gave the Americas the distinction of becoming the first European colonized region of the world to depart from the imperial umbrellas of Spain, Portugal, Britain, and France (the dominant European powers). The foundational elites of these new nation-states (23 by the second decade of the nineteenth century in Latin America alone) relied upon ecclesiastic and scientific discourses to rationalize—and racialize—population hierarchy and inequality in national law. Haiti and the United States, in particular, provide interesting points of comparison and insight into both the codification of racial and ethno-national hierarchy within individual nation-states, and more broadly, within the nation-state system itself.

Religious and scientific discourses rationalized the inferiority of Africans, Native Americans, and Asians, and in most cases women, regardless of national, regional, or presumed racial origin. The Catholic Church and its missionaries in Latin America devised the *castas* system, which fused ecclesiastic and colonial authority, to administer to a racial, phenotypic, and religious hierarchy that at once denigrated indigenous and African peoples and their customs while valorizing Christianity, Europe, and whiteness. This mode of ecclesiastic racism, which preceded scientific racism by two centuries, would prefigure subsequent reaction to the scientific racism of the nineteenth century when New World intellectuals began to ponder the implications of race mixing.

National intellectuals in the Caribbean and South America ranging from Gilberto Freyre, Nina Rodriques, Simon Bolivar, and Fernando Ortiz, worried about the consequences and implications of melding distinct populations from various parts of the world into a single nation-state. An additional worry expressed by Woodrow Wilson from the United States, Alexis de Tocqueville from France, and Edward Augustus Freeman from England was the prospect of being ruled by formerly enslaved Africans and their descendants (see De Tocqueville 2014; Wilson 1967; see also Hanchard 1998; Helg 1995; Hooker 2017; Mazower 2013; Miller 2009; Skidmore 1990). An examination of how governments and elites, at both national and local levels, responded to these anxieties provides opportunities to examine how racialized human borders and boundaries were constituted (in both the embodied and textual sense) and managed in the Americas and in modern Western politics more generally.

My specific contribution to this volume is an explication of how racial and ethno-national regimes have functioned within nominally democratic nation-states, not in opposition to democracy but in conjunction with state and elite aspirations to reap most, if not all, the benefits of a limited, democratic republicanism, while also denying marginalized populations the same rights and privileges. In all of the cases examined, racial and ethno-national regimes can be identified by the development and maintenance of formal and informal institutions to demarcate, restrict, and surveil the movement of racialized or ethno-nationally subordinated populations within a given nation-state. In many nominally democratic, republican, or democratizing polities, racial and ethno-national regimes developed in response to populations in society to whom ruling elites did not originally intend to grant citizenship.

Underpinned by norms, customs, and the rule of law, racial regimes perpetuate inequalities in the allocation and distribution of public goods and resources such as education, employment, housing, and social welfare, in addition to formal limitations upon suffrage, property ownership, and freedom of assembly. Racial regimes impact on domestic and foreign policy not only through the institutional measures noted just above, but through immigration policy and, in certain cases, the extension of internal boundary-making institutions (formal and informal) into territories occupied and administered by other nation-states.

Racial and ethno-national hierarchies within the nation-state system help complicate the analytic distinction offered in this volume between borders, which externalize difference between one nation-state and another, and boundaries, which symbolize and often maintain internal distinctions within a nation-state. Within the nation-state system, the internal boundaries separating majority and minority populations have often corresponded to more globalized understandings of racial hierarchy. The transnational dimensions of racial and ethno-national hierarchies are evidenced in the imperial templates of powerful European nation-states, as well as Japan and China.

Regimes and Racial Orders

In the social sciences, regimes are almost always characterized as structuring processes that guide actors toward specific objectives. In the case of labor regimes, incentives, reward, punishment, and coercion were imposed in a variety of productive forms (industrial and nonindustrial wages, or indentured and enslaved labor). Taylorist regimes, for example, were utilized in several plantation economies to extract the most productivity from slaves engaged in sugarcane and banana production. Any behavior considered by the architects and supervisors of the regime to be detrimental to its optimal functioning would be prohibited (see Holt 1992).

Rogers Brubaker (1992) reminds us that nation-states are not merely conjunctures of governments with a national citizenry inhabiting a formally recognized and demarcated territory. They are also ethical and political communities that are, in effect, instances of endogamy. Yet in order to identify and comprehend the multiregional and multinational dimensions of racist logics that privileged white people of European descent in the Americas, we must recognize that many governments of the Americas well into the first half of the twentieth century envisioned their countries as places where their notions of Europe (modernity, industry, order, and whiteness) could be articulated. Thus, Brubaker's description assumes that nation-states were—and are—discrete entities. Within these ethico-political communities, however, there is also a long history of national citizenries that evidence multiple affiliations that sometimes contradict if not undermine the premise of an internally coherent national community. Ethnic, religious, political and presumed racial affinities across the discrete boundaries of nation-states leads us to a reality that demonstrates that national citizenries are often composite communities. The prevalence of racial and ethno-national regimes across nation-states provides evidence of the affinities that cannot be explained simply through territory, sovereignty, or citizenship.

Racial and ethno-national regimes are not static institutions, and they develop in response to phenomena identified as a politico-administrative problem for state authorities and population management within a territory. They evolve and transform over time in response to shifting immigration and political and economic developments, and even sexual and marital relations between members of differentially situated groups. When specific populations are deemed a "problem" for governance, calls for immigration and employment controls, increased policing and surveillance, and even criteria for holding elective office were developed in response to the real or imagined increase in populations deemed unassimilable by society or the polity, or both.

Ethno-national and racial regimes can be identified across the continuum of modern Western politics, ranging from totalitarian and fascist governments to liberal and social-democratic government. I am most fascinated by the interrelationship of racial and ethno-national regimes and democratic polities. Much liberal scholarship in the social sciences (especially in political theory and American politics), but also in American studies and in US history, treat racism, gendered, and ethno-national chauvinism as somehow antithetical to democracy. The analysis offered here, part of a more broadly comparative research project on democracy and inequality, suggests that racial and ethno-national regimes have often served as barriers to political membership in democratic polities.

Closer examination of the dynamic interactions of states, dominant and subordinate political actors, and institutional settings reveal crises of statecraft, when political elites were confronted with the prospect of living amongst noncitizens who could potentially become citizens. The equalizing potential of full citizenship for noncitizen "others" generated debate and reactions amongst the citizenry in American nation-states, revealing anxieties about presumed racial and ethno-national difference in their societies and polities. In the perspective of many national elites in Latin America, the expansion of suffrage was equated not with the deepening of democracy, but with the devaluation of their own political, economic, and social privilege. As with the revolution in France, republican movements in the Americas revealed a similar hesitation—or an outright refusal—to allow colonial subjects, the enslaved, and the formerly enslaved to participate fully in politics. Ultimately, republican movements seeking to solve what was known as "the social question" often exacerbated the racial question.

Conservative Liberalism and Racial Regimes in Latin America

Benedict Anderson's synthetic treatment of nationalism as a cultural and material artifact of print capitalism reintroduces the concept of creole pioneers to a nonspecialist audience to characterize the political and economic activities of colonial elites in the Americas who were influenced by the republican ideologies of the French and American revolutions while at the same time ensuring their continued dominance (see Anderson 1983). Two key features characterize creole pioneers. First-generation descendants of Europeans, they considered it their providence to create independent nation-states with the laws and mores of the nation-states and societies of Western Europe, principally, Spain, Portugal, Britain, and France. Yet they were not physically in Europe, and as a result of their newly honed political affiliations and aspirations, no longer Europeans in a political sense. Their primary political affiliations lay with the societies and institutions they sought to create in the New World. Second, they were faced with the following political challenge: forging new societies premised upon the model of European nation-states with populations who were neither European nor necessarily interested in contributing to social, political, and economic systems that largely served to marginalize them.

Rather than merely extending republican ideals of direct, participatory democracy to the unenfranchised masses, these elites devised ingenious laws emphasizing literacy, property ownership, and other criteria as barriers to popular suffrage and polity participation. By contrast, popular egalitarian movements such as rebellions among the enslaved and indigenous, along with peasant uprisings, sought to abolish slaveholding regimes, serfdom, and tribute. Part of the political challenge of creole pioneers was to convince the enslaved and their descendants, along with indigenous populations and byproducts of miscegenation, that national independence was in the interest of both elites and the masses. In many cases, such as Colombia, Cuba, and the United States, the enslaved and indigenous participated in nationalist movements in the hope that their participation would bring about emancipation and suffrage.

The role of slaves, peasants, poor women, and indigenous populations in independence movements across a geographical span ranging from the United States to Argentina exemplify the challenges faced by *criollo* elites to transform colonial outposts into new societies and nation-states. These creoles were demographic minorities and thereby outnumbered in the majority of new nation-states, with the exception of the United States and Canada.

Creole nationalists shared at least one objective with their earlier Athenian counterparts' experiment in democracy: they proclaimed a democratic republic for a selected few, and the basis of their material wealth, if not their freedom, was coerced labor (slave, serf, and peasant). This will become evident below in the consideration of Simon Bolivar in his management of political crises in racial politics in Gran Colombia.

Consequently, creoles set limits upon the extension of the franchise in societies such as Cuba, Haiti, Argentina, Brazil, and Gran Colombia. The majority of American nation-states from Canada to Chile abolished slavery *after* obtaining formal independence. Even in instances where popular support from marginalized populations (the enslaved, freed persons, the indigenous, and the poor) was pivotal in the success of a revolutionary nationalist movement, freedom for slaves and their dependents was not simultaneous with national independence. Once independent, most American nation-states devised federal laws to limit (when not prohibiting completely) formerly enslaved populations and their descendants (Colombia, the United States, Paraguay, Uruguay, Argentina, and Brazil among them) from participating in civil and political society as citizens with suffrage and property rights, two significant attributes in the political cultures of liberal nation-states after the eighteenth century.

Creoles, often together with colonial loyalists, created novel criteria of political exclusion to ensure that former slaves did not wield the same political rights as their former owners. Institutionalized inequality was remade by the rule of law to adapt to new political prospects and dangers, namely the democratization of society to enable former slaves access to the polity, thereby making (along with women and foreigners) members of the polity and society one and the same. The political predicaments for creoles resulting from the prospect and actuality of freed slaves can be evidenced throughout the Americas.[1]

One significant example is included here from Spanish America to underscore the extent to which racial slavery and emancipation became a significant social and political challenge for white elites who sought to both institutionalize and secure their political and social privilege at the crucial moment of nation-state foundation. The dynamic interactions among slave owners, royalists, slaves, freepersons, indigenous people, their immediate descendants, and their "mixed" offspring helped produce, when codified in law, the definitions and categorization of both citizen and noncitizen.

Simon Bolivar—one of the most prominent advocates of Pan-Americanism in Latin America, and perhaps the most significant state-builder in the region during the nineteenth century—unified what came to be known as Gran Colombia in a successful war for independence from Spain. The French, American, and Haitian revolutions deeply impacted Bolivar, perhaps more so than any other nationalist of the Americas, because the fate of his nationalist and Pan-Americanist projects were directly impacted by the Haitian Revolution.

After two separate attempts to achieve independence from Spain were thwarted by royalist troops and lack of local support, Bolivar sought refuge in Jamaica and then Haiti. Jamaica was a British colony and a source of great wealth for the British Empire, its capitalists, and colonial elites, as well as a locale for British politicians and plantation owners to experiment with economic and social policy. Haiti provided a safe haven for Bolivar after Spain briefly reclaimed Gran Colombia in 1816. Alexander Petion, the Haitian monarch, provided Bolivar with sanctuary, money, weapons, and ammunition with one condition: liberty for all slaves within the territories of Gran Colombia.

Upon returning to Venezuela, Bolivar partially fulfilled his promise and therein revealed his distinctly creole political calculus, a combination of liberalism, monarchy, and racial rule. After Gran Colombia achieved independence from Spain in 1821, Bolivar and his followers drafted a constitution that combined French republican principles, British parliamentary democracy, and monarchial prerogatives to enable Bolivar to rule indefinitely and creole elites to inherit political offices. As part of the new constitution, all children born to slave mothers after 1821 were declared free.

As in Brazil's Lei Rio Branco (also known as Lei do Ventre Livre) of 1831, the 1821 manumission law of Gran Colombia did not actually outlaw slavery, but rather provided formal freedom to the unborn while keeping their mothers, as well as fathers and nonwhite relatives, in conditions of bondage or passive citizenship. Historian Aline Helg notes that the Colombian constitution, like other Latin American constitutions crafted after successful independence movements in the 1820s, "stressed its protections of Colombians' liberty, security, property and equality" (Helg 2004: 163). Property was at once an inclusionary and exclusionary criterion for active citizenship, since propertyless males were disqualified from active citizenship. The majority of slaves and freepersons could neither read nor write Spanish. Thus, Colombian constitutional criteria for citizenship effectively limited suffrage and active citizenship to creole elites and people of European descent in Venezuelan society, excluding blacks and zambos (so-called half-castes, of indigenous and African ancestry). Finally, "property" included slaves. Thus, citizenship laws based in whole or in part upon descent, literacy, and property requirements nevertheless served to limit the political access of people of African descent in the upper reaches of society, the polity, and economy of Latin America. They were, in effect, as in earlier, colonial times, relegated to the realm of labor, not the realm of rule (see e.g. Gordon 1998; Helg 1995; Hooker 2009).

Haiti

The Haitian Revolution, which began as a slave rebellion in the French colony of Saint-Domingue on Hispaniola in 1791, brought both the antinomies and ideals of the French Revolution to the forefront of debates in the colonies as well as the new nation-states of the Americas (see Gaspar & Geggus 1997). The slave rebellion in Saint-Domingue, France's most profitable colony before the French Revolution, generated intense discussion and ultimately fear among New World slaveholders about the moral, economic, and political costs of slavery. Jacobinism, along with other nationalist and revolutionary ideologies of the eighteenth and nineteenth centuries, critiqued aristocracy for its discouragement of status acquisition based on talent and achievement (meritocracy), not birth. Yet even the Jacobins of the French Revolution imposed limits upon who could be citizens of the new republic.

The apparent contradictions between French bourgeois claims of the rights of man and citizen on the one hand, and their reliance upon profits garnered from human trafficking and coerced labor on the other, resonated throughout the Americas and the Western imperial nation-states with colonial holdings and subservient populations. The prospect and eventual reality of an independent black republic led to changes in domestic policy in the United States and colonial policies regarding the institution of slavery and related trafficking and monitoring of slave populations (see Berlin 1998).

In his account of the Haitian Revolution, C.L.R. James wrote that slavery served to remind the Jacobins and their progressive and missionary allies of the colonial question—the spectre of the colony in their deliberations regarding republican freedoms. Yet with the exception of an organization devoted to the abolition of slavery, the Friends of the Negro, "everybody conspired to forget the slaves" (James 1989: 71). Referring to debates in the French Assembly at the moment when conflicts between Left and Right prompted the Thermidor reaction (the Terror) and the brutal countermeasures to follow, James concluded that "the colonial question again and again split the bourgeoisie, made it ashamed of itself, destroyed its morale and weakened its capacity to deal with the great home problems which faced it" (ibid.: 70).

The Jacobin Right strategized to forestall discussion of slavery, particularly at the moment when colonists in Haiti, Martinique, and Guadeloupe warned of the prospect of race war in the Francophone Caribbean if slavery was abolished and mulattos gained full political rights. Abolition advocates ranged from those who distinguished, in keeping with the forms of rights under consideration in France at the time of the Revolution, civil rights from political rights, to advocates like Sieyes and Condorcet who believed in full civil and political equality for freepersons and slaves. Pro-slavery advocates often referred to divine right, racial laws, or simply an assertion of their privilege as justification for the continued servitude of their black subjects.[2]

The rebellion and subsequent revolution on Saint-Domingue brought practical political and economic exigencies to the fore: the colony was far too profitable to simply relinquish. But what kind of compromise could enable poor whites to retain their status vis-à-vis the enslaved and mulattoes, allow slaves greater freedoms (if not full civil and political rights), and retain the monopoly of force of the maritime bourgeoisie and white elite to ensure their continued extraction of profit? Given the intensity of the conflicts in Saint-Domingue, could a compromise be reached among these contending positions? One participant in these discussions in France during the period was Pierre Gaspard Chaumette, a leading journalist and member of the Paris city government between 1790 until his date with the guillotine during the Terror in April 1794. He succinctly captured the problems not only of France, but of democracies more generally:

> Without speaking here of the danger and folly of slavery in democratic states, I could cite the history of all the peoples who have had slaves and depict the torments of the government whether it tries to keep them in a yoke that often quakes with their struggles and tries to diminish ... their too great population; or whether it tries to restrain the cruelty of the masters. I could cite the laws that rapidly succeed one another, the regulations that follow upon regulations. (quoted in Hunt 1996: 116–18)

This passage, taken from Chaumette's speech celebrating the abolition of slavery just two months earlier, encapsulates the problems of law, population management, and administration incumbent upon governments that administer democratic and enslaved institutions simultaneously. Saint-Domingue, the Demerara Revolt in Guyana, Harper's Ferry in Virginia, the Morant Bay Rebellion in Jamaica, and many other slave rebellions in the New World resonate with Chaumette's description of the consequences of a dualist regime that ultimately becomes untenable.

The colonists of Saint-Domingue, however, wanted nothing less than a maintenance of the dualist regime. They understood that any change in the racial order of the region would upend the colonial political economy and thus the basis of French colonial power, authority, and wealth. Whites in Saint-Domingue viewed black and mulatto political participation in colonial society as a threat to their very existence as a dominant racial, economic, and political force. Within Saint-Domingue, tensions between blacks, mulattos, and elite and non-elite whites during the period of the revolution further underscores how racial regimes became operative throughout the French empire: territorial France and its *départements* and colonies. If, as the Jacobins claimed, the French National Constituent Assembly's "Declaration of the Rights of Man and the Citizen" was a truly universal document, then shouldn't those rights proclaimed therein apply to slaves—and other people—as well? This point was raised by, among others, Danton, and was opposed by, among others, Robespierre. There was a political explanation for the tabling of this very particular "social question," the question of slavery: if the Jacobins amended the "Declaration of the Rights of Man and the Citizen" to include slaves, then it would be impossible to convince those recently empowered by citizenship that either God, nature, or pure coercion justified their subjugation and unremunerated toil. The source of wealth for a good portion of the French monarchy and the French maritime bourgeoisie would disappear. Consequently, the political rights eloquently proclaimed in the final document pertained to those already endowed with citizenship, whether residing in metropolitan or colonial France, and not the unenfranchised.

Recent scholarship on Saint-Domingue and the Haitian Revolution has provided insight into additional tensions not only between mulattoes, whites, and blacks, but among the category referred to as free "people of color" (*gens de couleur*), which included African-born women and men who somehow acquired freedom, as well as children who were the offspring of unions between slave owners and enslaved women. The boundaries created by whites within colonial society to restrict full economic and political participation of the enslaved, free blacks, and free people of color affirmed what critics of enslavement and colonialism have referred to as the "aristocracy of the skin." Laurent Dubois provides primary evidence of colonial laws devised to prevent free people of color "from practicing law and medicine, from holding local administrative positions, even from buying luxury clothes and furniture" (Dubois 2012: 25).

The political aspirations of the mulattos of Saint-Domingue generated the most anxiety among the *petit blancs* of the colony, because wealthy or well-off mulattoes had already become an economic force there. The repression of their political interests was accompanied by brutal repression of mulatto attempts at political and, ultimately, military mobilization. In a chapter appropriately titled "Parliament and Property," C.L.R. James provides a foreboding historical context to the eve of the revolution, as tensions between slaves, slave owners, *petit blancs*, and the maritime bourgeoisie reached the point of irreducible conflict: "It was the quarrel between bourgeoisie and monarchy that brought the Paris masses on the political stage. It was the quarrel between whites and mulattoes that woke the sleeping slaves" (James 1989: 73). The brutal repression and denial of citizenship by *petit blancs* in the colony of mulatto aspirations for political rights represented an attempt to maintain a racial regime that ensured white dominance and black, mulatto, and freeperson subordination during a period of intense political crisis and change, when the conditions of possibility seemed to suggest, at least in Paris, that active citizenship could be extended beyond the bourgeoisie to all members of society, not just members of the polity.

Despite enormous exogenous constraints and internal conflicts concerning color, caste, class, and agriculture, the newly formed Haitian state sought to unify disparate groups of people (mulattos, the Polish mercenaries who deserted the French imperial army, slaves) under the category of black peoples. For example, the Haitian Constitution of 1805 forbade whites from owning property in Haiti, a response to fears of French reoccupation through land ownership rather than military conquest. Foreign blacks were given special status under civil laws and were to be treated as Haitian citizens. Article 14 of the constitution required all Haitians, regardless of color, to be referred to as black (see Linstant 1886).

The constitutionally mandated citizenship granted to populations of African descent was an acknowledgement of this unprecedented imagined community, based largely in recognition of the widespread political repression of subjects of African descent the world over. Moreover, the constitution also authorized military operations against any and all nation-states and peoples who held people of African descent captives and profited from their labor. Making good on this constitutional prerogative, Boyer, the fourth emperor of Haiti, invaded the adjoining Spanish colony on Hispaniola (now the Dominican Republic) and successfully—albeit temporarily—freed slaves there. Additionally, the constitution declared any person of African descent a potential citizen of Haiti, and thus articulated an automatic law of the returnee (see Bellegarde-Smith 2004: 69).

Thus, "home" for Haitians, and by extension, blacks, was constituted in the act of sovereignty and the attendant claim of territorial dominion rather than place of origin; there was nothing natural or predetermined about this virtual space for politics created by mostly African-born slaves and their descendants in a territory formerly held and administered by the French Empire. Yet the Haitian instantiation of sovereignty was also a recognition of the racialized dimensions of the nation-state system, since it provided the possibility of citizenship for blacks from all parts of the world, and not just Haitian-born ones. The Haitian government's granting of citizenship to the Polish mercenaries who deserted the French imperial army to fight on the side of the Saint-Domingue rebellion delimited an exclusively racial criteria for citizenship, an acknowledgement that the mercenary's politico-military contributions to the revolutionary struggle warranted membership of the polity. Their color and nationality was of secondary importance to a new nation that needed loyal citizens who had already demonstrated their commitment.

For its efforts, the sovereign republic of Haiti was ostracized by Western powers. Not a single Western nation-state recognized Haiti's formal sovereignty after it gained independence in 1804. To put Haiti's nationalist and abolitionist efforts into perspective, Britain was the first imperial power to formally abolish the slave trade in its colonies in 1831, over 25 years after the declaration of Haitian sovereignty. France did not recognize Haiti formally until 1838, and only after imposing in 1825 the condition that Haiti pay an indemnity for the losses France incurred during the war. Haiti agreed to pay the indemnity, which further impoverished the financially weak state. Britain, Denmark, the Netherlands, and Sweden commenced diplomatic relations with Haiti soon after France's conditional recognition in 1825 (see Trouillot 1990: 49–51). The Vatican would not recognize Haiti as an independent republic until 1860.

The Vatican's refusal to institute an independent diocese in Haiti, one of the requisites of Vatican recognition, denied Haiti a system of formal education at a crucial moment in the new nation-state's development. The United States did not formally recognize Haiti until 1862, though both governmental and private business interests had engaged in trade throughout the period of isolation. Haiti's predicament, in this respect, foreshadowed the conundrum of Cuban–US relations in the latter half of the twentieth century, as the political logic of the major hegemon in the region greatly hindered the economic, political, and cultural access a small Caribbean nation-state and its peoples had with the rest of the world. As in the sixteenth and seventeenth centuries, through *asientos* (licenses granted by the Church to trade in enslaved Africans) and the *castas* system, the Catholic Church once again aligned itself with the imperial powers of the nation-state system to uphold the institution of slavery and the repression of black freedoms.

Haiti's sanctioning and isolation by Western states inaugurated the pattern of political marginalization of black political actors and states in the international political economy of the post-Westphalian era. Haiti's political behavior, however, would also serve as the archetype for future black political mobilization on a global scale, whether in Africa, the Caribbean, or points elsewhere over the succeeding century. As Trouillot notes, each Haitian state leader after 1802—L'Ouverture, Dessalines, Christophe, Pétion, and Boyer—all concurred that "slavery as an institution was to be forever abolished from Haiti" (Trouillot 1990: 48).

The embargos, sanctions, and retaliation against the republic of Haiti indicates the degree to which Western powers were quite hostile to the idea and practice of a black nation-state with the right of sovereignty and recognition in the international system of nation-states. Haiti was viewed as a threat to the geopolitics of Western colonialism and the fabulous profits and status privilege generated within them. A people who had overcome the institution of racial slavery and colonialism to create an independent nation-state and society could have been viewed as the heirs to the French and American revolutions. Instead, Haiti became the scourge of the nation-state system.

The Haitian Revolution in particular underscores how an analytic emphasis on the nation-state as the source of the distinction between borders and boundaries can obscure more transnational patterns of racial hierarchy and exclusion constituted within the nation-state itself. In these and other examples, governments extended their policies of racial, religious, and ethno-national preferences to locales and populations outside their immediate territorial dominion. In this sense, external borders were internalized and internal boundaries were externalized through the mandating of preferences for certain groups over others.

The United States

An analysis of federal and state law, policy, and juridical decisions in the United States in the period spanning the late eighteenth to the mid-nineteenth centuries provides an opportunity to locate the United States within the larger cluster of cases analyzed here. During this period, the French and Haitian revolutions prompted changes in US federal and state laws to heighten surveillance of republican-minded radicals with seditious ideas, and at the other end of the spectrum, to more closely monitor the trafficking of slaves brought to the United States from the Caribbean, the region where the Haitian Revolution took place.

State and federal laws concerning slavery and black insurrection in the nineteenth and twentieth centuries directly influenced the development of national immigration policy, restrictions on the internal movement of black peoples within the United States, and restrictions upon the travel and movement of black citizens or subjects of the United States in other polities. Movement restrictions upon African American slaves and freepersons made US African Americans native-born "foreigners." As will be explored below, legal determination of the status of US African Americans as slaves and freepersons often influenced the legal determination of the immigrant as a potential citizen of the United States.

The United States government responded to the French Revolution with the creation of the Alien and Sedition Acts of 1798. The acts sought, among other things, to stem the flow of European political radicals into the country. Regarding the Haitian Revolution, the US government was not only concerned with the spread of ideologies via elite discourse, but with the circulation of rebellious ideas among slave populations. Winthrop Jordan writes how white observers noted that US slaves grew more insolent with news of the Saint-Domingue revolt. Whites, especially in the Eastern seaboard states, were wary of the presence of West Indian slaves who accompanied their masters from Saint-Domingue and the possible synergies between the imported and established slave populations. The iconographic depiction of the contented black slave was replaced with the icon of what Jordan called the "Negro as potential rebel" (Jordan 2012: 386). State, local, and federal governments began to pay close attention to the types of slaves brought into the country (see Gaspar & Geggus 1997). The South in particular fed upon the rumors of rampant mayhem in Haiti as an example of what would happen if slaves were given their freedom.

The response of slave owners throughout the New World to the fall of Saint-Domingue to a group of rebellious slaves bears some similarity to the response of French Prime Minister Jacques Chirac after the World Trade Center attacks of September 11, 2001, in New York City: "We are all New Yorkers." Similarly, the rebellion in Saint-Domingue made all New World slave societies French. The exodus of French colonials and their slaves from the colony of Saint-Domingue began in 1793, two years after the revolt. Jordan (2012: 377) chronicles how US citizens and local governments, through philanthropy and governmental assistance, provided safe haven for some colonial refugees from Saint-Domingue, many of whom fled to Cuba before moving elsewhere. The major powers and industries that profited from the slave trade and plantation economies empathized with the calamity that bourgeois and maritime France experienced, which could happen to any world power with colonial political economies and subject populations.

The prospect of slave revolt led many state and municipal governments in the United States to adopt laws that tracked and monitored slave populations and their internal movement, as well as the influx of slaves imported from the Caribbean. South Carolina prohibited the importation of all slaves in 1792 and prohibited slaves from Hispaniola from entering the state in 1803, as did Georgia (Hunt 2006: 108). In Virginia, slave owners and importers had to take an oath that they had not imported any slaves from the West Indies or Africa; North Carolina imposed a similar statute in 1795 (Mullin 1992: 226).

Many Southerners believed that the Haitian Revolution was caused by an uncontrolled slave population; thus, prohibiting the slave trade was a direct result of the revolution and a concern for safety. Not surprisingly, West Indian slaves were considered more dangerous than African ones, and US slaveholders began to pay greater attention to ethnic distinctions among slave populations than they had done before, and as had been done in the Caribbean, where slave revolts, resistance, and rebellion were more frequent. Laws were devised to curtail and monitor the movement of black populations in many states and to prevent the arrival of French West Indian blacks. The increased attention to diversity within slave populations was an implicit acknowledgement of their internal ethno-national and regional variation. With increased fears of black revolt, freed blacks were in an even more precarious position. They were often re-enslaved for minor infractions of state law, or if they moved from one state to another (Stuckey 1987: 146). Runaway slaves were often captured in free states and brought back to the site of their enslavement.

Virginia was the only Southern state that did not adopt restrictive laws against the entry of West Indian slaves. A random, but nonetheless instructive, analysis of state legislation of slave and freeperson movement in the states of Philadelphia, Delaware, Mississippi, and Illinois demonstrates that all four states passed legislation prohibiting black migration into and within their territorial domain in the eighteenth and nineteenth centuries. Out of 686 statutes passed between 1788 and 1798 in Pennsylvania, four statutes pertained to free blacks, mulattos, and slaves. Two statutes, passed in 1788 and 1789 respectively, relate to the eventual abolition of slavery in the state and the formation of the Pennsylvania Society for Promoting the Abolition of Slavery (see Mitchell and Flanders 1896). Of the four statutes, only the 1795 statute pertains to slave movement, specifically slaves of colonial refugees from Saint-Domingue.[3] The statute, in tortuous language, makes a distinction between slaveholding and nonslaveholding refugees, and provided monetary relief of up to $2,500 for the latter. In other words, refugees who were not slave owners were granted greater monetary relief than the slave owners seeking compensation for their loss of property as a consequence of the revolution.

Delaware provides an interesting example because of its geographical location at the border between free and slave states. Between 1803 and 1813, seven acts directly related to free blacks, mulattos, and slaves were passed. Four of the seven regulated internal movement, emigration, or intermarriage of any member of the aforementioned population with whites. In the case of Mississippi, a slave state, eleven acts were passed between 1820 and 1830 concerning slave, mulatto, and black freepersons. The provisions of the adopted statutes include prohibition against the employment of a Negro in a printing office and the entry of slaves who have been convicted of a criminal offense. Even Illinois, a free state and the land of Lincoln, passed laws prohibiting and regulating slave and freeperson movement and migration. Of 22 acts passed between 1809 and 1818, only two concerned free blacks, mulattos, and slaves. One of these two, however, dealt expressly with the entry of free blacks and mulattos.

In the cases of Mississippi, Illinois, and Delaware, all passed statutes that required a kind of 'racial registry' whereby freepersons and mulattos had to register and, in some instances, pay a fee to reside and remain within the state. What all of this suggests is that a system of intrastate identification, registration, and surveillance was devised during the nineteenth century to monitor black and colored presence in both free and slave states. These racial registries have their sole parallel in immigration provisions and restrictions in state and federal law.

Inevitably, the retention of slavery necessitated the clarification of other federal laws and policies designed to distinguish people from commerce, the movement of actual or potential citizens, and slaves. Both state and federal law evolved to distinguish the transport of slaves from the emigration of freeborn persons. The ninth section of the first article of the US Constitution concerning Congress's ability to monitor immigration and slavery led to Supreme Court cases in which individuals and states challenged the federal capacity to tax foreign immigrants entering the United States, and to determine whether section 9 of the first article applied to slaves, immigrants, or both. Though these cases did establish the precedent of congressional ability to impose taxes upon slaves and immigrants after 1808, the larger distinctions between the importation of slaves and migration of immigrants were unavoidable. For this reason, laws and policies with respect to immigration evolved, in part, out of the acknowledgement of their presence within the nation and the need to distinguish black and slave status from free whites. In so doing, the United States government not only developed immigration policies for the entire population, but further underscored the distinctive marginality of the black population excluded from the category of citizen. At the same time, subsequent waves of immigration from Europe and Latin America would generate crises of racial and ethno-national classification; should these new immigrants be classified according to existing criteria? How close or how far away are they from our ideal citizen?

The decisions of the US Supreme Court with respect to the so-called "Passenger Cases," *Smith v. Turner* (1849) and *Norris v. the City of Boston* (1849), led to the emergence of federal immigration law.[4] At issue in these cases was the federal government's exclusive ability to impose taxes upon incoming immigrants, as well as a state's ability to levy duty charges upon slave traders who brought slaves into the country. In the decision, the Supreme Court declared that states, as a policing authority, could monitor the entry of paupers, convicts, and slaves. Slaves fell under the category of commerce, while paupers and convicts (whites) were considered public safety hazards. The entry of white men into a state, however, was distinct from the entry of paupers, slaves, and convicts because free white men were not restricted from citizenship.

What is significant about this ruling, in addition to its structuration of a formal immigration policy, is its classification of slavery, vagabonds, and paupers under the auspices of police authority and, hence, criminality, noncitizens whose entry "might trouble the internal tranquility and security of the state".[5] Thus slaves, vagabonds, and paupers would fall under criminal codes, while citizens and foreigners would be first classified under civil codes.[6] While the court's opinion acknowledged the right of individual states to devise laws to monitor public behavior, the power to tax the entry of foreigners resided with the federal government.

The decision regarding the "Passenger Cases" is significant for at least three reasons: its distinction between the criminal and the noncriminal, the distinction between slave and free persons, and the criminalization of undesirable populations that were free and unfree, white and nonwhite. The distinction between importation and migration acknowledged a wider distinction between voluntary and involuntary movement of persons across nation-state boundaries. The development of immigration and commerce law with respect to these populations became the federal government's way of maintaining the distinctions between them in jurisprudential and material terms.

A far better known case is the much-examined Dred Scott decision of the Supreme Court.[7] In the majority decision, Justice Roger B. Taney explained his rationale: Europeans were considered citizens by individual states before the formation of the United States, and subsequently in the crafting of the constitution. African-born or descended peoples, however, were slaves more often than not and consequently had no rights to citizenship under the US Constitution or in federal courts. Thus, Dred Scott did not even have the right to bring a case on his behalf before a federal court:

> The question is simply this: Can a negro, whose ancestors were imported into this country, and sold as slaves, become a member of the political community formed and brought into existence by the Constitution of the United States, and as such become entitled to all the rights, and privileges, and immunities, guaranteed by that instrument to the citizen?[8]

Taney's question frames the distinction between society and polity in the context of US politics, and, as a result, the Supreme Court decision, to remind his audience—jurists and non-jurists alike—of the stakes involved in the distinction.

Two ingenious, albeit perverse, rhetorical maneuvers underlie Taney's argument. First, Taney utilized a very Jacksonian understanding of the relationship between state's rights and federal law to argue for the supremacy of state law in adjudicating matters of race. Secondly, Taney argued that England, as a European nation, prohibited the political participation of a "degraded race" in its colonies, and concluded that the United States should be similarly consistent in its racial perspectives. The perverse nature of this argument is its rhetorical alliance in racial terms with the very imperial power it successfully freed itself from on the grounds of political repression, premised upon a political commonality across nation-states that was ultimately based upon a presumed racial commonality.

Taney's majority opinion in *Dred Scott v. Sandford* (1857) provides some ideational evidence of at minimum a multi-national racial ideal in which Anglo-Saxons (Taney's language) and Euro-Aryans or Aryans (Woodrow Wilson's language) represent the highest form of humanity—and by extension, political community—which becomes part of the basis for his determination of a very specific instance within a national territory of the suitability of a Negro to present his case before the highest judiciary of the land.

The conjuncture of racial regimes and immigration policy in the United States helps illustrate how ethnic and racial categorizations are dynamically related and ultimately determined in—and through—politics. A key to understanding the distinction between borders and boundaries involves comprehending more than their function, but the objects and subjects of their functioning. Since racial and ethno-national hierarchies within the nation-state system have informed the formation of both borders and boundaries, we might consider analytically the distinction between the two as, to paraphrase early twentieth century political scientist Charles Merriam, indices of difference (Merriam 1939: 24). The ethno-national and racial boundaries of dominant nation-states within the nation-state system have in certain cases helped constitute the ideological justifications for internal and external boundary and border constitution in other nation-states.

Roy Garis, an advocate of selective immigration in the 1930s, wrote that "historical facts thus seem to refute the contentions of the past and present advocates of unrestricted immigration that we have always welcomed the immigrant with outstretched arms" (Garis 1927: 33). The first US Congress of 1790 limited naturalization to "any alien, being a freeborn white person." Rather than review the literature on the racist underpinnings of US immigration law in the history of the United States, the next section will focus on the Immigration and Nationality Act of 1952, which will demonstrate how the more contemporary rhetoric of "shithole" countries, and more and less desirable immigrants coming into the US republic, have roots deeper than the present Trump administration.

Racialized Immigration Law and Policy: Echoes of the Not Too Distant Past

While often viewed by scholars of US immigration policy as a significant shift from a race-based immigration policy to quotas based upon national origin, the Immigration and Nationality Act (also known as the McCarran–Walter Act) of 1952 in some important respects continued to maintain the formal as well as tacit parameters of racial and ideological conformity of previous immigration laws. Although it erased the racial restrictions of the 1790 "freeborn white persons" edict, it nonetheless contained significantly higher entry quotas for North European immigrants while maintaining racial restrictions for Asian immigrants, specifically Japanese, Koreans, and Pacific islanders.

While no explicit restriction of other nonwhite immigrants was made in the 1952 act, quota restrictions of 100 people per year were levied upon entrants from the British West Indies—Trinidad, Jamaica, and the Virgin Islands. As islands of the British Commonwealth, proponents of this portion of the bill argued, its quota restrictions were components of Britain's national quota. The author of the bill argued that black immigrants from Haiti and the Dominican Republic were under no such restrictions, since they were sovereign nations and not colonies. Thus, it was argued, the bill did not have a racially discriminatory basis. Those opposed to the act, however, noted that no other immigrant population in the Western Hemisphere had similar quota restrictions.[9]

Most scholars of the Immigration and Nationality Act have emphasized its ideological underpinnings in the xenophobic, communist hysteria of the period. The bill's emphasis on quota restrictions, particularly with regard to Asian immigrants (northern and southern Asia, including Australia and New Zealand), was coupled with a desire for a "good neighbor" policy to halt the alleged spread of communism throughout Asia. Indeed, much of the debate surrounding the amendment of racial restrictions against Asia-Pacific Triangle peoples focused on the contradictions of excluding members of populations who, as naturalized citizens, had either fought in World War II on the side of the Allied Powers or were descendants of Asian Americans who had lived for several generations in the United States and its territories. Opponents noted the seeming paradox of advocating geopolitical consistency during the Cold War (the "good neighbor" policy) while at the same time upholding racialist criteria for entry into the country, the very criteria the act was supposed to abolish. Their criticisms obviated the need to think of immigration policy not in terms of rhetoric and slogans about democracy, but in the racialized underpinning of actual immigration legislation.

Throughout the debate preceding the House vote on the bill, the racialist and ideological intent of its crafters was made explicit through their rationalization of racial and national restrictions. The significant bias toward northern and western European immigration (84 percent of the total immigration quota per year) was justified by several congressmen with the claim that these immigrants proved to be the most productive citizens, while southern and eastern Europeans were overwhelmingly represented in degenerate, illicit, and ideologically radical acts. For example, in the discussion of an amendment presented on April 23, 1952, to give nations with a quota under 7,000 the unused portions of quotas from nations with greater quota allotments, Representative Wood of Idaho stated that while he was not a follower of Hitler, the idea of racial superiority had some validity. Metaphorically referring to the idea of Aryan racial supremacy, Wood stated:

> We cannot tie a stone around its neck and dump it into the Atlantic just because it worked to the contrary in Germany ... I believe that possibly statistics would show that the Western European races have made the best citizens in America and are more easily made into Americans.[10]

With the unfounded assertion that "possibly statistics" would prove him right, Wood's preference for maintaining lower quotas for nonwhite immigrants had blatant echoes of *Herrenvolk* ("master race") notions of national unity. The amendment was rejected by a vote of 70 to 25.

Conclusion

My contribution here has sought to demonstrate how racial and ethnonational regimes developed in conjunction with democratic, republican polities in the Americas, serving as barriers to polity membership within those nominally democratic polities. Secondly, racial hierarchy and immigration policy have often been conjoined within laws of individual nation-states, and also evidenced by their similarity in multiple nation-states. By paying closer attention to what political scientist Charles Merriam referred to as the "indices of difference," the forging and maintenance of hierarchies by translating social differences into political differences, we can better identify and examine how racial and ethno-national regimes generate inequalities within nominally democratic polities and societies. The presence of these regimes also demonstrate the existence of multiple forms of governance and political rule, often in dynamic tension with each other.

On the one hand, nation-states are discrete sovereignties within the global system of nation-states. On the other hand, nation-states, like the populations that inhabit them, are also regionally, economically, and racially coded, with certain populations and states more likely to find affinities with one another than among other nation-states, often with proclamations of kinship and common origins, when in fact there are none.

Notes

1. For country-specific and regional accounts of these dynamics in early nineteenth-century independence movements, and in the region more generally, see Andrews (2004), Helg (1995), Jordan (2012), Rout (1976), Scott (1985), and Wright (1990).
2. See Lynne Hunt's nuanced introduction, which contextualizes key themes in debates and primary texts on the topic of human rights in the French Revolution (Hunt 1996).
3. See An Act to Afford Relief to Certain Distressed French Emigrants of 1795, in Mitchell and Flanders (1896).
4. Smith v. Turner, Norris v. City of Boston, 48 US 283 (1849). Reprinted as *Opinions of the Judges of the Supreme Court of the United States, in the Cases of Smith vs Turner, and Norris vs. the City of Boston* (Washington, DC: Office of the Printer to the Senate, 1849).
5. Smith v. Turner, in *Opinions of the Judges*, p.168.
6. Mr. Justice Wayne states, "The States have the right to turn off paupers, vagabonds, and fugitives from justice, and the States where slaves have a constitutional right to exclude all such as are, from a common ancestry and country, of the same class of men" (in *Opinions of the Judges*, pp. 170–1).
7. Dred Scott v. Sandford, 60 US 393 (1857).
8. Dred Scott v. Sandford, p.403.
9. See Revision of Immigration, Naturalization, and Nationality Laws: Hearings before the US Senate Committee on the Judiciary, 82nd Cong., 1st sess., 1952.
10. 16 Cong. Rec. 4314 (1952).

References

Anderson, Benedict. 1983. *Imagined Communities: Reflections on the Origins and Spread of Nationalism*. London: Verso.
Andrews, George Reid. 2004. *Afro-Latin America, 1800–2000*. New York: Oxford University Press.
Bellegarde-Smith, Patrick. 2004. *Haiti: The Breached Citadel*. Toronto: Canadian Scholars' Press.
Berlin, Ira. 1998. *Many Thousands Gone: The First Two Centuries of Slavery in North America*. Cambridge, MA: Belknap Press.

Brubaker, Rogers. 1992. *Citizenship and Nationhood in France and Germany.* Cambridge, MA: Harvard University Press.
De Tocqueville, Alexis. 2014 [1835]. *Democracy in America.* New York: Sheba Blake Publishing.
Dubois, Laurent. 2012. *Haiti.* New York: Metropolitan Books.
Garis, Roy L. 1927. *Immigration Restriction: A Study of the Opposition to and Regulation of Immigration into the United States.* New York: Macmillan.
Gaspar, David Barry, and David Geggus (eds). 1997. *A Turbulent Time: The French Revolution and the Greater Caribbean.* Bloomington: University of Indiana Press.
Gordon, Edmund T. 1998. *Disparate Diasporas: Identity and Politics in an African Nicaraguan Community.* Austin: University of Texas Press.
Hanchard, Michael. 1998. *Orpheus and Power: The Movimento Negro of Rio de Janeiro and São Paulo, Brazil 1945–1988.* Princeton: Princeton University Press.
Helg, Aline. 1995. *Our Rightful Share: The Afro-Cuban Struggle for Equality, 1886–1912.* Chapel Hill: University of North Carolina Press.
―――― 2004. *Liberty and Equality in Caribbean Colombia, 1770–1835.* Chapel Hill: University of North Carolina Press.
Holt, Thomas C. 1992. *The Problem of Freedom: Race, Labor, and Politics in Jamaica and Britain, 1832–1938.* Baltimore: Johns Hopkins University Press.
Hooker, Juliet. 2009. *Race and the Politics of Solidarity.* Oxford: Oxford University Press.
―――― 2017. *Theorizing Race in the Americas: Douglass, Sarmiento, Du Bois, and Vasconcelos.* Oxford: Oxford University Press.
Hunt, Alfred N. 2006. *Haiti's Influence on Antebellum America: Slumbering Volcano in the Caribbean.* Baton Rouge: Louisiana State University Press.
Hunt, Lynne. 1996. *The French Revolution and Human Rights: A Brief Documentary History.* New York: Bedford Books.
James, C.L.R. 1989. *The Black Jacobins: Touissant L'Ouverture and the San Domingo Revolution,* 2d ed. New York: Vintage Books.
Jordan, Winthrop D. 2012. *White Over Black: American Attitudes toward the Negro, 1550–1812,* 2nd ed. Chapel Hill: University of North Carolina Press.
Linstant, Pradine. 1886. *Recueil général des lois et actes du gouvernement d'Haïti depuis la proclamation de son indépendance jusqu'à nos jour.* Paris: A. Durand.
Mazower, Mark. 2013. *No Enchanted Palace: The End of Empire and the Ideological Origins of the United Nations,* Vol. 1. Princeton: Princeton University Press.
Merriam, Charles. 1939. *The New Democracy and the New Despotism.* New York: McGraw Hill.
Miller, Marilyn Grace. 2009. *Rise and Fall of the Cosmic Race: The Cult of Mestizaje in Latin America.* Austin: University of Texas Press.
Mitchell, James T., and Henry Flanders (eds). 1896. *The Statutes at Large of Pennsylvania from 1682–1801,* Vols. 2–14. Harrisburg: State Printer of Pennsylvania.
Mullin, Michael. 1992. *Africa in America: Slave Acculturation and Resistance in the American South and the British Caribbean, 1736–1831.* Urbana: University of Illinois Press.
Rout, Leslie B. 1976. *The African Experience in Spanish America, 1502 to the Present Day.* Cambridge: Cambridge University Press.

Scott, Rebecca. 1985. *Slave Emancipation in Cuba: The Transition to Free Labor, 1860–1899*. Princeton: Princeton University Press.

Skidmore, Thomas. 1990. "Racial Ideas and Social Policy in Brazil, 1870–1940." In Richard Graham (ed.), *The Idea of Race in Latin America*, 37–70. Austin: University of Texas Press.

Stuckey, Sterling. 1987. *Slave Culture: Nationalist Theory and the Foundations of Black America*. New York: Oxford University Press.

Trouillot, Michel-Rolph. 1990. *Haiti, State against Nation: The Origins and Legacy of Duvalierism*. New York: Monthly Review Press.

Wilson, Woodrow. 1967. *The Papers of Woodrow Wilson*, Vol. 2, ed. Arthur Stanley Link. Princeton: Princeton University Press.

Wright, Winthrop R. 1990. *Café con Leche: Race, Class, and National Image in Venezuela*. Austin: University of Texas Press.

9
The Outlawed
Landscapes of Human Rights

Tugba Basaran

> Before the Law stands a doorkeeper.
> —Franz Kafka, *The Trial*

In this chapter I propose engaging with the technique of outlawing, an ancient legal tradition that, in a modified version, is still relevant today and used to govern in violation of human rights and contrary to prevailing legal norms. The outlawed are people strategically portrayed to be *outside* of the remit of the law, thus creating people subject *to* law, but not full subjects *of* law. In its ancient as well as contemporary formations, outlawry remains one of the severest forms of socio-legal exclusion. As *homo sacer* in Roman law or *vogelfrei* in medieval German law, being outlawed was equivalent to societal expulsion and effectively amounted to a death sentence. In its more recent imperial formations, the legal technique of outlawing was not used to ban people from society but, on the contrary, to incorporate slaves and colonial subjects as an important productive force within society, whilst also limiting their rights. This chapter will engage with contemporary configurations and techniques of outlawing and explore how people are portrayed to be outside of the reach of law. A priori, it is important to underline that the outlawed are in reality never outside the law, but the outlawed are constituted through law, embedded within law, and set outside its protection through law. This is the paradoxical state of affairs.

While great strides have been made in the course of the twentieth century toward eliminating the outlawed by guaranteeing access to the law to everyone, the legal technique of outlawing, that is portraying a person strategically to be outside of the law, continues to be used primarily as a strategy of social exclusion and securitization toward non-citizens. In this chapter, I propose analyzing how contemporary techniques of outlawing operate through legal geographies and legal borders. I will proceed as follows. I start with precedents of nonadmission to the law and the right to be recognized as a person before the law. I then go on to look at how nonadmission to the law has become dependent on state borders in the twentieth century. Next I explore practices of legal bordering and the production of the outlawed as a result thereof, and then I engage with the construction of the symbolic outside of the law, a vision that relies on particular forms of imagination, distinctions, and politics. Finally, I look at the relation between legal geographies, borders, and social boundaries in the twenty-first century.

Before the Law

The edifice of rights rests on admission to the law. That everybody has the right to be recognized as a person before the law is often disregarded as an evident statement. History, however, is filled with people who were denied access hereto. People degraded to the status of objects were vivid in the minds of the drafters when they prepared the Universal Declaration of Human Rights (UDHR), adopted by the United Nations General Assembly in December 1948.[1] They had witnessed how millions of lives could be eroded with the stroke of a pen.[2] Hence, the UDHR stresses that "Everyone has the right to recognition everywhere as a person before the law."[3] Everybody should be recognized as a person before the law. Nobody is outside the law. The recognition of legal personality is a necessary condition for all other human rights. Hereby, two components stand out: first, that admission to the law must be guaranteed to everyone, without exception, and second, that admission to the law must be guaranteed everywhere, again without exception.[4] The past and the present are filled with exceptions, however. Law has never been "accessible to every man and at all times" (Kafka 1998: 213).

The right to be recognized as a person before the law is one of the most important acknowledgements of the twentieth century. "Without this right, the individual could be degraded to a mere legal object, where he or she would no longer be a person in the legal sense and thus be deprived of all other rights, including the right to life" (Novak 2005: 369). The denial of legal personality was a common legal currency of history, with two primary formations of nonadmission to the law.

One form was through expulsion from citizenship. In ancient and medieval times, former citizens were outlawed, as *homo sacer* in Roman law, *caput luminum* in medieval English law, or *vogelfrei* in medieval German law. The outlawed were banned from society and had all their rights revoked, and the body of the outlawed was rendered open to all forms of punishment with impunity, effectively amounting to a death sentence. An individual who had lost the right to life survived by the benevolence of others, hence the expression "bare life" (Agamben 1998). Here outlawry was equivalent to expulsion, and may be most closely related today to the revocation of citizenship and denationalization (Arendt 1973; Perett 2015). Expulsion was historically not only restricted to individuals punished for their deeds, but groups of citizens could equally be banished from their society. As such, while the Nuremberg Laws were remarkable for the facility of stripping people of their citizenship and for the ensuing genocide, they were hardly a historical aberration.

Another form was based on legal status: many were designated not citizens but subjects by birth, a legal practice most recently and notoriously deployed in the age of empire for institutions of slavery and colonialism. Various forms of slavery and serfdom from Roman law to modern incarnations in the twentieth century relied upon the denial of legal personality to slaves, and occasionally even their legal objectification as a form of property. Admission to the law was never meant to be for everybody, but reserved for a class of citizens, often male property holders. Equally, colonialism had at its foundation the colonial subject, differentiated through manifold legal configurations from the citizen (Burbank & Cooper 2011; Ruskola 2013). The slave and the colonial subject were not banned from society, however, but were on the contrary an important productive force within it, whilst partially or entirely denied admission to the prevalent law available to citizens as part of a political-economic order.

Redressing historical conditions of liminality began with the recognition of individuals as legal persons, that is the individual as a bearer of rights and duties. Nonrecognition as a person before the law could amount to, as many have pointed out, not only any social boundary, but the harshest form thereof, reducing individuals to mere life, a civil and/or social death (Agamben 1998; Patterson 1982). To this effect, the preliminary draft of the UDHR prepared by the Secretariat stressed that "Everyone has the right to a legal personality. No one shall be restricted in the exercise of his civil rights except for reasons based on age or mental condition or as a punishment for a criminal offense."[5] The recognition as a person before the law is a non-derogable right.[6] Human beings acquire legal personhood at birth, which serves as the prerequisite to legal capacity—that is, the ability to amend rights and obligations.[7]

It remains important to point out here that nonrecognition before the law was not always equivalent to having no rights at all, but may have provided for some form of lesser rights. Whilst *homo sacer* had all rights revoked, often people had access to parts of the law but not its entirety, common under conditions of racial segregation and apartheid, or they were governed by laws designated particular to them, providing them with the rights of a slave or the rights of a native. It is in this sense that Article 6 of the UDHR on the right to recognition before the law must be read jointly with Article 7 on equality before the law, as a statement on the equal protection of laws: "All are equal before the law and are entitled without any discrimination to equal protection of the law. All are entitled to equal protection against any discrimination in violation of this Declaration and against any incitement to such discrimination."[8]

Before the Border

While great strides have been made in the course of the twentieth century toward guaranteeing access to the law to everyone, the core obstacle for access to rights now more than ever is that they are not guaranteed everywhere. Shortly after the adoption of UDHR, it was undeniable that the law continued to be inaccessible to many. People on the move between states fell through the cracks of sovereignties in the international system. As Hannah Arendt pointed out in relation to the stateless:

> We became aware of the existence of a right to have rights ... and a right to belong to some kind of organized community, only when millions of people emerged who had lost and could not regain these rights because of the new global political situation ... Only with a completely organized humanity could the loss of home and political status become identical with expulsion from humanity all together. (Arendt 1973: 177)

The recognition of human rights required state implementation, as the preamble to the UDHR underlines, and hence drew against its very universal claims questions of the scope of responsibility and implementation. Further, channeling issues of scope was the discrepancy between the right to leave and return to one's own country without a corollary right to enter another, leading to the destitution of those condemned to move in a situation where there was no state to welcome them.

Even now, lives not admitted to the law continue to be present around us. Detainees, whether refugees, migrants, or combatants, can be allocated to particular places designated as "not yet admitted to the law," and these become determinative of their rights. These can be encountered under rendition and extradition regimes, established in the name of anti-terrorism, where detainees at sites such as Abu Ghraib, Bagram, Guantanamo or black sites (Bigo & Tsoukala 2008; Gregory 2006) are strategically portrayed as being outside the law. Nonadmission to the law is also used for anti-immigration measures (Kneebone 2010; Ryan 2010). Refugees arriving in Australia by boat have been sent for indefinite detention to Nauru and Papua New Guinea, and Haitian and Cuban refugees destined for the United States have been sent to the leased lands of Guantanamo. These sites, located outside national territory, are used as part of an effort to place people outside the reach of the law. Those held at these locations may change, but the designation of being outside of the law remains. Guantanamo Bay is a particularly relevant example here. The site of a refugee camp in the 1990s, it was transformed at the beginning of the twenty-first century into a detention camp for combatants, relying upon the longstanding jurisdictional status of Guantanamo Bay. Lives not admitted to the law are not only encountered outside a state's territory, however, but also lived within it. Only lawful entry guarantees access to the law. Mere physical presence in a state's territory is often regarded as insufficient to access the law in its entirety (some rights may apply depending on the state). Referred to as unlawful, irregular, or illegal migrants, many are precluded from even the basic rights provided by the law (Ngai 2014). The desperate situation of the stateless, incisively underlined in Arendt's remark that "Only as an offender against the law can he gain protection from it" (Arendt 1973: 286), still remains valid for those who cannot access the protection of the law.

Lives outside of the law remain precarious and vulnerable, often at the mercy of others and exposed to flagrant rights violations. Even though portrayed as lives outside of the law, none of the outlawed are actually outside of the law, however. Their lives are governed by the law, but they are not (or only partially) protected by it. Important variations are present amongst those outlawed. Some people do not have the protection of any laws, they can never reach the law, as in the case of black sites; others can only benefit from laws especially designed for them, as in the case of

Guantanamo; others have access to particular laws only and may only be able to access emergency healthcare and educational services, as with the case of irregular migrants. How lives outside of the law are governed, their relation to the law, changes constantly. In some circumstances, partial access to lawyers and courts, and limited types of legal protection may be available, even though these are not equivalent to access to the full range of fundamental rights.[9]

Operations of states across the globe demonstrate how state power can be deployed to limit human rights by narrowing access to the law. Particular conceptions of territory, its delimitations as well as the scope of rights, have allowed for exemptions from national laws, and by implication constitutional rights, and permitted human rights to be ignored (Gregory 2006). As location has become determinative of rights, borders have gained new significance in contemporary politics for the allocation of rights. Borders can bar admission to rights, and/or provide possibilities for creating subjects of lesser rights. Currently, nonrecognition before the law usually is directly related, and one may even argue an outcome, of the significance of borders.

The significance of space in contemporary politics cannot be simply attributed to state practices and power politics, however, but is ingrained in public international law. Public international law carries a number of assumptions on the role of the state and promotes a particular vision that recognizes the state as the locus of politics. It dictates a politics of congruence between territory, sovereignty, and state, and proposes a politics of strong legal and political delimitations (Basaran forthcoming; Walker 1993). In accordance with this vision, the scope of human rights instruments, particularly their geographical scope, has traditionally been read conservatively, and territory has been considered instrumental in defining the borders of rights, state accountability, and responsibility. International conventions, for example, have largely been read in a territorial context, neglecting or limiting questions of human rights outside state territory but within state jurisdiction. Even for the recognition of a person before the law, territorial interpretations have been influential, in spite of the fact that the UDHR states that admission to the law must be guaranteed everywhere. The word "everywhere" was retained, despite dissent from the British delegation, in the International Covenant on Civil and Political Rights of 1966, which proclaims, "Everyone shall have the right to recognition everywhere as a person before the law."[10] Nonetheless, it is common among human rights lawyers to agree that inclusion of the word "everywhere" does not "permit the conclusion that by way of art. 16 states parties have assumed obligations regarding international cooperation going beyond the territorial scope of application set down in Art. 2(1)" (Novak 2005: 371). Equally, national jurisprudence on jurisdiction has usually been conservative, limiting access to the adjudication of rights, posing restrictions on the right to hear cases to a particular geography, reinforced by legislative and executive claims that court jurisdiction should not apply to human rights and questions of security abroad—relevant examples being Guantanamo and Australian offshore processing.

The territorial principle, hardly of relevance to private international law, continues to be a central, if increasingly contested, tenet of public international law and human rights instruments. This is not intended to imply that other forms of nonadmission to the law do not continue to occur in practice. Contrary to these state practices, however, the premises of public international law contribute to the normative acceptance and legitimation of nonadmission to the law, as long as nonadmission takes place before the borders. Due to its normative acceptance, nonadmission to the law before borders remains a very hard case to contest. That said, during the recent past the territorial scope of human rights instruments has increasingly been questioned, and the scope of human rights instruments contested. Important here have been regional human rights conventions that underline jurisdiction rather than territory, such as the European Convention on Human Rights, which extends state obligation to "everyone within their jurisdiction,"[11] and the American Convention on Human Rights, which applies "to all persons subject to their jurisdiction."[12] In spite of jurisprudence of regional courts, and here especially the European Court of Human Rights, with an increasingly expansive human rights jurisdiction (Guild et al. 2018), territory largely remains an accepted symbolic border for justifying differential treatment in terms of human rights. The territorial principle continues to determine the scope of state obligations and the scope of human rights, allowing for differential treatment of people at borders. Therefore it is important to note that claims to territoriality do not solely rely upon physical territory and territorial borders, but upon legal borders and the distinction between lawful and unlawful. This leads us to the next section, on the formation of legal borders, in which I seek to understand the distinction between inside and outside that is so crucial for human rights and fundamental freedoms.

At the Legal Border

Contrary to much of the literature on borders, which has focused on the territorial borders of the state, border politics are precisely effective as they are based on bordering practices of law, not on territorial borders. For human rights, techniques of legal bordering allow the creation of disjunctures between legal borders of policing and legal borders of rights, and allow for these to be created anywhere. They create the outlawed—subject to the state's jurisdiction, subject to the state's power, but without corollary rights.

Legal borders authorize things in two ways (Basaran 2010). First, legal borders authorize and legalize the expansion of the state's policing powers beyond its territory. Here we find a variety of approaches, including local, national, transnational, and international instruments. Most common is the establishment of transnational policing through bilateral approaches, including bilateral agreements, but also the exchange of diplomatic notes, memoranda of understanding, and even oral agreements. These have been used to interdict refugee and migrant boats between Haiti and the United States as well as for detention (offshore processing) between Australia and its Pacific neighbors. There are some unilateral approaches, including specific readings of international law or proclamations, but these are seldom used. Against common perceptions, it is rare to find a unilaterally acting sovereign in modern times. The expansion of policing has not only relied on interstate cooperation, but increasingly also public–private cooperation. This includes for-profit and nonprofit organizations, particularly carriers and airlines, international organizations, and humanitarian organizations, and is often referred to as delegation, outsourcing, or externalization. Both state and non-state cooperation, delegation, and externalization do not only expand the scope and depth of policing and possibilities of intervention, but also dilute responsibilities for policies and acts through the symbolic uses of the territory as the outer limit of state responsibility. The separation of policy-making from delegated policy implementation allows for a dilution of state responsibilities.

Second, legal borders allow for the restriction of human rights, even within the physical territory of states. Thus, for restricting rights and liberties, an important legal technique applied is the distinction between physical and legal presence. This is especially important at ports of entry, such as airports, harbors, and train stations, but also territorial waters and sometimes land territory. Another technique is the limitation of the scope of laws through geographical or status-based exemptions. While the legal framework for the constitution of these spaces varies, dependent upon domestic laws, their common characteristic is the suspension or limitation of human and constitutional rights, even if taking place on the physical territory of a state. The status "unlawful" can be carried within the state's physical territory. The unlawful, the irregular, and the illegal remain as such within a territory because the border crossing was not recognized as lawful. People can carry the status of being outside borders even when they are physically inside them. Hence, the 100-mile border zone inside the United States in which Border Patrol agents can operate immigration controls, or waiting zones in France that are physically in the territory of the state, but where constitutional rights have limited application, or excised islands in Australia, where physical arrival is not equivalent to legal arrival. Nonetheless, territory continues to retain a legitimizing function. It serves as the alibi for the restriction of rights. The politics of contestation by human rights lawyers is more effective when human rights violations take place in a state's territory; equally, claims to extraterritoriality are most effective when a state's acts (those of its agents or by delegation) occur outside the state's physical territory, on the high seas, or in third countries.

Legal borders are crucial for nonrecognition before the law. They produce disjunctures between the expanding powers of the state, including policing powers, and restrictive interpretations of human rights. Contrary to a material understanding of borders, legal borders are not lines in landscapes or fixtures; they cannot be pinned down geographically or temporally, and they lack the visual permanence of borders found on maps. Legal borders are plural, dynamic, and selective, temporally and spatially flexible, largely independent of physical territory, existent in a legal space. They allow for modifications, for expansions, and for multiplications. For analyzing legal landscapes, it is important to keep in mind that there never was a unitary state, or a uniform scope of state jurisdiction. The state is not a unitary actor. Various related practices of boundary- and border-making need to be analyzed simultaneously because multiple boundaries of jurisdiction and multiple boundaries of law coexist. These can be in conflict with each other, making it impossible to determine a state's jurisdiction, but they give rise, through their disjunctures, to human rights violations. Boundary variations may arise between the different powers that prescribe the rule of law (legislative), enforce this (executive), and adjudicate this (judicial). Courts may exercise self-restraint, limiting judicial jurisdiction in spite of the presence of executive jurisdiction. Legal landscapes and disjunctures are set through a combination of practices by the legislature, the executive, and the courts: legislative practices can be unilateral, multilateral, or international; the executive usually relies on bilateral and multilateral approaches; adjudication can include national court decisions as well as regional and international courts. Analyzing legal borders helps establish the legal landscapes of the state, how inside and outside distinctions are created, how we can reenvision the state, its legal geographies, its borders, its jurisdiction, and its responsibilities. They illustrate the fragmented legal infrastructure of the state and illustrate how simple differences in legal boundary-making have the potential to create legal disjunctures and limit human rights.

Images of the Outside

The particularity of those not admitted to the law, the outlawed, is that they are claimed to be outside the law. But what does it mean to be outside the law? How does the symbolic power of the law operate in the construction of the outlawed, produce an inside and an outside, allocate some people inside and others outside, and what are the implications of this? Crucial to nonadmission to the law is the imagery of the outside. This image provides legitimation to politics that otherwise would be regarded as contrary to the liberal democratic credo. Three important points should be noted: the vision of the outside, its implication for human rights, and the importance of visible and invisible circuits of power.

First, the vision of the outside. Outside of the law, even if it does not exist, is a very important and advantageous symbolic construction nonetheless. A sharp distinction between inside and outside of the law is drawn (see also Walker 1993). The inside is equated with lawfulness, whereas the outside is equated with a lack of law, as if such a condition could exist in modern life where subjectivities, materialities, and even physical landscapes have become products of the law, deriving their identity, sense, and purpose largely from legal frameworks. The outside is often equated to the state of nature, associated with lawlessness, chaos, and a lack of security (particularly if one reads about people trying to cross borders). Human destinies of the outlawed are portrayed as taking place in an alternative, naturalized environment, in a state of nature in which life is, as Thomas Hobbes famously put it, "solitary, poore, nasty, brutish and short" (Hobbes 2006: 62). It appears as if here it is forces of nature that kill, not legal or political power. By implication, power can be disassociated from responsibility (Basaran 2015). Ultimately, what is portrayed as outside of the law is not outside of the law, however. These spaces contain those people without a willing state or powerful state to make their claims heard (Agamben 1998; Arendt 1973). Being outlawed, condemned to be symbolically outside of the law, is the ultimate punishment. The distinction between being inside and outside of the law is geographically indeterminate as we know from the figure of the outlawed and from modern legal bordering practices, but in its modern formations it is imagined as a geographical concept nonetheless.

Second, visions have an important political purpose for the liberal conception of human rights and governing modern societies (Dean 1999; Foucault 1991; Scott 1998). Assumptions of territoriality allow liberal democracies, states that perceive themselves as defenders of human rights, to limit human rights, and by implication their political project as guarantors of human rights, to their (symbolic) territory. The sharp distinction at the border authorizes and legitimates the differential treatment of people, some according to human rights and others not. Liberty is seen as part of a spatial, territorial order under the authority of the state. With places of sovereign responsibility and rights allocated to the inside, charity and humanitarianism at best are reserved for the outside. What happens there (however "there" is defined), is no longer the responsibility of the state. Hence, when people die there, nobody is held responsible—whether they be refugees on the high seas or enemy combatants in Guantanamo or Afghanistan. Like any other boundary, the boundary of politics, with its imaginary physical location through the conjuncture of state, territory, and law, serves and reinforces a particular political purpose. It justifies the political form of government and confines its scope of application, or as some may say, the moral scope of the state.

Third, symbolic landscapes fulfill an important function, legitimizing a political order within which different formations of state power can take place, but only some remain visible, "conceal[ing] multiple phenomena in a claim to unity" (Walker 2017: 13). The relation between the symbolic and practices, between the visible and the invisible, between the territorial and the extraterritorial, takes an important role and, one could even say, allows a particular form of governing through disjunctures. Invisible legal borders are most effective when operating within symbolic orders, in this case in relation to territory and territorial borders. Here, starting from a statist viewpoint, the symbolic reference point remains territoriality, even though the legal practices of states indicate a wide array of fragmentations, pluralities, and formations, dependent on institutional actors but largely independent of territory. The statist vision and divisions, contrasted with its practices, point toward disjunctures as an important means of governing. This allows states to achieve their unrestrained potential outside of their symbolic territory. It provides them with the inherent potential to be more forceful outside of the symbolic territory, where there are less counterbalances, less judiciary restraints, and more jurisdictional questions.

Thus, states can create the outlawed as a result of modern forms of governing. The symbolic construction of law's outside enables a facile justification of illiberal practices in liberal democracies, maintaining human rights within, whilst denying them outside.

Reflections on Borders and Boundaries

An important historical evolution of the twentieth century has been that admission to the law became guaranteed widely to everyone. Historical fault lines for rights, differential rights, as under colonialism, apartheid, and slavery, can no longer be normatively justified and have been largely, even though not fully, eradicated in practice. Difference can no longer be justified through a different legal status, but must be perceived as contrary to the law. With the expansion of citizenship, the once common distinction between citizens and subjects can no longer be normatively sustained, but new fault lines for the differential government of people have been created through legal geographies and the imposition of the distinction between inside and outside. The principal problem for admission to the law is no longer whether the law covers everybody, but whether it operates everywhere. Space rather than status has become determinative for admission to the law. Nonadmission to the law now requires an outside to normatively justify differential treatment and the violation of human rights. Particular places, designated as "not yet admitted to the law," have become determinative of the rights of those detained there. Even though contestations are mounting, these are minor compared to the wide acceptance of the spatial determination of rights. As states, sovereignty, and rights have become more inclusive through the enlargement of citizenship, this process has been accompanied by borders as the mechanisms of exclusion and nonadmission to the law, with practices of legal bordering opening up possibilities for borders anywhere. Borders have become of increasing importance in creating contemporary social boundaries.

What are the boundaries of nonadmission today? Boundaries imposed through borders have a set of particularities. Lives outside the law could be present anywhere. De facto, the outlawed are not a random selection of people, however, but have a number of common characteristics that make them vulnerable. Crucially, all are foreign nationals (or in some cases ascribed the status of the foreigner, even if they are residents or citizens). Effectively, not every foreign national is prone to being outlawed, however, but only those who come from particular countries, which are economically, and hence politically, less powerful than the destination countries. National selection criteria are usually complemented by existing social boundaries within the place of origin and the destination society, including class, ascribed race, ethnicity, religion, and gender. Differences and inequalities in the implementation of the law affirm, reflect, and at times emphasize some of these boundaries, depending on the destination country. Simply, not every Mexican is stopped at the US–Mexican border, not every Syrian is stopped at European borders. The arrested and detained are usually foreigners without sufficient economic, cultural, and social capital, the poorer segment of society not seen as worthy of protection and often even discriminated against in their own country, leading to their willingness to migrate. Hence, class, in a broad sense, is an important determining factor in access to mobility and rights (see also Baumann 1998; Ypi 2018). It is under a combination of these conditions that one is rendered unlawful or illegal and condemned to being outlawed in the present situation. The law thus has a triple function: affirming, creating, and amplifying social boundaries. The particularities of these are dependent of each border and impossible to represent in a generic fashion.

To analyze contemporary legal landscapes of human rights, it is helpful to "look at repertoires of imperial power—at the different strategies empires chose as they incorporated diverse peoples into the polity while sustaining or making distinctions among them" (Burbank & Cooper 2011: 2). We need to consider how empires provided for politico-legal distinctions between citizens and subjects. These also help us understand how previous forms of nonadmission through racial categories and colonies have entered modern conceptions of nation and citizenship.[13] Empires provided for and required complex spatio-legal assemblages, dependent upon a combination of geography as well as status. A variety of distinct territories with different rights and obligations, with different levels of citizenship and subjectification, coexisted in them. It is in this sense that imperial lawscapes that configured and distinguished amongst their parts and populations cannot be separated from the general development of law, its distinctions and categorizations. Imperial lawscapes required legal cartographies, mechanisms of legal bordering within the empire. It is within this context that we need to understand arising notions, such as the state, territory, sovereignty, and strict territoriality, not as originary of law, but as statements of law that seek to protect imperial lawscapes. Decolonization may have flattened and transformed many of these lawscapes, but imperial, colonial, and neocolonial laws remain implicitly and explicitly relevant for contemporary configurations of law and power nonetheless (see also Merry 1988; Tamanaha 2008). Past governing strategies have been incorporated into contemporary global configurations through fragmented legal infrastructures of the state.

Lives outside of the law are only the most recent incarnations of a recurrent liberal technique that seeks to uphold human rights for some while violating them for others. The paradox of the situation is that these violations take place in established liberal democracies. Whilst liberal democracies operate to a greatest extent under the rule of law and the values of fundamental rights, these cornerstones of their regime are restricted or even suspended for a specific category of people in specific places. A dual state arises that simultaneously respects rights and violates rights. History shows that this situation is not new. Empires governed people differently, foreseeing different forms of governing for different populations, between metropole and colonies, between citizens and subjects, in complex spatio-legal formations. Contemporary states continue this legacy. While imperial forms of denying recognition through social structures and subservient institutions of slavery and colonialism may have widely vanished, vertical legal hierarchies have been substituted through a distinction between inside and outside, and the impossibility of entering from an unlawful outside to the lawful inside. In understanding modern forms of outlawry as a form of governing, we cannot ignore its legal proliferation as a product of empire. Governing people differently, once the rationale of empires, has now, for contemporary states, mutated into governing people differently at legal borders. Some people continue to remain unrecognized "before the law"; these are now people before the borders, modern outlaws.

Conclusion

Admission to the law must be guaranteed to everyone, without exception, and, admission to the law must be guaranteed everywhere, again without exception. Admission to the law has always been a political and economic way of governing, however, whether employed during slavery for economic benefits, or as a means of exclusion from society. Nonadmission to the law does not occur by chance; it is a political strategy, deployed to keep people at a distance with as few rights as is convenient, and it is utilized often as a practice of security (Balzacq et al. 2010). This is not astounding. In liberal democracies, this political strategy has taken on a new format and requires a new form of justification through geographies and symbolic images of the outside. In its new configuration, it allows liberal democracies to govern in a way that exempts them from their own constitutional obligations. Strategically portraying people as outside of the law, as (not yet, never or no more) admitted to the law, allows governments to govern, at worst without, at best with, less than normal restraints on matters of life and death.

Notes

1. Universal Declaration of Human Rights (UDHR), 1948 (available at: https://www.ohchr.org/EN/UDHR/Documents/UDHR_Translations/eng.pdf, accessed July 31, 2019).
2. The Nuremberg Laws of 1935 (the Reich Citizenship Law, the Law for the Protection of German Blood and German Honor and subsequent decrees) declared only those of German or related blood to be Reich citizens, and stripped people defined as Jews, Romanies, and blacks of their citizenship, legally clearing the path for subsequent deportations and genocide.
3. UDHR, art. 6.
4. This right is also enshrined in the International Covenant on Civil and Political Rights, 1966 (art. 16), the International Convention on the Protection of the Rights of All Migrant Workers and Members of their Families, 1990 (art. 24), as well as regional human rights instruments, including the American Convention on Human Rights, 1978 (art. 3), the African Charter on Human and Peoples' Rights, 1986 (art. 5), and implicit in the European Convention on Human Rights, 1953.
5. UN Commission on Human Rights Drafting Committee, "Draft Outline of International Bill of Rights," art. 12 (available at: https://www.un.org/en/ga/search/view_doc.asp?symbol=E/CN.4/AC.1/3, accessed July 31, 2019).

6. International Covenant on Civil and Political Rights (ICCPR), art. 4.2 (available at: https://treaties.un.org/doc/publication/unts/volume%20999/volume-999-i-14668-english.pdf, accessed July 31, 2019).
7. It should be noted that to be a person before the law is not equivalent to the capacity to act. The latter poses limitations based on age (children and juveniles) and mental condition.
8. UDHR, art. 7. The equal protection of laws is likewise incorporated into the ICCPR (art. 26), the American Convention on Human Rights (art. 24), the African Charter on Human and Peoples' Rights (art. 3), and the European Convention on Human Rights (protocol 12).
9. See e.g. the determinative outcomes of the US court case Boumediene v. Bush, 553 US 723 (2008) for Guantanamo, and the European Court of Human Rights case of Amuur v. France, Application No. 19776/92 (1996) for French waiting zones.
10. ICCPR, art. 16.
11. European Convention on Human Rights, art. 1 (available at: https://www.echr.coe.int/Documents/Convention_ENG.pdf, accessed July 31, 2019).
12. American Convention on Human Rights, art. 1 (available at: https://www.oas.org/dil/treaties_B-32_American_Convention_on_Human_Rights.pdf, accessed July 31, 2019).
13. See the chapters by Munshi and Ngai (this volume) for the crucial link between law, race, and nation.

References

Agamben, Giorgio. 1998. *Homo Sacer: Sovereign Power and Bare Life*, trans. Daniel Heller-Roazen. Stanford: Stanford University Press.
Arendt, Hannah. 1973. *The Origins of Totalitarianism*. San Diego: Houghton Mifflin Harcourt.
Balzacq, Thierry, Tugba Basaran, Didier Bigo, Emmanuel-Pierre Guittet, and Christian Olsson. 2010. "Security Practices." In Robert Denemark and Renée Marlin-Bennett (eds), *International Studies Encyclopedia Online*. Available at: https://oxfordre.com/internationalstudies/view/10.1093/acrefore/9780190846626.001.0001/acrefore-9780190846626-e-475?result=3&rskey=PWKsbW (accessed July 31, 2019).
Basaran, Tugba. 2010. *Security, Law and Borders: At the Limits of Liberties*. New York: Routledge.
—— 2015. "The Saved and the Drowned: Governing Indifference in the Name of Security." *Security Dialogue* 46(3): 205–20.
—— Forthcoming. "A Journey through Law's Landscapes: Close Encounters of the Scalar Kind." In C. Greenhouse, K. Scheppele and C. Davis (eds), *Landscapes of Law*. Philadelphia: University of Pennsylvania Press.
Bauman, Zygmunt. 1998. *Globalization: The Human Consequences*. New York: Columbia University Press.
Bigo, Didier, and Anastassia Tsoukala (eds). 2008. *Terror, Insecurity and Liberty: Illiberal Practices of Liberal Regimes after 9/11*. New York: Routledge.

Burbank, Jane, and Frederick Cooper. 2011. *Empires in World History: Power and the Politics of Difference*. Princeton: Princeton University Press.

Dean, Mitchell. 1999. *Governmentality: Power and Rule in Modern Society*. New York: Sage.

Foucault, Michel. 1991. "Governmentality." In Graham Burchell, Colin Gordon, and Peter Miller (eds), *The Foucault Effect: Studies in Governmentality*, 87–104. Chicago: University of Chicago Press.

Gregory, Derek. 2006. "The Black Flag: Guantánamo Bay and the Space of Exception." *Geografiska Annaler: Series B* 88(4): 405–27.

Guild, Elspeth, Didier Bigo, and Mark Gibney (eds). 2018. *Extraordinary Rendition: Addressing the Challenges of Accountability*. New York: Routledge.

Hobbes, Thomas. 2006. *Leviathan*. London: A&C Black.

Kafka, Franz. 2019. *The Trial*. London: Penguin.

Kneebone, Susan. 2010. "Controlling Migration by Sea: The Australian Case." In Bernard Ryan and Valsamis Mitsilegas (eds), *Extraterritorial Immigration Control*, 341–68. The Hague: Nijhoff.

Merry, Sally Engle. 1988. "Legal Pluralism." *Law and Society Review* 22(5): 869–96.

Neal, Andrew. 2009. *Exceptionalism and the Politics of Counter-Terrorism: Liberty, Security and the War on Terror*. New York: Routledge.

Ngai, Mae M. 2014. *Impossible Subjects: Illegal Aliens and the Making of Modern America*, 2nd ed. Princeton: Princeton University Press.

Novak, Manfred. 2005. *UN Covenant on Civil and Political Rights: CCPR Commentary*, 2nd ed. Kehl: N.P. Engel.

Patterson, Orlando. 1982. *Slavery and Social Death: A Comparative Study*. Cambridge, MA: Harvard University Press.

Perret, Sarah C. 2015. "Legiferer en matiere de naturalization ou construire l'immigration comme enjeu de securite." Available at: https://www.academia.edu/28536004/L%C3%A9gif%C3%A9rer_en_matiere_de_naturalisation_ou_construire_limmigration_comme_enjeu_de_s%C3%A9curit%C3%A9 (accessed July 31, 2019).

Ruskola, Teemu. 2013. *Legal Orientalism: China, the United States, and Modern Law*. Cambridge, MA: Harvard University Press.

Ryan, Bernard. 2010. "Extraterritorial Immigration Control: What Role for Legal Guarantees?" In Bernard Ryan and Valsamis Mitsilegas (eds), *Extraterritorial Immigration Control*, 1–37. The Hague: Nijhoff.

Scott, James C. 1998. *Seeing Like a State: How Certain Schemes to Improve the Human Condition Have Failed*. New Haven: Yale University Press.

Tamanaha, Brian Z. 2008. "Understanding Legal Pluralism: Past to Present, Local to Global." *Sydney Law Review* 30(3): 375–411.

Walker, R.B.J. 1993. *Inside/Outside: International Relations as Political Theory*. Cambridge: Cambridge University Press.

—— 2017. "Only Connect: International, Political, Sociology." In Tugba Basaran, Didier Bigo, Emmanuel-Pierre Guittet, and R.B.J. Walker (eds), *International Political Sociology: Transversal Lines*, 13–23. London: Routledge.

Ypi, Lea. 2018. "Borders of Class: Migration and Citizenship in the Capitalist State." *Ethics and International Affairs* 32(2): 141–52.

PART III

Creating Spaces

10

Protection
Sanctuary and the Contested Ethics of Presence in the United States

Linda Bosniak

In debates over irregular immigration in liberal destination states, it is the fact of immigrants' physical presence in a state's territory that organizes the conversation. On the one hand, and most obviously, the person's bodily presence within that territory is designated by the state as an offense or a wrong against the state itself (Bosniak 2016a). This offense, in turn, is invoked to justify both forcible removal of the person from the territory and imposition of repressive treatment and legal disadvantage during such time as the person remains present. Stated another way, the territorial presence of these immigrants is illegalized, and that illegalized presence is invoked to justify both their legal subjection within and physical removal from this same territory.

On the other hand, the territorial presence of illegalized migrants is not merely the occasion for subjugation. Rather, in nominally liberal national polities, this presence in the territory is also precisely what grounds a range of claims made both by them and on their behalf for protective treatment at the hands of the state. Territorial presence engenders legal and ethical prerogative; it constitutes a basis for individual rights and immunities within and against the state.

Claims for protection based on a person's territorial presence arise in two distinct, though often overlapping, settings. First, the fact of presence is invoked to champion the immigrant's basic treatment, while present, under general law. In liberal democratic states, persons within the territorial jurisdiction of the state are theoretically due basic legal protections qua persons. A person's presence "on the soil" of a state generally occasions that state's responsibility as a matter of law to guarantee her minimum standards of treatment.[1] Note that these territorial rights exist notwithstanding that person's status under, and subjection to, the same state's immigration laws. Those laws inevitably undercut, but do not extinguish, the rights of territorial personhood (see Bosniak 2007).[2]

Second, it is precisely irregularized migrants' territorial presence over a span of time which becomes the basis for their claims for protection against deportation or removal. Territorial presence, that is, serves as the ground for their claims for the right to stay. Whether taking the discursive form of legalization, amnesty, *in situ* asylum, or some other mechanism, regularization claims always presuppose, and pertain to, a population that is already "here." Indeed, migrants and their advocates specifically invoke that already-hereness as the foundation of the claim.[3]

Understanding that territorial presence imposes constraints upon, as well as opportunities for, the exercise of state power—or, stated conversely, understanding that territorial presence provides legal ballast for migrants as well as grounding their legal vulnerability—helps explain why states engage in often drastic efforts to prevent noncitizens from physically touching their territory at all. Likewise, it accounts for why migrant-receiving states employ various convoluted legal fictions, including pronouncements of territorial excision (Phippin 2016), and why they deploy various off-shoring detention and rendition practices. The goal is to render persons—whether constructively or actually—as beyond or outside national soil for legal purposes, and thereby, to evade the juridically acknowledged responsibilities associated with a person's territorial "hereness."

In short, I begin with the thesis that a person's territorial presence is double edged. Debates over irregular migration within broadly liberal democratic states are comprised by competing and crosscutting struggles about the meaning of such presence, with that presence understood as both ground for subjection and the basis of protection.

This chapter analyzes this paradoxical constellation of subjection and protection as a contested ethics of presence. By this phrase I refer to a set of institutional and discursive struggles over the meaning and import of immigrants' territoriality. These are struggles which have, for decades, structured nationally framed liberal-legalist politics. The chapter begins by briefly surveying the contours of liberal-legalist territorialism. It then attempts to characterize what is now an unfolding moment of legal and political transformation. At the time of writing (early 2018), the political landscape that has produced this constellation is under acute pressure by increasingly authoritarian and nativist forces. The chapter thus reflects on the conflicting meanings of territoriality over the last period, together with some of the transformational pressures to which this regime appears to be presently subject.

To set the scene, I begin the discussion with an overview of the recent drastic intensification of internal border enforcement practices brought to bear against illegalized immigrants in the United States. These practices have two features: ever-greater criminalization of immigrant presence, and escalated efforts to terminate that presence, both through traumatization to induce "self-deportation," and through direct forms of expulsion. I examine how these practices both arise from, and simultaneously threaten, the precarious liberal nationalist settlement that has characterized immigration politics in the U.S. in recent decades.

In the second part of the chapter I proceed to reflect on the unfolding moment of popular resistance to this new phase of enforcement. What interests me is the resistance's unfailing invocation of immigrants bodily presence as the ethical ground for rights and protection. I note that in many settings these protective efforts take the form of—or are characterized under the umbrella term of— "sanctuary" politics. I reflect on the idea of sanctuary and consider the relationship between sanctuary and an emancipatory ethics of presence. I conclude by examining some of the risks and opportunities associated with presence-based ethical arguments.

Unleashing the Border

As is now well known, assaults on the liberal democratic order in the United States have ranged almost indiscriminately across domains since the 2016 presidential election. Even so, immigration stands out. From early in the campaign, it was Trump's showcase issue, and it remains the foremost site in which the new America-First, nativist shock politics are being enacted.

We have seen a number of different initiatives. The campaign against immigrants began with repeated incantations about "the Wall"—a wall to be built, it was declared, along the 2,000 mile length of the US–Mexico border.[4] This was quickly followed by the attempted implementation of a ban on the admission of people from several Muslim-majority nations.[5] But it is a third dimension of the nativist agenda,[6] one comprising an amplified surge in the interior enforcement of immigration laws, that interests me here. Rhetorically, the objects of this surge include the long-targeted—and transparently racialized— categories of "illegal aliens," "criminal/terrorist aliens," and "chain migrants." But now, in addition, the targets are said to be "bad hombres," "violent animals," and, most vividly, persons hailing from "shithole countries."[7] The inflammatory rhetoric does plenty of work on its own, no doubt. But the interior enforcement surge takes a material form as well, by way of a range of specific aggressive policing practices.

It is possible to read this interior enforcement campaign as a project intended to perform a racial purging of the national political body. That is surely its manifest content. And yet, beyond the fantasy of mass cleansing via ejection, we have to recognize that the internalized border surge is something more: it functions as a highly repressive and terrorizing mode of governance within the national territory.

Before describing the nature of this recent escalation in interior governance, let me first emphasize that none of these policy initiatives originated with Trump.[8] Versions of walls and bans and migrant chain-cutting have all been championed and implemented before, as have dehumanizing racial rhetorics; each has its own thick and twisted history. This is likewise true of internalized border enforcement via repressive internal immigration policing, which is my focus here. That is to say, it would be badly misleading to think of interiorized borders as a particular feature of this demagogic authoritarianizing moment. Rather, the internalized enforcement of national borders—under which rubric fall arrests, detentions, and deportations—is a constitutive feature of various modes of relatively liberal governance (Bosniak 2006; Kanstroom 2007). Nor can we forget that President Obama earned—not unfairly—the moniker "deporter in-chief" during his eight-year tenure; and to be perfectly clear, Obama was himself no outlier from liberal practice or common sense. Conventional liberals—and here I include both activists and theorists—have long generally accepted the legitimacy of deportation in principle, as long as it is done selectively, with due process, and some degree of humanitarian discretion (Bosniak 2016a). Getting tough on immigrants convicted of crimes and suspected of terrorism—each itself a racializing project (Armenta 2017; Volpp 2002)—has consistently been conceded by liberals, even if sometimes reluctantly, as the necessary cost of pursuing more generous policies for more apparently deserving immigrants.

Nevertheless, I will argue that the landscape is shifting—indeed, shifting tectonically—under the Trump administration. Today's interior enforcement policies depart from prior practices in respect to the aggressiveness of their scope and their permeating intensity. Previously, certain protective administrative norms and practices involving selectivity, due process, and humanitarian discretion served to partially constrain the border enforcement regime; these have now been very specifically and publicly jettisoned. In their place, we see a perfusion of border logic and enforcement activity into more domains, more locations, and more moments of people's existence in the territorial interior. This is border *ubiquitization*, which operates in symbolic registers, but is also performed materially by way of reinterpreted statutes, rewritten administrative regulations, and turbo-charged policing.

This process, in turn, is transmuting the deep structure of immigration law and policy as it has developed under US law for several decades. It has begun to upend a kind of dynamic settlement that—I have elsewhere explained—had broadly characterized the status of irregular immigrants in the United States for decades.

In order to make the argument that we are facing true legal and political rupture and not merely continuity in slightly modified garb, I must first say something more about the legal structure of the liberal national immigration regime from which this moment is departing. Here is a brief synopsis. In liberal democratic states, "the border"—which is as much a modality of regulation as a set of physical boundaries—is generally understood to operate beyond the reach of liberal democratic governance. The institutional and normative exceptionalism of the border is not generally regarded as contrary to liberal democratic values; instead, the border is treated as exceptional because it is commonly understood as preconditional for the very existence of democratic states—indeed, as necessarily constitutive of the sovereign space *within which* liberal democracy is supposed to unfold. Thus, borders of liberal democracies are deemed to be necessarily outside of, and prior to, liberal democracy itself.

That said, keep in mind that national borders do not merely operate at the liberal state's territorial edges.[9] Borders operate inside the territorial liberal state as well, and their entailed authority is understood to properly include state power to arrest, detain, and deport noncitizens from the territory. And in this mode, too, border regulation is exempted from ordinary constitutional constraint.

What is notable is that such relatively unconstrained interiorized border enforcement is not controversial per se in liberal democracies. Indeed, in both theory and practice, liberals ordinarily accept the functioning of the nondemocratic border on the territorial inside, including the practices leading to and culminating in the deportation of noncitizens. Certainly, they often champion greater protections for noncitizens—protections derived from norms of due process and humanitarian discretion. Most liberals want border control confined as much as possible to the state's territorial edges, precisely because they wish to promote a more egalitarian interior.[10] But they do not object to the interior enforcement of borders in principle.

Border interiorization, therefore, is a longstanding element of the interior liberal national immigration landscape, with such (largely non-democratically constrained) borders functioning always in tandem with regulation at the nations' territorial perimeter.

Yet that is only half the story. Because when we step back to examine the entirety of irregular immigrants' status in the state's internal legal landscape, we see that they are governed internally by various regimes and logics of legality, of which the interior border regulation is only one. Internal borders have had to coexist with, and sometimes accommodate to, other governing logics, including certain egalitarian and democratic rules, practices, and norms, which fundamentally structure their experience.

Two strands of alternate rules and norms are relevant here. One set provides rights and recognition to territorially present persons. The other mandates divisions and separations of institutional powers. While critiques of formalism apply in both cases, and while liberal individualist rights and institutional checks and balances sometimes have more symbolic consequence than concrete effect, it would be wrong, analytically, to minimize them. Avowed norms of liberal liberalism of both sorts have had real protective consequence (Bosniak 2006).

Most significantly for my current argument, these norms have functioned to place constraints on—and sometimes impose robust firewalls against—the reach and effect of interiorized border enforcement. It is precisely pursuant to these norms that many undocumented immigrants have been able carve out sometimes significant spaces in which to conduct fairly ordinary lives in civil society—as homeowners, spouses, parents, churchgoers, consumers, students, employees. These spaces in civil society have often remained partially insulated from the reach of interior border enforcement as a consequence (Bosniak 2010).

This is why the internal national space of liberal democratic states as it applies to irregular immigrants is best conceived of as governed by overlapping and often non-convergent regulatory regimes. The interplay between them—the dynamic map of their respective and competing jurisdictions—is exceedingly byzantine and contested, and it plays out differently across settings and over time. But there are structural commonalities across them. To put it succinctly, internal liberal national spaces are characterized by an equilibrated war of position between borderist and liberal legalist impulses. In this dynamic constellation, the interior border is sometimes constrained by liberal norms, and liberal norms are sometimes undercut by sovereign border imperatives. Neither routinely "trumps" the other. In broad form, this is what liberal nationalism—or a nationally framed liberal legalism—has looked like.

Now we can return to the argument I am developing here. The concerted shift toward illiberalization I have described is beginning to transform this constellation. The Trump administration's launch of an affirmatively bellicose campaign of interior border pervasion threatens to undo the constraints on state power that individual rights and rule of law commitments, as well as humanitarian discretion, have sometimes heretofore provided. What we see now is a thoroughgoing blasting of border logic into more domains, more locations, and more moments of existence. This process began as a matter of aggressive rhetoric, but has steadily taken material form, and now threatens to upend the precarious liberal-nationalist settlement that had structured the lives of irregular immigrants for decades.

Border Pervasion On the Ground

Trump's Executive Order, titled "Border Security and Immigration Enforcement Improvements," issued days after his inauguration, begins with this declaration of purpose:

> Interior enforcement of our Nation's immigration laws is critically important to the national security and public safety of the United States. Many aliens who illegally enter the United States and those who overstay or otherwise violate the terms of their visas present a significant threat to national security and public safety.[11]

The specific policy initiatives that have flowed from this and other declarations include the following.

Widening the enforcement net

First, the Trump administration formally eliminated tiered and protective discretion in immigration enforcement and is now mandating enforcement against any and all suspected immigration law violators. This departs from prior policy, including the policy of the Obama administration, which had expressly de-prioritized immigration enforcement against certain irregular immigrants with no criminal record, and had affirmatively declined to enforce immigration law against certain categories of irregularly present noncitizens—the sick, children, military veterans, and people pursuing civil rights claims, among others. As noted above, Obama's policy was to instead focus the government's enforcement arsenal on people characterized as "criminal aliens." While this focus on criminality was itself problematic— especially given the ever-broadening legislative definition of crimes triggering deportation—the prior policy did leave more or less alone millions of undocumented persons who the government had characterized as "otherwise law-abiding" (Nakamura 2014). Moreover, the Obama administration undertook affirmative policies to protect, ex ante and en masse, some classes of irregular migrants—for example through the Deferred Action for Childhood Arrivals (DACA) program (ibid.).

However, the Trump administration has expressly rescinded these policies of de-prioritization and selective shelter. Trump's one-time secretary of homeland security, John Kelly, made the following announcement just days after the president's inauguration:

> Effective immediately ... Department personnel shall faithfully execute the immigration laws of the United States against all removable aliens ... [P]rosecutorial discretion shall not be exercised in a manner that exempts or excludes a specified class or category of aliens from enforcement of the immigration laws.[12]

Since then, immigration officers have been arresting, charging, and deporting the formerly tolerated: undocumented children, sick people, young mothers, military veterans, cooperating witnesses and others.[13] Additionally, after months during which Trump personally professed assurances to, and sympathy for, DACA's beneficiaries, his administration rescinded the program. This means that 800,000 undocumented young people will lose their permission to remain and work in the United States and will soon become deportation priorities if the courts do not intervene.[14] The administration has also announced the termination of temporary humanitarian protection programs for hundreds of thousands of persons, including those from Nicaragua and Haiti.

The requirement that "all removable aliens" be subject to enforcement without exemption or exclusion represents a massive widening of the enforcement net. And since, in practical terms, it is commonly people who "look foreign" who are deemed to be potentially out of status, the order effectively functions as further license for an already pervasively racialized immigration enforcement practice.

Heightened criminalization of immigration violations

Add to this that many immigration violations have been redefined as criminal violations over the past few years.[15] Previously, basic immigration offenses (such as "entry without inspection" and "reentry after removal") were treated as civil offenses. Earlier administrations had begun to criminalize the field. But Trump's first attorney general Jeff Sessions specifically instructed federal prosecutors to "increase [their] efforts … [in] making immigration offenses higher priorities" for criminal enforcement.[16] In a 2017 Department of Justice press release, Sessions stated: "Under the President's leadership and through his Executive Orders, we will secure this border and bring the full weight of both the immigration courts and federal criminal enforcement to combat this attack on our national security and sovereignty."[17]

Expanding domains of immigration enforcement

Another of the Trump administration's significant innovations is the radical expansion of the domains and loci of immigration enforcement. Immigration and Customs Enforcement (ICE)—the internal immigration enforcement arm of the Department of Homeland Security—has launched a comprehensive campaign of investigations and arrests in venues which, under previous administrations, had been treated as "sensitive locations." These venues were previously treated by the state as off-limits as a matter of discretion. Under the current administration, however, ICE agents have all but abandoned this policy of restraint. Arenas once relatively insulated are now affirmatively fair game.[18] Most controversially, ICE has launched a campaign of enforcement efforts in local courthouses, where individuals are engaged in proceedings over non-immigration matters, such as child custody, domestic violence, and housing disputes (see e.g. Spaggett 2018). ICE officers have also arrested people in hospitals and clinics, in school drop-off zones, in public libraries and neighborhood centers, and in food pantries—again, all previously treated as sensitive, and therefore off-limit, enforcement locations.

Meanwhile, the administration has mandated detention for virtually all noncitizens who have been arrested and placed in immigration proceedings. To house the now soaring numbers, it is reverting to reliance on private detention companies—a practice Obama had ordered discontinued at the end of his term.[19]

Expanding the number of law enforcement entities

Finally, and significantly, the federal government is seeking to expand the number and categories of the interior border's enforcers. First, states and localities are being enlisted by both invitation and coercion to partner with the federal government in enforcing immigration law.[20] Some are eager to team up, while others are refusing to assist or even cooperate, leading to various unfolding struggles over so-called "sanctuary city policies."[21] Second, the administration has sought massive hiring of officials for ICE and Customs and Border Protection (CBP)—among other things, conducting extensive recruitment on college and university campuses (see Moran 2018). Add to this the Trump administration's efforts to promote private immigration enforcement. The US government has had a "tip line" that private parties can call to report suspected undocumented immigrants, but it had long laid dormant. The line has been revived and publicly showcased, and its use is being encouraged by Trump's base. For example, the far-right agitator Milo Yiannopoulos reportedly urged the crowd at a 2017 speech at the University of New Mexico to "purge your local illegals" and gave out the tip line number (Hadfield 2017). Vigilante border "militias" that forcibly detain immigrants have found tacit, and sometimes express, encouragement as well (see Grant & Miroff 2018).

What all of the foregoing amounts to is this: more immigration enforcement in more domains against more individuals at more times by more and more diverse agents, all undertaken with more dehumanizing justifying rhetoric. This is what I mean by border pervasion. And while it remains the case that persons who are territorially present are entitled to some protections in some domains against the force of border law, it is also true that the insulated spaces of liberal individual protection are being drastically narrowed.

Courts may push back to some degree. For example, if authorities were to enter a primary or secondary school to enforce immigration law, courts would likely enjoin because the US Supreme Court held in the case *Plyer v. Doe* (1982) that, as a matter of constitutional equal protection, undocumented children are entitled to access to education—although even here, the Trump administration is signaling a testing of limits (see Klein 2018). Moreover, the federal judiciary has long understood its reviewing role in the immigration sphere as limited, and themselves as properly deferring to the political branches. Without electoral reversals, the institutional constraints on increasing border pervasion will be limited.[22]

Resistance and "Sanctuary"

These recent developments have taken us from what was already a grim situation for irregular immigrants in the United States to a real siege condition. Yet the enforcement surge is by no means going unchallenged. Resistors of various stripes have worked to challenge policy, block enforcement actions, and shield and protect immigrants.

A large share of this opposition is taking place in the legal domain—with judicial challenges to the travel ban, to federal coercion of states and localities, and to child detention predominating, alongside the ongoing defensive legal work involved in individual immigration cases. Other resistance takes political and civic form: lobbying, marching, letter-writing, fundraising, as well as other acts of protest and solidarity, including humanitarian aid and civil disobedience.

Many have characterized the various strands of immigration resistance as part of a broader politics of "sanctuary."[23] The term is often invoked to label municipalities that decline to cooperate with federal immigration authorities. Houses of worship are re-embracing provision of physical refuge to individual families under the banner of sanctuary. Some university campuses and private businesses have declared themselves sanctuaries, or have debated doing so,[24] and the idea of sanctuary has entered the curriculum, with one group of faculty and students recently publishing an extensive "sanctuary syllabus" that "introduce[d] readers to the intellectual and social histories that have given life to today's sanctuary movement."[25] A broad national network of activists and faith groups working on behalf of immigrant justice have titled their efforts a "New Sanctuary Movement."

One might well ask what these various sanctuary-denominated initiatives have in common. To be clear, "sanctuary" is a term of art, not a technical term. In the US context it has become an umbrella concept covering a broad array of protective stances—some more affirmative, some more defensive, some publicly proclaimed, some unspoken—undertaken by a diverse range of parties and entities. Still, I would submit that these invocations contain a common normative thread. In all of its incarnations, sanctuary entails some commitment to contain, constrain, or abridge the scope of the border's operation. Perhaps most significantly, the sanctuary impulse endeavors to *insulate* certain domains and spaces and moments from the reach of the interior border. Sanctuary both insists upon, and evokes, jurisdictional bulwarks or force fields between the state's immigration enforcement apparatus and various domains of civil society in which immigrants conduct their lives. In this way, we might say that sanctuary stands against border totalitarianism. It demands that borders themselves be bounded.

Yet why should they be bounded? What is the underlying ethical vision that sanctuary embodies, and what grounds the impulse that animates its insistence on border containment?

It often appears that sanctuary discourse and activism are motivated by an array of normative logics. The first and most obvious of these is a natural law-grounded humanitarianism. This understanding is implicit in the very term "sanctuary," which doubles as a word describing a hallowed space of worship. Earlier movements of immigration sanctuary in the US were directly religious and church-led, and associated with a "welcome the stranger" faith-based biblical imperative. There are, as well, increasingly secular versions of a humanitarian-motivated sanctuary, which emphasize secular norms of human dignity or an ethics of hospitality, or both.

Notably, earlier humanitarian-based sanctuary movements were centered on the persecuted—on refugees or asylees or fugitives from "unjustice" (Emanuel 2017). For more recent sanctuarists, shielding people who have specifically fled persecution is not the central motif. Instead, the humanitarian imperative—proclaimed by some universities, for example—is articulated in terms of protecting one's own de facto community members, or the vulnerable in general. This protective discourse is often coupled with a call to shelter people who are "Americans in all but name," thus appending to humanitarian appeals the idea of a shared national civic identity.

On the other hand, a different strand of sanctuary discourse explicitly invokes instrumental rationalities of community self-interest. We hear this increasingly, from many cities and local police departments, which declare that *non*cooperation with federal immigration authorities is essential to the protection of their own communities. To successfully fight crime, per this argument, you have to maintain relations of trust between community members, law enforcement personnel, and local social-service providers. And to do that, noncitizens cannot be afraid that the police or providers are working hand-in-hand with ICE. The position, in short, is that the internalized border must be constrained to ensure the well-being of the rest of us (Lancer Julnes & Gibbs 2017).

Often linked with this community safety discourse, though distinct, are the logics of localism. These involve invocations of principles of democratic self-rule, of states' rights, city autonomy, and—per constitutional federalism principles—claims against central government commandeering. The juridical fight over sanctuary has taken this form; at stake is local power as against national power, and the scope and limits of federal coercion of local action. Many sanctuary advocates find themselves enthusiastic state- and local-rights advocates in this domain (Kwong & Roy 2018).[26]

These, then, are some of the normative strands embedded in sanctuary politics in the United States. But beyond humanitarianism, pragmatic self-interest, and autonomism, what else can we find? Specifically, I want to ask: Is sanctuary a politics of justice? And if so, how? There is no question that a great many people who currently support or participate in sanctuary efforts understand themselves to be engaged in a justice-pursuing practice for, and on behalf of, illegalized immigrants. But what is the conception of immigrant justice that animates them? Or to pose the question inversely: What is the nature of the *injustice* that these irregular immigrants are understood to experience? What is the wrong at stake that the new sanctuarists oppose and seek to redress?

It seems to me that current mobilization around the idea of sanctuary carries forward much of the ideological work that the immigrant justice movement had undertaken during the Bush, and especially Obama, administrations. In that period, young undocumented activists, sometimes referred to as DREAMers, were publicly "coming out" and declaring themselves "undocumented, unafraid, and unapologetic."[27] And they did so to great political effect because, although the DREAM Act (which would have provided regularization for undocumented youth) failed as a legislative project, the activism of young immigrants began to transform popular consciousness, and was powerful enough to later ensure administrative passage of DACA. Today, in the wake of the current interior border enforcement rampage and DACA's rescission, the undocumented are structurally less able to take a frontally "unapologetic", yet many continue to speak publicly. Notably, they don't use the language of sanctuary—perhaps because the term seems to connote a condition of beneficent protection that would need to seek from others. Instead, they make a self-authorizing demand: they declare that they are HereToStay.[28] Through this challenging slogan—which has been posted all over social media, emblazoned on banners at demonstrations, and elsewhere—they publicly perform the presence that they claim is theirs, by right, to retain (see e.g. Guillen et al. 2017).

And while a HereToStay politics might, at first, appear to exceed the ethics of sanctuary, my view is that it precisely captures the justice impulse that this new sanctuary movement embodies. Claims of sanctuary are becoming more affirmatively and more trenchantly political, pressing increasingly toward a demanding ethics of territorial justice.

Let us consider more closely what a HereToStay political ethics entails. It is a declaration of entitlement to continue to maintain bodily presence and/or residence in the national territory. The fact is that #HereToStay is, at its core, an anti-deportation politics. It is a politics that regards forced removal or deportation as itself an injustice.[29]

And in virtue of what is deportation an injustice? Motivating such a conviction is what I have called an ethics of presence (Bosniak 2007). By "the ethics of presence," I refer to justice claims that are based on a person's extant territorial presence—based on the fact that they are *already here*. The conviction is that a person's already-hereness is a stake to defend, and that an injustice would be committed if it were to be forcibly disrupted and she were to be uprooted and expelled.

Let's be clear that defending current presence as the basis for continuing presence going forward, and treating state interference with, or rupture of, that presence as an injustice, represents a highly demanding politics. Even in less draconian political times, an anti-deportation stance was indisputably radical. As I noted earlier, liberals usually concede the legitimacy of deporting some immigrants in some circumstances, so long as it is undertaken with a modicum of due process. They defend border laws in principle, if not in execution, and regard many irregular immigrants as culpable offenders. They maintain that deportation becomes ethically unjustifiable only after an "otherwise law abiding" (that is, not criminally convicted) person has lived in the country for some years, and/or when they were "not at fault" for their presence, either because they were brought by their parents as children or because they were fleeing persecution.[30] Presence per se does not ground the right against removal.

A here-to-stay stance, in contrast, does not count years (although in this discourse, the length of time present is sometimes treated as implicitly strengthening the claim). Nor do its supporters accept the implied concession embedded in standard legalization discourse that irregular immigrants must be forgiven an earlier wrong—wrongful entry, wrongful visa violation—or that the wrong must be forgotten via an official act of oblivion (Bosniak 2013). HereToStay is, in this respect, a deeply non-repentant politics. Immigrants make this claim because, when it comes down to it—and to paraphrase another key immigrant justice slogan—"No One (here) Is Illegal" (Chacon & Davis 2017).

Many young sanctuary activists—particularly those on college and university campuses (who are usually themselves not undocumented but self-identified "allies")—are embracing a HereToStay politics grounded in an ethics of territorial presence. It is in their literature; it is on their banners. Meanwhile, immigrant activists seem glad to ally themselves with the idea and politics of sanctuary, where sanctuary is now understood to extend beyond compassionate protection—beyond a bid for shelter or mercy—to stand for a justice-based politics (Ticktin 2015).

A sanctuary movement ultimately motivated by an anti-deportation politics represents an invigorating departure from the standard pragmatic border and rights balancing that characterizes so much liberal legal policy discussion on immigration. It is particularly powerful in the way that it reverses the standard culpability premise in this domain by insisting that the wrongful party in the situation is not the targeted immigrant but the deporting state. The discursive power of this shift is immeasurably freeing for noncitizens here.

And yet, refreshing as this departure from standard liberal feasibilism is, it is also true that a politics organized around the right to stay itself represents an ethically confining political imaginary. For one thing, the scope of its justice claim remains territorially and nationally endogenous. It grounds itself entirely in the fact of these persons' extant presence inside the territory—meaning the theater of justice remains nationally insular. Second, a HereToStay politics sidelines the reality that gaining access to hereness in the first instance is itself violently policed and restricted. "Getting here" in the first instance is not on the agenda. Finally, a HereToStay sanctuary ethos is temporally presentist, with its focus the fact of the person's current presence. On its own, it fails to register the historical and structural antecedents to the current constellations of hereness. A claim that invokes a person's already achieved and ongoing territorial presence as the stake to be defended fails to look beyond the here and now to inquire about territoriality's own geopolitical and social determinants.

In short, there is something both incomplete and incoherent about focusing only on the right-to-stay side of things, without critiquing the initial constraints on getting to the place one demands to stay—without interrogating the regime that has long forcibly coercively structured access to territory in the first place. An anti-deportation position alone does not address those who were stopped from being here, nor does it speak for those who were once here and departed on their own or after forced deportation—unless a politics of presence becomes a politics of "once having been here."[31] And it does not speak for those who never came or never tried to come. Nor finally, does the HereToStay position have the ballast, at least on its own, to challenge the subordinated status experienced by territorially present noncitizens while they remain territorially present. Even if they were to be shielded from physical ejection, the claim to retain hereness on its own is not inconsistent with ongoing precarious status while here. In this respect, a politics of presence is not quite a politics of inclusive, democratic citizenship.

For this reason, I would suggest that we open up the conversation about immigration justice and add to #HereToStay two additional critical approaches. The first would link immigrants' current territorial presence to specific geopolitical and economic histories. From this perspective, coming "here" in the first instance has to be understood as the product of or subsequent to past forms of domination by the destination state or elements thereof. In part, this notion is captured in another immigrant justice dictum—one that has so far had more purchase in Europe than in the United States: "We are here because you were there" (Delano 2018). In this framing, the HereToStay claim is based not specifically in the intrinsic significance of current bodily presence, but represents one mode, among others, of redressing forms of historical injustice on the part of actual or functional colonial states (Bosniak 2016a). Part of this redress would include the right of those affected and their descendants to enter, remain, and be incorporated into the former colonial nation.

The other possible approach would be a wholesale border abolitionist position, such as that followed by various "no border" networks. No Borders politics embody a different strand of radical immigration politics, common especially in Canada and in some European countries. This is a politics that stands for freedom of movement, but in its progressive incarnation this is not a claim for market freedom but for liberty of movement across a more justly organized planet. It is an anti-nationalist, globalization-from-below stance.[32]

Both corrective justice and border abolitionist approaches would, in principle, be more satisfying and more critically trenchant than here-to-stayism, both because the gaze of each is less spatially and temporally insular and because each has the potential to critically scrutinize the broader global migration system and the set of economic and social relations over time in which it is embedded.

On the other hand, let us return to the earlier discussion about sanctuary. If such reparative and abolitionist political framings were to become more salient in immigrant justice activism and theorizing, where would that leave claims articulated in the idiom of sanctuary? Does the idea of sanctuary have the capacity to follow?

Notably, there are some voices in activist circles that now seek to harness the justice-linked undercurrent of the sanctuary idea by extending it beyond the immigration setting altogether.[33] In this approach, sanctuary would "tackle not just immigration-related ... policy but also policies related to issues like law enforcement, education, labor, gender, and economic justice," thereby "bringing more people under [sanctuary's] dome" (Farman 2017). These invocations of "extended sanctuary" are intriguing and provocative, though one might reasonably wonder whether such extension would not diminish the concept's political potency in addressing migrant-targeted oppression. On the other hand, extension of the term's usage in this way could productively enlarge our current migrant-focused political imaginations by linking various other struggles for social justice with those of immigrants. That would seem appropriate, since sanctuary's historical lineages both precede and exceed the migration setting (see e.g. Krauthamer 2017; Smart 2013).

But let's put such "extended" invocations of sanctuary aside for now. I want to conclude by reflecting briefly on both potentials and limitations of conducting oppositional *immigration* politics under the banner of sanctuary.

First of all, sanctuary performs protection through the insulation of spaces and places and persons. The term designates refuge or immunity from some official force or authority. In this respect, we must think of sanctuary not as challenging state power frontally but as shielding against incursions of power. It is protective and defensive. This means that the political valence of sanctuary will depend in any given case on who is being shielded, against what and whom, and by what means.

Here, I wish to emphasize that precisely because sanctuary is a politics of boundary maintenance, it is to this extent quintessentially liberal in nature and impulse. Liberalism stands for a politics of jurisdictional separation; it demands the division of spheres and powers. In political theorist Michael Walzer's terms, liberalism *is* "the art of separation" (Walzer

1984).[34] And indeed, as I argued earlier, jurisdictional sphere separation has been enormously protective for noncitizen immigrants in liberal democratic states like the United States. Liberal legalism has imposed crucial constraints on the jurisdiction of interior border enforcement. It has embedded pockets of sanctuary into the regulatory landscape. That this is so becomes particularly clear in moments like the present one, in which the state is smashing through prior jurisdictional boundary settlements and extending the interior border to reach an ever wider set of spaces and moments and subjects. Which is to say: the aggressive processes of border pervasion unleashed by the Trump administration represent a systematic attack upon, and partial dismantling of, certain sanctuarist elements endemic to liberal legalism.

Therefore, to insist on immigration sanctuary is, in one respect, to insist on liberal legalist constraints on borders within the liberal national setting. On the other hand, we have also seen that sanctuary politics grounded in a HereToStay commitment stands significantly *against* a core feature of the liberal nationalist settlement to the extent that it challenges the legitimacy of interiorized immigration enforcement via deportation. Read in this way, sanctuary continues to shield and protect, but what is shielded and protected against is state invasion of people's territorial presence. In this understanding, *the national territory as a whole becomes the sanctuary*. Conceived as such, sanctuary now repudiates a defining feature of the standard liberal-national settlement, which either tacitly or affirmatively accepts the legitimacy of forcible removal of persons from territory.

It is powerful to conceive of the national territory as a whole to be the rightful locus of sanctuary. Yet, once again, it is a conception with normative limits. Perhaps we might say, by way of analogy, that immigration sanctuary in its HereToStay mode resembles that strand of protective anti-slavery activism which shielded free or escaped persons against physical removal to slavery. It provides a kind of asylum via a logic of safe harbor. But the idea of immigration sanctuary would stop short of demanding the equivalent of abolition of the slave system altogether. Fighting for the idea of border abolitionism—pitching one's politics around No Borders—requires a figurative sword, not only the (valiant) shield that sanctuary embodies. Ironically, while sanctuary's critics caricature the project as committed to an anti-border or open borders stance, sanctuary's animating impulse is, as I have said, about protecting people *from* border power not deconstructing or destroying it. Sanctuary demands that borders be bounded. In the long run, this might be regarded as a concessionary stance. In the current moment, however, it is a vital ethical project.

Notes

1. Note also that international law imposes responsibilities on all sovereign states, liberal or otherwise, for the treatment of territorially present noncitizens (that is, citizens of other states). This is not merely a function of individual human rights obligations arising post-World War II, but of a legal regime grounded in states' responsibilities to other states—including the "host" state's responsibility to the state of which the territorially present noncitizen is a national. See Spiro (2011).
2. As noted later in the chapter, the fact that territorially present noncitizens are also subject to immigration regulatory action inside state territory functions, in various ways, to curtail the potential and actualization of basic personhood rights. It remains the case, though, that rights of territorially present persons, by virtue of that territoriality, are endemic to liberal legalism and at times can be deployed to circumscribe state border power and protect irregular immigrants.
3. Occasionally, claims are made on behalf of those already deported and thus no longer present—on grounds that their prior presence was wrongfully taken from them via wrongful deportation. These people seek restoration of that presence. See Bosniak (2016a).
4. This is a structure which Trump long claimed Mexico would pay for—but now the government claims it will be financed by a tax on remittances by Mexican immigrants to their country.
5. The addition of Venezuela and North Korea to the list of precluded states was invoked to bolster the administration's argument that it was not a specifically anti-Muslim animus that motivated the policy.
6. The concept of "nativism" is itself both contested and internally complex. See Bosniak (1997).
7. The quoted phrases are taken from Dawsey (2018), Price (2017), and a White House "3 minute read" of May 21, 2018 titled, "What You Need to Know about the Violent Animals of MS-13" (available at: https://www.whitehouse.gov/articles/need-know-violent-animals-ms-13/, accessed August 1, 2019). See also Smith (2012).
8. As Tsai and Terbeek (2018) make clear, the discursive elements of Trumpism have national antecedents.
9. If they did, then when a person physically entered the territory of such a state, they would thereby be beyond the reach of that state's border control authority.
10. They ideally champion what I have called a hard-on-the-outside, soft-on-the-inside vision of national polity—though in fact they concede the legitimacy of (admittedly "hard") border interiorization where necessary (see Bosniak 2007).

11. Executive Order No. 13767, January 25, 2017 (https://www.whitehouse.gov/presidential-actions/executive-order-border-security-immigration-enforcement-improvements/, accessed August 3, 2019).
12. Secretary of Homeland Security, "Enforcement of the Immigration Laws to Serve the National Interest," memorandum, February 20, 2017 (available at: https://www.dhs.gov/sites/default/files/publications/17_0220_S1_Enforcement-of-the-Immigration-Laws-to-Serve-the-National-Interest.pdf, accessed August 2, 2019).
13. Meanwhile, the government has been engaged in a massive hiring of Border Patrol and ICE personnel—the only area of federal government that is not being cut back, with widespread recruitment occurring, including on college campuses (Katz 2018; O'Toole 2017).
14. Even before their permits expire, scores of DACA holders have been targeted for deportation in the wake of minor traffic violations and status technicalities (Rodriguez 2017).
15. Here, I must note that the statutory infrastructure permits this. The underlying statute delegating enforcement power to the executive branch offers the new administration plenty of room to proceed. That is, much of what Trump is doing is entirely consistent with the statute. See e.g. AIC (2018).
16. Office of the Attorney General, "Renewed Commitment to Criminal Immigration Enforcement," memorandum, April 11, 2017 (available at: https://www.justice.gov/opa/press-release/file/956841/download, accessed August 1, 2019).
17. Sessions is also reported as saying: "For those that continue to seek improper and illegal entry into this country, be forewarned: This is a new era. This is the Trump era. The lawlessness, the abdication of the duty to enforce our immigration laws and the catch and release practices of old are over" (quoted from "Attorney General Jeff Sessions Announces the Department of Justice's Renewed Commitment to Criminal Immigration Enforcement," press release, Department of Justice, April 11, 2017; available at: https://www.justice.gov/opa/pr/attorney-general-jeff-sessions-announces-department-justice-s-renewed-commitment-criminal, accessed August 1, 2019).
18. The ICE website states that it maintains a "sensitive locations" policy, though in narrowed form (see https://www.ice.gov/ero/enforcement/sensitive-loc). In practice, the policy is often breached. Thus far, however, immigration enforcement actions have not been carried out in places of religious worship.
19. Indeed, the stock of the former Corrections Corporation of America, recently rebranded as CoreCivic, more than doubled in value immediately after the election (Long 2017).
20. For reportage on recent Section 287(g) agreements and efforts to penalize "sanctuary cities," see e.g. Casteel (2017).
21. Those who have not cooperated justify their refusal in the idiom of public safety, arguing that when undocumented immigrants fear encounters with the police as crime victims or witnesses, communities suffer. The Trump administration, in turn, is seeking to force compliance by threatening to withdraw federal funding. Whether such coercion is constitutionally permissible is being litigated in the courts (see Gerstein 2018).

22. Electoral reversals are of course ever more difficult to achieve in the face of the partisan gerrymandering and judicial affirmations of voter suppression laws (see e.g. Liptak 2018).
23. John Washington, "Another Way To Keep Families Together: Join The New Sanctuary Movement." *The Nation*. June 28, 2018. (accessed August 1, 2019).
24. Some universities embrace protective stances but have been unwilling to deploy the sanctuary term, either because they regard it as politically inflammatory or because they say it misleadingly suggests provision of greater protection to the undocumented than is actually on offer. For a general discussion of the politicization of the sanctuary term, see Farman (2017). For consideration of private-entity proffered sanctuary, see Gulasekaram and Villazor (2018).
25. "Sanctuary Syllabus," Public Books, December 5, 2017 (available at: http://www.publicbooks.org/sanctuary-syllabus/, accessed August 1, 2019).
26. Advocates also urge businesses to invoke common law property rights and constitutional and privacy rights to insulate themselves from liability for sanctuary-like protections they might choose to extend (Gulasekaram & Villazor 2018).
27. The DREAM (Development, Relief, and Education for Alien Minors) Act is a legislative initiative that would have regularized hundreds of thousands of undocumented youth. Congress came close to passing the legislation more than once, and the Obama administration supported it, but it ultimately failed. It was in response to that failure that Obama implemented DACA. For a discussion of the meaning of the "unapologetic" strand in this area, see Bosniak (2016b).
28. See https://weareheretostay.org/ (accessed August 2, 2019).
29. "Not One More" is a slogan the immigrant justice movement has been pressing for several years. See e.g. the home page of Not1More (http://www.notonemoredeportation.com/, accessed August 2, 2019).
30. As the liberal political theorist Joseph Carens puts it when arguing on behalf of "amnesty" for some undocumented immigrants, "The longer the stay, the stronger the claim" (Carens 2013: xxx). The implicit corollary, of course, is: the shorter the stay, the weaker the claim (Bosniak 2015).
31. In fact, some legal challenges to wrongful deportation could be said to entail this position. See Bosniak (2016b).
32. E.g., NoBorder Network, http://www.noborder.org/ (accessed August 1, 2019).
33. As one commentator has put it, "black people need sanctuary cities too" (Bonsu 2017).
34. "Liberalism is a world of walls, and each one creates a new liberty" (Walzer 1984: 315).

References

AIC (American Immigration Council). 2018. "The End of Immigration Enforcement Priorities under the Trump Administration." Available at: https://

www.americanimmigrationcouncil.org/research/immigration-enforcement-priorities-under-trump-administration (accessed August 1, 2019).

Armenta, Amada. 2017. "Racializing Crimmigration." *Sociology of Race and Ethnicity* 3(1): 1–14.

Bonsu, Janae. 2017. "Black People Need Sanctuary Cities Too." *Essence*, March 10. Available at: https://www.essence.com/news/politics/sanctuary-cities-black-families-immigrants/ (accessed August 1, 2019).

Bosniak, Linda. 1997. "Nativism: The Concept." In Juan F. Perea (ed.), *Immigrants Out! The New Nativism and the Anti-Immigrant Impulse in the United States*, 279–99. New York: New York University Press.

—— 2006. *The Citizen and the Alien*. Princeton: Princeton University Press.

—— 2007. "Being Here: Ethical Territoriality and the Rights of Immigrants." *Theoretical Inquiries in Law* 8(2): 389–410.

—— 2010. "Persons and Citizens in Constitutional Thought." *International Journal of Constitutional Law* 8(1): 9–29.

—— 2013. "Amnesty in Immigration: Forgiving, Forgetting, Freedom." *Critical Review of International Social and Political Philosophy*, special issue, 16(3): 344–65.

—— 2015. "Review of J. Carens, *The Ethics of Immigration*." *Ethics* 125(2): 571–6.

—— 2016a. "Wrongs, Rights and Regularization." *Moral Philosophy and Politics* 3(2): 187–222.

—— 2016b. "Unapologetic." Paper presented at the Institute for Advanced Study, Princeton, February 2016.

Carens, Joseph. 2013. *The Ethics of Immigration*. Oxford: Oxford University Press.

Casteel, Kathryn. 2017. "While Some Communities Become Sanctuaries, Others Are Happy to Help with Trump's Immigration Crackdown." *Five Thirty Eight*, August 10. Available at: https://fivethirtyeight.com/features/while-some-communities-become-sanctuaries-others-are-happy-to-help-with-trumps-immigration-crackdown/ (accessed August 1, 2019).

Chacon, Justin Akers, and Mike Davis. 2017. *No One Is Illegal: Fighting Racism and State Violence on the US–Mexico Border*. Chicago: Haymarket Books.

Connolly, William E. 2017. *Aspirational Fascism: The Struggle for Multifaceted Democracy under Trumpism*. Minneapolis: University of Minnesota Press.

Dawsey, Josh. 2018. "Trump Derides Protections for Immigrants from 'Shithole' Countries." *Washington Post*, January 12. Available at: https://www.washingtonpost.com/politics/trump-attacks-protections-for-immigrants-from-shithole-countries-in-oval-office-meeting/2018/01/11/bfc0725c-f711-11e7-91af-31ac729add94_story.html?noredirect=on&utm_term=.b2b8e02ca3e8 (accessed August 1, 2019).

Delano, Alejandra. 2018. *From Here and There: Diaspora Policies, Integration and Social Rights Beyond Borders*. Oxford: Oxford University Press.

Emanuel, Gabrielle. 2017. "Religious Communities Continue the Long Tradition of Offering Sanctuary." *NPR*, March 14. Available at: https://www.npr.org/2017/03/14/519307698/religious-communities-continue-the-long-tradition-of-offering-sanctuary (accessed August 1, 2019).

Farman, Abou. 2017. "In Defense of Sanctuary." *The Baffler*, April 6. Available at: https://thebaffler.com/latest/in-defense-of-sanctuary-farman (accessed August 1, 2019).

Gerstein, Josh. 2018. "Justice Threatens Subpoenas in Sanctuary Cities Funding Fight." *Politico*, January 24. Available at: https://www.politico.com/story/2018/01/24/sanctuary-cities-justice-department-subpoenas-365465 (accessed August 1, 2019).

Grant, Mary Lee, and Nick Miroff. 2018. "US Militia Groups Head to Border, Stirred by Trump's Call to Arms." *Washington Post*, November 3. Available at: https://www.washingtonpost.com/world/national-security/us-militia-groups-head-to-border-stirred-by-trumps-call-to-arms/2018/11/03/ff96826c-decf-11e8-b3f0-62607289efee_story.html (accessed August 28, 2019).

Guillen, Itzel, Irving Hernandez, Allyson Duarte, and Justino Mora. 2017. "'We're Here to Stay." *Guardian*, December 11. Available at: https://www.theguardian.com/us-news/2017/dec/11/guardian-guest-edit-dreamers-us-edition-editorial (accessed August 1, 2019).

Gulasekaram, Pratheepan, and Rose Cuison Villazor. 2018. "The Case for Nongovernmental Sanctuary for Immigrants." *Los Angeles Times*, April 5. Available at: https://www.latimes.com/opinion/op-ed/la-oe-gulasekaram-villazor-immigrant-sanctuary-network-20180405-story.html (accessed August 1, 2019).

Hadfield, Jack. 2017. "Milo Gives ICE Hotline to UNM Students: 'If You See Something, Say Something'." *Breitbart*, January 28. Available at: https://www.breitbart.com/social-justice/2017/01/28/milo-unm-heres-ices-phone-number-use-wisely/ (accessed August 1, 2019).

Kanstroom, Daniel. 2007. *Deportation Nation*. Cambridge, MA: Harvard University Press.

Katz, Matt. 2018. "ICE Gets Cold Shoulder from Rutgers, Backs Out of Career Fair." *WNYC*, February 22. Available at: https://www.wnyc.org/story/ice-gets-cold-shoulder-rutgers-backs-out-career-fair/ (accessed August 1, 2019).

Klein, Rebecca. 2018. "Betsy DeVos Stirs Uproar by Saying Schools Can Call ICE on Undocumented Kids." *Huffington Post*, May 23. Available at: https://www.huffingtonpost.com/entry/betsy-devos-uproar-schools-call-ice-undocumented-kids_us_5b05a297e4b05f0fc8441ce3 (accessed August 1, 2019).

Krauthamer, Barbara. 2017. "Sanctuary Cities Have Historical Roots in Slavery-Era US." *Portside*, February 27. Available at: https://portside.org/2017-02-27/sanctuary-cities-have-historical-roots-slavery-era-us (accessed August 1, 2019).

Kwong, Christine, and Marissa Roy. 2018. "Local Action, National Impact: Standing Up for Sanctuary Cities." *Yale Law Journal Forum*, January 20. Available at: https://www.yalelawjournal.org/forum/local-action-national-impact (accessed August 1, 2019).

Lancer Julnes, Patricia de, and Jennifer C. Gibbs. 2017. "Does Cooperating with ICE Harm Local Police? What the Research Says." *The Conversation*, April 24. Available at: https://theconversation.com/does-cooperating-with-ice-harm-local-police-what-the-research-says-76072 (accessed August 1, 2019).

Liptak, Adam. 2018. "Supreme Court Upholds Ohio's Purge of Voting Rolls." *New York Times*, June 11. Available at: https://www.nytimes.com/2018/06/11/us/

politics/supreme-court-upholds-ohios-purge-of-voting-rolls.html (accessed August 1, 2019).

Long, Heather. 2017. "Private Prison Stocks up 100% Since Trump's Win." *CNN Business*, February 24. Available at: https://money.cnn.com/2017/02/24/investing/private-prison-stocks-soar-trump/index.html (accessed August 1, 2019).

Moran, Greg. 2018. "ICE Looks to Private Sector to Help Hire Nearly 6,000 Workers to Support the 10,000 New Agents Trump Wants." *San Diego Union-Tribune*, February 1. Available at: https://www.sandiegouniontribune.com/news/watchdog/sd-me-ice-hires-20180201-story.html (accessed August 1, 2019).

Nakamura, David. 2014. "Obama Acts on Immigration, Announcing Decision to Defer Deportations of 4 Million." *Washington Post*, November 20. Available at: https://www.washingtonpost.com/politics/obama-acts-on-immigration-announcing-decision-to-defer-deportations-of-4-million/2014/11/20/9a5c3856-70f6-11e4-8808-afaa1e3a33ef_story.html (accessed August 28, 2019).

O'Toole, Molly. 2017. "Trump Administration Seeks to Loosen Hiring Requirements to Beef Up Border Patrol." *Foreign Policy*, February 25. Available at: https://foreignpolicy.com/2017/02/25/trump-administration-seeks-to-loosen-hiring-requirements-to-beef-up-border-patrol/ (accessed August 1, 2019).

Phippin, J. Weston. 2016. "Australia's Controversial Migration Policy." *The Atlantic*, April 29. Available at: https://www.theatlantic.com/international/archive/2016/04/australia-immigration/480189/ (accessed August 1, 2019).

Price, R. Darren. 2017. "Trump on NYC Subway Bombing: 'End Chain Migration.'" *NBCDFW*, December 12. Available at: https://www.nbcdfw.com/news/politics/President-Trump-Chain-Migration-Port-Authority-Bus-Terminal-Bombing-Explosion-463482233.html (accessed August 1, 2019).

Rodriguez, Nicole. 2017. "Trump Administration Has Illegally Attempted to Deport DACA Recipients, Advocates Say." *Newsweek*, December 2. Available at: https://www.newsweek.com/trump-administration-has-made-illegal-attempts-deport-daca-recipients-724842 (accessed August 1, 2019).

Smart, Anthony. 2013. "Review of *Sanctuary and Crime in the Middle Ages 400–1500*." *Journal of Legal History* 34(1): 117–20.

Smith, David Livingstone. 2012. *Less Than Human: Why We Demean, Enslave and Exterminate Others*. New York: St. Martin's Press.

Spaggatt, Elliot. 2018. "ICE Formalizes Plans for Courthouse Arrests." *Chicago Tribune*, January 3. Available at: https://www.chicagotribune.com/nation-world/ct-ice-plans-courthouse-arrests-20180131-story.html (accessed August 1, 2019).

Spiro, Peter. 2011. "A New International Law of Citizenship." *American Journal of International Law* 105(4): 694–746.

Ticktin, Miriam. 2015. "The Problem with Humanitarian Borders: Toward a New Framework of Justice." *Public Seminar*, September 18. Available at: http://www.publicseminar.org/2015/09/the-problem-with-humanitarian-borders/ (accessed August 1, 2019).

Tsai, Robert, and Calvin Terbeek. 2018. "Trumpism before Trump." *Boston Review*, June 11. Available at: http://bostonreview.net/politics/robert-tsai-calvin-terbeek-trumpism-trump (accessed August 1, 2019).

Volpp, Leti. 2002. "The Citizen and the Terrorist," *UCLA Law Review* 49: 1575–1600.

Walzer, Michael. 1984. "Liberalism and the Art of Separation." *Political Theory* 12(3): 315–30.

11
Ruination and Rebuilding
The Precarious Place of a Border Town in Gaza

Ilana Feldman

Beit Hanoun, a town located along the northern edge of the Gaza Strip, was "particularly badly hit" in the summer 2014 Israeli assault on Gaza and "70 per cent of its housing became uninhabitable" (Loewenstein 2016). According to a report from November 2016: "today, sand, rubbish and discarded clothes remain strewn across the ground ... [Many people] live in shoddy caravans that are bitterly cold in the winter and extremely hot in summer" (ibid.). Rebuilding has been impeded by strict Israeli controls on the goods that can enter Gaza.[1] Throughout Gaza people live with the residues, and often amidst the ruins, of past attacks and in fear of the next assault. Israel has attacked Gaza three times in the last ten years. The current cycle of attack and pause—what Israelis refer to as "mowing the lawn"—is the latest iteration in a long history in which Beit Hanoun has been at the epicenter of destruction. According to an American Friends Service Committee (AFSC) aid worker who visited the empty town after its destruction in the course of the war during the establishment of Israel in 1948:

> the village was systematically and completely destroyed by burning each individual home. The roofs of wood and thatch were of course consumed quickly and the heat of the burning destroyed the texture of the mud walls so that with time and rain they have been pretty much washed away.[2]

This initial destruction coincided with the establishment of a militarized boundary within the former Gaza district of Palestine.[3]

Beit Hanoun is located in a distinctive sort of borderland. Rather than marking the territorial differentiation of two independent states, whether symmetrical or asymmetrical (Nugent, this volume), the armistice demarcation line between Gaza and Israel is a boundary of conflict and occupation. From 1948 to 1967 it marked an uneasy truce between two warring states, Egypt and Israel, and it was a securitized border keeping Palestinian refugees away from their lands and homes on the other side. Directly connected to the managed instability of this line, the United Nations played a role in border control, through the UN Truce Supervision Organization and, after 1957, the UN Emergence Force. Since 1967, when Israel occupied Gaza, the line's status has changed over time as Israel's policies toward Palestinians (and Palestinian political practice) has shifted. It went from being relatively open in years before the first intifada—with Palestinian laborers and visitors crossing north and Israeli consumers and settlers going south—to nearly hermetically sealed since the second intifada. Gaza is often described as "the world's largest open-air prison."[4] Due to its location along the borderline, Beit Hanoun has been especially vulnerable to repeated assault and destruction.

The changing status of the borderline intersects with reconfigurations in Gaza's social boundaries. There were many Palestinian population distinctions before 1948, along lines of lifestyle and livelihood (city-dweller, peasant, Bedouin), religion, class, and political affiliation. The end of the British Mandate in Palestine, which marked the establishment of the state of Israel, produced the displacement and dispossession of the majority of Palestine's native population. The Nakba ("catastrophe"), as these events are known in Arabic, dispersed Palestinians and created the new category of the refugee. In the West Bank and Gaza, where people were displaced within the territory of historic Palestine, after 1948 there was a new internal population distinction between refugees and natives. This distinction was especially important in Gaza where around 250,000 refugees from other parts of Palestine outnumbered the 80,000 original inhabitants. The refugee influx created social and economic tensions within the population and concerns for the governing authorities. These tensions were felt across the Gaza Strip.

Managing an unsettled population of natives and refugees required significant government action in the areas of both service and security. Services were provided both by the governing Egyptian administration and by the UN Relief and Works Agency for Palestine Refugees. Questions regularly arose about which party was responsible for a given service matter. Beit Hanoun's border geography created additional challenges. The mechanisms that were available in other locales in Gaza to generate resources and organize service delivery were impeded by Beit Hanoun's location. As an Egyptian administration official commented about a failed public works project in the village, "the weakness of the economic conditions and the village's location along the border make it difficult to establish a council and to impose direct taxes on the residents."[5]

One way of distinguishing between borders and boundaries is that the former are territorial and geopolitical markers of external difference and the latter are social categories of internal differentiation. Gaza's perimeter shows how a physical demarcation can be both internal and external, both as a territorial matter and in reference to the differences it marks. Gaza's borderline is a physical boundary that cuts within the territory of historic Palestine, separating people from their homes and lands. It has functioned as an internal line of control—territorially delineating populations who live under different legal regimes and have different rights, even as they are governed by a single state. Gaza's boundary line is not an officially recognized international border, but it operates as such when permits and documentation, along with encounters with personnel of multiple states (or quasi-states), are needed to cross it. These alternating conditions have significant consequences for the people living in the shadow of this border. This chapter takes the case of Beit Hanoun as a means to explore some of those consequences, looking particularly at the centrality of (repeated) ruination and (repeated) rebuilding in Palestinian experience. It tells the nested stories of a small town with a precarious place on the border; of the Gaza Strip, all of which might be considered a borderland; of Palestine in the twentieth-century; and of globally resonant late colonialism and securitized imperialism.

From "No-Man's-Land" to Borderland

What makes a borderland? Proximity to a border is obviously important, but what gives shape to a space as a borderland are the radiating effects of that proximity. In contexts of relatively open borders these might include densities of commerce and tourism. In conflicted borderlands, ruination, and only sometimes rebuilding, is a key feature of the landscape. Yael Navarro-Yashin describes the Cyprus borderland as an "abjected space" (Navarro-Yashin 2012: 148) that is "filled with ruins and rubbish" (ibid.: 147). In the aftermath of the 1948 war that established Israel, created the

Gaza Strip, and displaced the majority of the Palestinian population, Beit Hanoun remained in a state of ruination. During the Mandate (1920 to 1948), in contrast, the area was a productive agricultural zone. According to a local history of the Gaza region, the village was prosperous enough to support the salaries of two teachers for its local school (Skeik 1981: 89).

The terms of the February 1949 armistice agreement between Egypt and Israel stipulated that "Egyptian forces shall nowhere advance beyond their present positions, and this shall include Beit Hanun and its surrounding area from which Israeli forces shall be withdrawn to north of the Armistice Demarcation Line."[6] Beit Hanoun thus became a no-man's-land, technically located within the territory of the new Gaza Strip, but inaccessible to both Egyptian authorities and Gaza's inhabitants. In addition to the legal prohibition, a large number of mines in the vicinity discouraged visits to the area. But it quickly became clear that these conditions created a problem, not just for the people denied access to their homes and lands, but for Egypt and Israel. The existence of the no-man's-land, designed to create a cushion between the two parties, resulted in an area that could only be tenuously controlled.

Despite the prohibition, refugees from villages on the other side of the armistice line continued to cross to retrieve food and possessions from their former homes (Feldman 2006). Complaints about Israel shooting at returning refugees were regularly brought to the UN's Mixed Armistice Commission.[7] The no-man's-land also served as a conduit for smuggling operations between Gaza and Hebron, about forty miles away and under Jordanian control. As long as Egyptian forces could not enter the area, it proved impossible to halt this smuggling.[8] This uncontrolled situation was concerning to both Israel and Egypt. In October 1949 the Egyptian delegation submitted a proposal to the UN Conciliation Commission that "the inhabitants of the northern part of the Gaza strip whose lands lay within 'no-man's-land' should be authorized to cultivate their lands in that area."[9] Israel proposed that part of this territory be attached to the Gaza Strip and part ceded to Israel in exchange for other territory near Khan Yunis. On the first anniversary of the armistice signing, the two sides reached an agreement that they would have, as the *New York Times* put it, "nothing more than a straight line between them" (Anon. 1950c). As an Israeli official reported on the agreement, "the original inhabitants of the Egyptian section of the neutral zone are entitled to resume residence and civilian occupation of that area."[10]

Their desires were not the motivating reason for the border reconfiguration, but Beit Hanoun's residents were eager to return. In order for return to be possible, ruination had to be replaced with rebuilding. The near-total destruction of the village, and the continued mine problem, posed potential obstacles. Despite these impediments, people began to return as soon as the road that led to town was reopened. The AFSC, which had been commissioned by the UN to provide relief to refugees in Gaza, had a keen interest in the fate of Beit Hanoun.[11] Despite many challenges, it viewed the return to Beit Hanoun as "a major rehabilitation opportunity" since "for the first time we are actually seeing Arab families returning to their former village in considerable numbers."[12] The AFSC proposed first to establish a tent camp at the edge of the village to house people until the buildings could be reconstructed. Further, it decided it would "bring rations to the village on the regular bi-weekly scale ... [and] a clinic service."[13]

Excitement about return appears to have been widely shared. The local Gazan press reported on plans for the return with evident delight. *Sawt al-'Uruba* stated: "It has become very easy for us to reassure all the people that a joyful surprise will be coming soon and we will be gladdened by the return of the Arab refugees to their towns and villages" (Anon. 1950a). It reported that the inhabitants of Beit Hanoun would be returning to their homes "after this wide agricultural area is cleared of mines (ibid.)." The article went on to detail the AFSC plans, and to note that the Egyptian administration was establishing a police station. A local bus company was ready to provide transportation "when the orders to return the people to this village are published (ibid.)." In a follow up piece, the paper reported that there were plans to build a "model village" in Beit Hanoun (Anon. 1950b)—a model of a successful return to a destroyed village.

Whatever hopes the return to Beit Hanoun may have engendered in Gaza's other refugees, it turned out to be not the first return but the only one. At about the same time that the people of Beit Hanoun returned to their village, the inhabitants of the village of Majdal, which lay on the other side of the armistice line in Israeli controlled territory, were being expelled from theirs.[14] It was the forced depopulation of Majdal, and not the repopulation of Beit Hanoun, that proved to be more of a harbinger of the fate of Palestinians after 1948. But the experience of Beit Hanoun has been emblematic of the Palestinian experience in other ways. As a borderland town, Beit Hanoun has been on the frontline of confrontation—until 1967 between Israel and Egypt, and thereafter between Israel and Palestinians.¹⁵ After the town was first repopulated it became a stop on a "political tourism" trajectory, as Egyptian officials brought foreign delegations there to see the armistice line and the Israeli flag flying on formerly Palestinian land on the other side. When UN peacekeepers were deployed after the 1956 four-month Israeli occupation of Gaza, the quarters of the Danish–Norwegian contingent were located just outside of town.

The return of Beit Hanoun's displaced inhabitants in 1950 immediately raised internal boundary questions. As long as they remained outside the town, Beit Hanoun people were refugees, and therefore recipients of UN humanitarian aid. When they returned home, they would cease to have refugee status but, as the AFSC acknowledged, "it will probably be some time before the crops and flocks can again support them and some form of rations will have to be continued for a time."¹⁶ The additional fact that the agreement that determined which lands would fall within Gaza "has resulted in all the large estates and orange groves being so included, while a great proportion of small holdings of individual fellaheen [peasants] are still across the line in Israel,"¹⁷ ensured that most of the returnees would remain dispossessed. Along with creating the distinction between refugees and natives, 1948 and its aftermath had the effect of exacerbating existing class distinctions within the native Gazan population and producing a category of newly landless peasants.

All these distinctions were connected to both persons and places. After 1948, Gaza's internal geography included eight refugee camps, three cities (Gaza City, Khan Yunis, and Rafah), and many small towns like Beit Hanoun. In theory, camps are refugee-only spaces, and this was largely the case in Gaza, even as it has become increasingly less so in other places of Palestinian life. Only about half the refugees ever lived in camps, however, so cities and towns have always been mixed environments. This mixing produced problems of governing jurisdiction. The entirety of the Gaza Strip was administered by Egyptian authorities, but many services for the refugee population (rations, education, healthcare, shelter, sanitation) were addressed by the UN Relief and Works Agency for Palestine Refugees (UNRWA).

The challenges that sometimes arose from the multiplicity of population kinds and service providers in Gaza was evident in Beit Hanoun. After its repopulation the town's inhabitants included both natives and refugees. Some services—such as medical care, rations provision, and education—were attached to persons. Refugees could get these services from UNRWA wherever they lived, and natives could get them from the government (with food support also from private agencies such as CARE). Housing was a somewhat more complicated category, involving judgments of both person and place. Shelter was available from UNRWA only for refugees in camps. Land for housing was offered by the Egyptian administration to any Gazan civil servant (refugee or native) who did not already own property. But there was no jurisdictional debate here. Sanitation and infrastructure was another matter, and became a source of contention in places where both refugees and natives lived.

In September 1957, the Egyptian administration's director of public health wrote to the director of municipal and village affairs asking that the poor state of Beit Hanoun's water supply be addressed as a vital public health concern.[18] The latter responded that the matter should be addressed to UNRWA since many of the inhabitants were refugees "who carry rations cards," and UNRWA "is responsible for service for them, just as for the remainder of refugees."[19] When the government and UNRWA proved unable to resolve this debate, residents took action on their own. The mukhtars (village leaders) and a'yan (notables) rented some of the village land to a private farmer, on the condition that he provide free water to the people for the 27-year duration of the contract.[20] However, lacking enforcement power, such as might have been provided by a village council, when the farmer did not fulfill his obligations, the mukhtars were forced to ask the UN Emergence Force (UNEF) for water and seek enforcement assistance from the governor general.[21] The a few years later, the village residents made an ultimately successful request to establish a local council.[22]

Governance, jurisdiction, and service provision were not the only matters that forced a grappling with the sometimes muddied character of population distinctions. So too did conditions of life in Gaza. Despite the tensions, and sometimes even hostility, that existed across these categories, that Gazans do now consider themselves part of one community is beyond dispute—even as distinctions between natives and refugees continue to matter within the community. The fact that this community has developed in spite of all of the tensions and divisions shows the power of time and of the accumulated habits of living and working together in both conflict and cooperation, and through ruination and rebuilding. At the same time it should be remembered how much work—local, regional, international—goes into producing the conditions that enable such habits to unfold. When I conducted research in Gaza in the late 1990s, people repeatedly told me that, whatever criticisms they may have had about it, the Egyptian administration expended considerable effort to constitute a Gazan community of people from many places in Palestine.

This rule ended with the June War of 1967. In what proved to be the final weeks of the Egyptian administration, when UNEF forces withdrew from Gaza at Egypt's request, Gaza's refugees and dispossessed natives hoped that they might regain their lands. In May 1967 the *New York Times* reported from Beit Hanoun: "Excited Palestinians trained for war today in this village near the Israeli frontier, believing they were on the brink of recovering the land they lost 19 years ago. Soldiers of the Palestine Liberation Army lay in trenches formerly manned by United Nations troops" (Anon. 1967). Contrary to their hopes, Israel occupied the Gaza Strip (along with the West Bank, Golan Heights, and the Sinai). For Beit Hanoun, the June War did not mean ruination, but incorporation, along with the rest of the Gaza Strip, into the matrix of Israeli control.

Between Border and Boundary

The Israeli occupation of the West Bank and Gaza Strip reached its fiftieth year in June 2017. Over this long time span the character of the borderline between Gaza and Israel—a line that cuts through the interior of historic Palestine—has been through many permutations, and has had varying degrees of permeability. These transformations highlight how a single demarcation line can have many different effects on people's lives and can carry multiple affective charges. It has gone from border to boundary, and back. It has been a threshold for travel and a site of heightened vulnerability to attack. It has been transformed from a passable space to a zone of immobility, although the tunnels that have been built below, and across, the border have made it possible for goods and fighters to move. As a zone of contested occupation, the changes in Gaza's borderland have been acute.

Israeli occupation was met with considerable resistance in Gaza in its first years, but that resistance was largely quashed by Ariel Sharon by 1971. And for the next twenty years, the boundary was relatively open. It was never fully obscured, as happened with the Green Line in the West Bank for many years. Passage was freely available for Gazans to enable them to work in Israel, for refugees to visit their lost homes, and for Israelis to travel to Gaza for its widely renowned (for quality and price) car mechanics. During this period, Israel's economy came to depend heavily on Palestinian labor. Sara Roy describes Israel's policy toward Gaza during this period as one of "de-development" (Roy 1995). Gaza's population had access to income opportunity through work in Israel, but efforts to pursue independent economic activity were impeded.

The first phase of occupation—when Israel claimed to be conducting a "benign" occupation—ended when the first intifada began, on December 9, 1987, in the Jabalia refugee camp in the north of Gaza. The immediate spark for the uprising was the killing of four Palestinians by an Israeli military jeep, but its deeper cause was the already long-standing occupation of Palestinian territories, theft of Palestinian land, and the refusal to grant Palestinians desired freedoms. The protests in Jabalia quickly spread across Gaza and the West Bank, launching a popular uprising that lasted for years. Pictures of Palestinian youth throwing stones at Israeli tanks are among the famous intifada images, but stone-throwing was only one of many forms of opposition. Palestinians refused cooperation with the occupation machinery in multiple fields: police resigned their positions, entire towns engaged in tax strikes, and consumers boycotted Israeli goods. Within Palestinian society, people observed a general strike (with shops closing first at 1 p.m. and later at 3 p.m. daily) and refrained from holding major celebrations. Palestinian women famously would claim any young man as their son, in an effort to protect them from pursuing Israeli soldiers. And, at least for a time, the intifada upended traditional hierarchies of Palestinian society, as women went into the streets and youth led the movement. Resistance reworks boundaries.

The occupation had never been benign, but its cruelty had not always been globally visible. The violent Israeli response to the intifada—captured in Yitzhak Rabin's notorious policy of breaking the bones of demonstrators in an effort to halt the uprising—and the Palestinian refusal to give up in the face of this violence irrevocably changed the conversation. In addition to its military response, Israel responded to the intifada by curtailing Palestinian movement. The first step in what has become a decades-long policy of immobilization was the requirement that Gazans have an entry permit—"magnetically encoded cards" (Anon. 1989)—to cross into Israel. According to news reports, residents of Beit Hanoun and the nearby village of Beit Lahiya were the first to get the cards, as the army lifted a curfew for these two villages alone to permit their registration. The process of controlling people's movement out of Gaza was also a process of reinscribing the armistice line as a border. This transformation was materially marked by the expansion of the infrastructure of inspection at the crossing point.

This process was sped up by the signing of the Oslo Accords in 1993 and 1995, which people had hoped might lead to the establishment of two states and actual borders. During the Oslo period, movement through the Erez crossing to Israel or the West Bank became impossible for most Palestinians. The agreement's deadline for final status resolution passed in 1999 without any real progress toward Palestinian independence. After the outbreak of the second intifada—whose immediate spark was a deliberately provocative visit by Ariel Sharon to the Haram al-Sharif in Jerusalem; the cause was dismay and disillusionment with the Oslo process—Gaza's isolation became more severe. Entrance to Gaza by non-residents was heavily curtailed and controlled by Israel. The number of Gazans granted permits plummeted even further.

During the second intifada large portions of Beit Hanoun were once again reduced to rubble. As a site from which Qassam rockets were launched at nearby Israeli towns, the village was subjected to repeated and sustained invasion and destruction. A May 2003 Médecins Sans Frontières report described the effects of one invasion: "Large swaths of orchards had been razed, the bridge on the main road had been destroyed once again and several streets torn up ... In some cases, the families inside the [destroyed] houses were given no warning and had to jump out of windows in order to save themselves."[23] A report in *Haaretz* in July 2004 described the demolition of a vegetable packing plant in the village and reflected, "It is difficult to shake the impression that the IDF [Israeli Defense Force] has undertaken a 'scorched earth' policy in the [Gaza] Strip" (Anon. 2004).

This policy, and repeated attacks on Beit Hanoun, have been a hallmark of the three Israeli wars on Gaza over the last decade (2008/9, 2012, 2014). Another feature of these wars has been new twists in the work of border-making, this time through squeezing territory. In the summer 2014 attack, for example, Israel created a 3 kilometer "buffer zone" all along Gaza's boundaries and told people who live in this area to leave. Beit Hanoun fell within this zone. A *Christian Science Monitor* article from late July reported on an extended Beit Hanoun family that was seeking shelter with relatives in Gaza City: "We have lost everything ... We have big homes and fields in Beit Hanoun. Now we are considered as refugees. No one can protect us, because we are not Israelis, we are Palestinian" (Chick 2014). Moving out of the buffer zone was no guarantee of safety; large portions of Gaza City were targeted for assault. In this case, as before, Beit Hanoun's displaced residents returned as soon as they could:

With shocked looks, residents who had fled their houses, as instructed by the Israeli army forces ... took in the sight of entire clusters of houses destroyed by shells and bombs. To many, it seemed as if an earthquake had hit the farming community of 30,000, where dead donkeys, horses and birds littered the ground—along with unexploded Israeli ordinance. (Anon. 2014)

Cycles of Ruination and Rebuilding

In his account of Palestinian lives and identity, Edward Said reflects that "each Palestinian structure presents itself as a potential ruin. The theme of the formerly proud family house (village, city, camp) now wrecked, left behind, or owned by someone else, turns up everywhere in our literature and cultural heritage" (Said 1986: 38). The destruction not only of homes but of entire towns is a central feature of the Palestinian experience. More than 400 villages were destroyed in 1948. In some places the buildings remained intact and the villages were reinhabited and remade as Israeli Jewish communities. Other villages were reduced to rubble. The experience of Beit Hanoun shows that a ruin can sometimes have a future, that it is not always doomed to remain wrecked or lost forever. Even if returning to homes lost in 1948 has not been a regular part of the Palestinian experience, rebuilding has.

Such rebuilding occurs across the landscape of Palestinian dispersal. The refugee camps where many Palestinians have lived since 1948 have been regular targets of state and militia violence. Some camps have been destroyed and disappeared (such as Nabatiyah and Tel al-Zaatar in Lebanon), but many have been rebuilt by their inhabitants as soon as fighting ceased (such as Ein el Hilwe, Shatila, and Burj al Barajneh in Lebanon).[24] And it is not only camps that people rebuild as quickly as possible. When I went to Ramallah in the summer of 2003, only a few months after the Israeli invasion and reoccupation of the city that had severely damaged much of its downtown area, I was struck by the fact that everything had already been repaired. Repair has become exceedingly difficult in Gaza because of Israeli restrictions on the entry of construction materials, but even under these conditions it happens.

In Beit Hanoun the cycles of ruination and attempted rebuilding have sped up in the first decades of the twenty-first century. Beit Hanoun suffered mightily in the three major offenses against Gaza that began in 2009. In these assaults the entire Gaza Strip came under attack, whether along the border or in the interior—and no place in Gaza is very far from the border. But in the years before these attacks, beginning during the second intifada, Beit Hanoun and other border locations such as Rafah were repeatedly targeted. As one report from these destructions described, "The worst collective punishment on Beit Hanoun, however, is the destruction of more than 70 per cent of its citrus groves since the beginning of the uprising 32 months ago" (Ghazali 2003). Another report gives some sense of the consequences of living in perpetual awareness of more devastation to come. In 2003, in advance of a proposed truce, the mood was glum:

> To a casual observer, the northern Gaza farm community of Beit Hanoun should be giddy with relief over the prospect of Israeli military withdrawal ... But the dour townsfolk are resigned to their own grim reality: Even if the fragile truce efforts bear fruit, Beit Hanoun will remain fruitless for a generation to come. (Potter 2003)

In its response to Hamas's firing of Qassam rockets from Beit Hanoun and environs, the Israeli military had destroyed most of the area's citrus trees.

But if the lull in destruction that came with the truce did not bring joy, it did, just as in earlier periods, bring return as soon as possible. As soon as Israeli troops pulled out, "The sandy highway through Beit Hanoun was packed with bikes, cars and donkey carts as Palestinians tasted one of the first rewards of the Israeli withdrawal from Gaza: The reopening of roads that had long been blockaded" (Bell 2003). Trees cannot be regrown as quickly as buildings can be rebuilt, but they can be regrown. In 2005 a reporter talked with a farmer in Beit Hanoun about his efforts. Having lost 1,250 trees to Israeli bulldozers, he showed the reporter the hundreds of seedlings he had ready for planting as soon as it was possible: "It will take seven years before the first oranges ripen and many more before these seedlings match the bounty of the mature groves that once were. These future groves will be for his children, all but one of whom remain in Beit Hanoun" (Anon. 2005). And lest it be forgotten that property is not the only target of attack, a report from the aftermath of yet another Israeli incursion, in November 2006, described the burial of a 13-year-old girl who was killed by an Israeli sniper while inside her home (McCarthy 2006). Similar reports accompanied the assaults of the past decade (Marlowe 2014). For Beit Hanoun, as for Gaza in its entirety, the twenty-first century has been marked by a tremendous speeding up in the cycles of ruination and rebuilding that were already central to the Palestinian experience. And rebuilding has become ever more difficult as Israeli restrictions on goods entering the Gaza Strip create perpetual shortages of construction materials. But here too Palestinians are creative, and Gazans have been making cement from the rubble of destroyed buildings (Kabariti 2017).

Boundary-Making as Colonization

When we think about borders, we often think of them as mechanisms to define space, separate people, and regulate movement. As the Palestinian experience confirms, border-making is also a central mechanism of colonization. The primary means of land acquisition for early Zionist settlement in Palestine was purchase. By 1948 around 6 percent of the territory of Mandate Palestine was owned by Jews and Jewish communities. Thereafter the primary means of acquisition became confiscation and boundary-making. Palestinians who were displaced across what became the armistice lines with Jordan, Egypt, Syria, and Lebanon were dispossessed of their property (Fishbach 2010). So too were many who remained within the borders of the new state of Israel. Termed "present-absentees," many people who had fled their villages during fighting, but who had stayed close by, were not permitted to return to their homes and lands. These lands, like those of other "absentees," were appropriated under the terms of the new Law of Absent Property (Cohen 2002). In this case both borders (the provisional territorial lines of the state) and boundaries (the differential categorization of people within the state of Israel) were deployed for colonization. When Israel occupied the West Bank and Gaza in 1967 it used the guise of "security" to appropriate land for soldiers and settlers (Lustick 1981).

As important as the theft of land is to any colonial enterprise, it is not the only way that settler-colonial societies take control of territory. In the case of native North America, Patrick Wolfe has described how after removal, the US used assimilation—"a paper-trail of tears that penetrated Indian life in the form of Bureau of Indian Affairs officials rather than the US Cavalry" (Wolfe 2011: 13–14)—through allotment (the dispersal of communal property to individual owners) and blood quanta (the arithmetic of identity) in its project of the "elimination of the native" (Wolfe 2006). In the Palestinian instance:

the settler colonial structure undergirding Israeli practices takes on a painful array of manifestations: aerial and maritime bombardment, massacre and invasion, home demolitions, land theft, identity card confiscation, racist laws and loyalty tests, the wall, the siege on Gaza, cultural appropriation, dependence on willing (or unwilling) native collaboration regarding security arrangements, all with the continued support and backing of imperial powers. (Salamanca et al. 2012: 2)

And boundary-making has been important to this project.

The Palestinian collective experience of dispossession over the course of the past 100 years has included an ever expanding denial of access to territory. During the Mandate this occurred at a relatively small scale, as Palestinian peasants were expelled from lands they had long occupied and worked but did not formally own. After 1948 the armistice lines were internationally recognized barriers to entry. In the occupied territories after 1967, and especially after closure was first imposed in 1990, codified by the first Oslo Accord in 1993, and accelerated again during the second intifada, an explosion of internal boundaries in the form of checkpoints, "flying checkpoints" (army jeeps blocking a road), and unwatched barriers (usually stones placed across a road) served to further alienate the Palestinian population from their territory. The Qalandia checkpoint near Ramallah in the West Bank is a case in point. The boundary it marks is not along the green line. That is at ar-Ramm, a ways down the road to Jerusalem. Rather, the Qalandia checkpoint was set up inside the West Bank during the second intifada, initially as an ad hoc barrier. In the years since, it has been transformed into a permanent-looking "border crossing," its growth matched by the construction of the wall that snakes across Palestinian territory (Tawil-Souri 2010). The border- and boundary-making work of establishing and solidifying Qalandia is part of the work of colonization.

In Gaza it is not only the land, but also the sea to which Palestinians are denied access. Fishing has long been a central part of the Gazan economy and seafood a highlight of Gazan cuisine. The Oslo Accords delineated a coastal zone of 20 nautical miles for Gazan fisherman, but in practice Israel has never permitted access beyond 12 nautical miles. Since the second intifada Israel has progressively diminished the area in which it will permit them to fish, reducing the limit to sometimes 6 nautical miles and more frequently 3 nautical miles (Smith 2016: 760). The imposed limit can vary with little or no warning, and Gazan fishing vessels regularly come under attack by the Israeli navy. In such cases, their boats are often confiscated and held until the fishermen pay a fine. This "marine siege" (ibid.: 759) constitutes a denial of both livelihood and way of life.

In this variegated landscape of colonization through making borders and boundaries, Beit Hanoun has the distinction of being in proximity to the border of the Gaza Strip and located next to or within (depending on Israeli military decisions) the No Go Zones in Gaza. As Ron Smith and Martin Isleen (2017) explain, these closed military areas range from 1 to 3 kilometers from the border. When they are extended to 3 kilometers—as was done during the 2014 Israeli assault on Gaza—the entirety of Beit Hanoun lies within the No Go Zone. Even when the areas are more narrowly circumscribed, they contain farmland that is crucial to the livelihood of farmers and to the sustenance of Gazans more generally. In his research with farmers who returned to work their land despite these restrictions, Smith describes a determination to continue "in spite of the constant harassment and violence meted out to them by Israeli military forces" (ibid.: 457). But even as some farmers do persist—a quite remarkable feat—more still are denied access. Even after the pullout of settlers and soldiers from Gaza in 2005, Israel has continued to colonize its territory and dispossess its people.

The fragmented history of Beit Hanoun from no-man's-land to border town, from ordinary space to monument of loss, reveals a place that has been at once a historical exception, a site of enactment of a national drama, and a space of interaction of social and political forces with significance for a wider region. Without the events of 1948 Beit Hanoun would not only have had a different history, it would have had a different sort of history. Since the Nakba, Beit Hanoun has existed in the shadow of a shifting, often threatening, demarcation line. And the shifts have only sometimes been geographic. More commonly it has been the character of the line itself—border or boundary, passable or blocked, safe or under attack—that has changed. The destruction and loss that have been central to Palestinian history since 1948 has accumulated in layers in Beit Hanoun. But this place has never been simply a repository of the past and its sorrows. As return and rebuilding highlight, the future, even if not always legible, has remained on the horizon. Living in Beit Hanoun, like living elsewhere in Gaza and in Palestine more generally, is both an enactment of ongoing connection to place and an act of defiance in the face of persistent and repeated threats of dispossession.

Notes

1. This is managed through the Gaza Reconstruction Mechanism, which many observers have noted puts the United Nations in the position of policing and punishing Gazans.
2. Letter from Paul Johnson, field director, to Bronson Clark, Palestine desk, 13 March 1950. American Friends Service Committee (AFSC) Archives, #215 FS Sect., Palestine 1950, Refugee Project: Correspondence. He goes on to say: "There are in the village perhaps six intact shells of building, all concrete. All doors and window frames are of course gone. These include the mosque, the school buildings, one residence and a coffee house or two. The motor from the village well is gone, but the well was not defiled."
3. The administrative boundaries of Palestine's districts changed over the course of the Mandate. Originally there was a Gaza district and Beersheba district, which later became sub-districts of the larger Southern district.
4. For a discussion of related processes in the West Bank, see Medzini (2016).
5. Letter from administrative commissioner to director of municipal and village affairs, January 28, 1960. Israel State Archives (ISA), RG 115, box 2056, file 27.
6. Egypt-Israel General Armistice Agreement. United Nations (UN), S/1264/Corr.1, February 23, 1949.
7. Report on activities of the Mixed Armistice Commissions, February 20, 1950. UN, S/1459.
8. Anon. (1950c) and Report on activities of the Mixed Armistice Commissions, February 20, 1950. UN, S/1459.
9. United Nations Conciliation Commission for Palestine, "Note on the secretary-general's draft report on the work of UNRPR," October 27, 1949. UN, A/AC.25/W/28.
10. Letter from Gideon Rafael to chairman of commission (part of exchange of letters between UNCCP and Israel), February 28, 1950. UN, A/AC.25/IS.46.
11. Prior to the establishment of UNRWA in 1950, relief to Palestinian refugees was funded by the United Nations, but delivered by private organizations. The AFSC was responsible for Gaza, while the International Committees of the Red Cross (ICRC), and the League of Red Cross Societies (LCRS) provided aid in other areas.
12. Letter from Paul Johnson, 13 March 1950. AFSC, #215.
13. Letter from Paul Johnson, 13 March 1950. AFSC, #215.
14. Majdal, which lay north of Gaza in territory that was under Israeli control, became Ashkelon. Benny Morris recounts that "the bulk of the town's population had fled to Gaza in 1948, and in the course of 1950 its remaining Arab inhabitants were transferred to the Strip" (Morris 1993: 111).
15. The armistice agreement stated quite explicitly that it "is not to be construed in any sense as a political or territorial boundary, and is delineated without prejudice to rights, claims and positions of either Party to the Armistice as regards ultimate settlement of the Palestine question" (Egypt-Israel General Armistice Agreement. UN, S/1264/Corr.1, February 23, 1949).

16. Minutes, camp leaders meeting, February 28, 1950. AFSC, #152 FS Sect. Palestine 1950.
17. Letter from Paul Johnson, 13 March 1950. AFSC, #215. Johnson went on to say, "I have no special comment on this fact except to say that it speaks for itself."
18. Letter from director of health to director of municipalities and village affairs, September 29, 1957. ISA, RG 115, box 2056, file 27.
19. Letter from director of municipalities and village affairs to director of health, October 26, 1957. ISA, RG 115, box 2056, file 27. Exact statistics for refugees versus natives in Beit Hanoun are not available. In 1981, Ibrahim Skeik, a local historian, suggested that nearly one-quarter of the town's then 5,800 residents were refugees (Skeik 1981: 143).
20. Rental contract, December 1957. ISA, RG 115, box 2056, file 27.
21. Letter from Beit Hanoun mukhtar to governor general, March 11, 1958. ISA, RG 115, box 2056, file 27.
22. Letter from director of Mabahith al-'Amma [Criminal Investigation Bureau] to director of interior and public security, May 21, 1964. ISA, RG 115 box 2007, file 16[b].
23. Médecins Sans Frontières, press release, May 23, 2003 (previously available at: http://www.msf.org/countries/page.cfm?articleid=C863A318-DE0C-409F-A0C98AA34DA5DF49).
24. Humanitarian actors have directed the rebuilding of more recently demolished camps such as Jenin in the West Bank and Nahr el Bared in Lebanon. These projects have taken longer.

References

Anon. 1950a. "'Awda al-Laji'in al-'Arab l-baladuhum" [The return of the Arab refugees to their villages]. *Sawt al-'Uruba*, March 16, p. 1.
Anon. 1950b. "Akhbarna al-Mahaliyya" [Our local news]. *Sawt al-'Uruba*, April 14, p. 2.
Anon. 1950c. "Egypt, Israel Push Moves for Peace." *New York Times*, February 25, 1950, p. 5.
Anon. 1967. "Liberation Army Prepares." *New York Times*, May 28, p. 3.
Anon. 1989. "Israel Orders Passes for Palestinians in Gaza." *Globe and Mail*, June 7.
Anon. 2004. "Scorched Earth in Gaza." *Haaretz*, July 27. Available at: https://www.haaretz.com/1.4767672 (accessed August 2, 2019).
Anon. 2005. "In an Orange Grove, New Seeds of Hope." *Toronto Star*, January 21.
Anon. 2014. "Families Return to Rubble That Was Once Home." *The Star* (South Africa), August 6.
Bell, Stewart. 2003. "Roadblocks Start to Fall on Long Road to Peace." *National Post*, July 2.
Chick, Kristen. 2014. "One Gaza Family's Dinner in a Brief Moment without War." *Christian Science Monitor*, July 26. Available at: https://www.csmonitor.com/World/Middle-East/2014/0726/One-Gaza-family-s-dinner-in-a-brief-moment-without-war (accessed August 2, 2019).

Cohen, Hillel. 2002. "The Internal Refugees in the State of Israel: Israeli Citizens, Palestinian Refugees." *Palestine–Israel Journal of Politics, Economics, and Culture* 9(2): 43–51.

Feldman, Ilana. 2006. "Home as a Refrain: Remembering and Living Displacement in Gaza." *History and Memory* 18(2): 10–47.

Fishbach, Michael. 2010. *Records of Dispossession: Palestinian Refugee Property and the Arab–Israeli Conflict*. New York: Columbia University Press.

Ghazali, Sa'id. 2003. "Crushed: The Farmers Caught between the Israeli Army and Hamas." *Independent*, May 21. Available at: https://www.independent.co.uk/news/world/middle-east/crushed-the-farmers-caught-between-the-israeli-army-and-hamas-105593.html (accessed August 2, 2019).

Kabariti, Ahmad. 2017. "Engineers in Gaza Convert the Rubble of War into Concrete for Rebuilding." *Mondoweiss*, February 20. Available at: http://mondoweiss.net/2017/02/engineers-concrete-rebuilding/ (accessed August 2, 2019).

Loewenstein, Antony. 2016. "Lives in Ruins: The Human Tragedy Unfolding in Gaza." *The National*, November 2. Available at: https://www.thenational.ae/arts-culture/lives-in-ruins-the-human-tragedy-unfolding-in-gaza-1.185047 (accessed August 2, 2019).

Lustick, Ian. 1981. "Israel and the West Bank after Elon Moreh: The Mechanics of De Facto Annexation." *Middle East Journal* 35(4): 557–77.

Marlowe, Lara 2014. "Gaza Family Devastated by Series of Attacks: Decomposing Bodies Remain Unburied in Rubble of Destroyed Building," *Irish Times*, September 8. Available at: https://www.irishtimes.com/news/world/middle-east/gaza-family-devastated-by-series-of-attacks-1.1920797 (accessed August 2, 2019).

McCarthy, Rory. 2006. "As Israelis Pull Out, Town Seeks Space to Bury Its Dead." *Guardian*, November 8.

Medzini, Arnon. 2016. "Life on the Border: The Impact of the Separation Barrier on the Residents of Barta'a Enclave Demilitarized Zone." *Journal of Borderland Studies* 31(4): 401–25.

Morris, Benny. 1993. *Israel's Border Wars, 1949–1956: Arab Infiltration, Israeli Retaliation, and the Countdown to the Suez War*. Oxford: Clarendon Press.

Navarro-Yashin, Yael. 2012. *The Make-Believe Space: Affective Geography in a Postwar Polity*. Durham, NC: Duke University Press.

Potter, Mitch. 2003. "Anxiety Grips Gaza Town." *Toronto Star*, June 25.

Roy, Sara. 1995. *The Gaza Strip: The Political Economy of De-Development*. Washington, DC: Institute for Palestine Studies.

Said, Edward. 1986. *After the Last Sky: Palestinian Lives*. New York: Pantheon Books.

Salamanca, Omar Jabary, Mezna Qato, Kareem Rabie, and Sobhi Samour. 2012. "Past is Present: Settler Colonialism in Palestine." *Settler Colonial Studies* 2(1): 1–8.

Skeik, Ibrahim. 1981. *Ghazzah 'Abr Al-Tarikh: Al-Mujtam'a Al-Ghazzi*. N.p.: self published.

Smith, Ron. 2016. "Isolation through Humanitarianism: Subaltern Geopolitics of the Siege in Gaza." *Antipode* 48(3): 750–69.

Smith, Ron, and Martin Isleen. 2017. "Farming the Front Line: Gaza's activist Farmers in the No Go Zones." *City* 21(3/4): 448–65.

Tawil-Souri, Helga. 2010. "Qalandia Checkpoint: The Historical Geography of a Non-Place." *Jerusalem Quarterly* 42: 26–48.

Wolfe, Patrick. 2006. "Settler Colonialism and the Elimination of the Native." *Journal of Genocide Research* 8(4): 387–409.

——— 2011. "After the Frontier: Separation and Absorption in US Indian Policy." *Settler Colonial Studies* 1(1): 13–51.

12

Symmetry and Affinity
Comparing Borders and Border-Making Processes in Africa

Paul Nugent

Some of the most contentious issues of our times are framed by international borders where acute asymmetries of wealth and power are reproduced through systematic practices of exclusion.[1] Such is the case along the external borders of the European Union (EU) at the interface with Africa and the Middle East, and on the border between the United States and Mexico. In these paradigmatic instances, we can see two kinds of border effect at work. On the one hand, there has been a leveling process on the more endowed side of the line as once neglected border towns and regions have benefited from their insertion into larger territorial constellations. On the other hand, material deprivation on the opposite side has been entrenched by hard lines of separation whose explicit purpose is to prevent people from crossing over. The border simultaneously serves to remake social boundaries between populations who are either favored or stigmatized through a process of profiling and filtering that is simultaneously gendered, racialized, and ethnicized. Although the processes of patrolling borders and defining boundaries takes place in other locations as well, most notably at airports, the effects tend to be especially evident at the physical margins.

In sub-Saharan Africa, stark asymmetries are rather exceptional in border regions. Although there are economic hotspots centered on resource extraction, standards of living generally tend to be comparable as between states. As is well known, the largest oil producers—Nigeria, Angola, and Chad—manifest some of the highest levels of poverty. Moreover, the enclave character of the oil industry means that relatively little employment is generated. The partial exception to the continental norm lies at the interface between South Africa and its neighbors. The mining industry in the former historically drew heavily on migrant labor from neighboring states, but numbers employed in this area have greatly reduced since the 1990s—with severe consequences for labor-exporting countries like Lesotho, where rural populations depended on mine wages (Crush et al. 1991). Nevertheless, the diversity and relative strength of the South African economy has continued to lure migrants from neighboring countries, most notably Zimbabwe, in the direction of the main cities and farming areas like the Cape wine lands. But at the borders themselves, South African towns are almost as unprepossessing as the settlements next door. Across the continent, the manifestation of very similar modes and standards of living at the border reflects the reality that populations on either side fashion a living from its existence.

But for all the apparent symmetry, a closer examination does reveal significant border effects in Africa as well. Physical (in)security creates dynamics that are comparable to the effects of asymmetry where the border clearly delineates a zone of endemic violence from one where relative peace prevails. In these cases, the two sides of a border typically assume different physical aspects. Across Africa, borders also serve to differentiate populations in more or less subtle ways, albeit with much greater scope for negotiation. As I will demonstrate, the inscription of multiple social boundaries is intimately bound up with flows of people and goods through territorial borders. In this chapter, I deploy a reading of asymmetrical borders in other parts of the world as a foil for mapping out some of the variations across Africa, but with a view to distilling lessons of broader relevance. I take asymmetry to refer to disparities of wealth and power rather than to the numerical dimensions of the population living in the border zone, although I consider this as an important border effect that is worthy of closer consideration. By invoking affinity, I seek to escape a purely state-centered perspective and to focus upon some of the ways in which populations conceive of, and act upon, the relationships that cut across borders. Although border-making might appear to be quintessential state work, it may more accurately be regarded as the coproduction of an extended cast of state and non-state actors. And it is precisely for this reason that border- and boundary-making processes are so deeply entangled.

Framing Symmetry and Asymmetry

In order to prepare the foundations for a comparative discussion, I begin by teasing out four variations that are generally associated with the operation of asymmetrical borders. The first concerns uneven levels of state presence. Along highly securitized borders there is likely to be a high level of visibility regardless of whether there is relative parity between the parties (as was initially true of North and South Korea) or a clear asymmetry (as was historically the case with the Russian–Finnish border). But where asymmetry reigns there is typically an interest on the part of the more endowed country in enforcing its physical presence at the border, which may not be shared by the other party. This is clearly the case around the Spanish enclaves of Ceuta and Melilla in North Africa and on the US–Mexico border. Alongside the rather crude symbolism of border fences, there has been a re-enchantment with technological solutions to issues of surveillance. At the same time, a veritable "illegality industry" (Andersson 2014) has grown up around the spectacle of surveillance and control (De Genova 2012). The less-endowed countries sometimes feel the need to keep up the appearance of sovereign equality by mirroring the presence of state agencies on their side of the line, but they have less invested in regulating border flows—unless they have been incentivized by the dominant neighbor to cooperate.

The second variation turns on the proliferation of networks of evasion feeding off the rents that are created by the creation and enforcement of hard borders. The activities that steal the headlines involve networks that are oriented toward the infiltration of elements that wealthier states are intent on excluding at any cost—namely people and narcotics. As a general rule, the harder the border, the greater the risks associated with crossing it, the higher the rents, and the more hierarchical the networks. But clearly the nature of what is being transported also has a bearing on the configurations. Drug cartels in South and Central America are highly monopolistic in nature and have been maintained through the active threat of violence (Payan 2006). The trafficking of people and drugs across the Sahara is somewhat more loosely organized, although the "mafias" are closely connected to the cartels in South America (Scheele 2012: 94–124).

The third variation is a peculiar form of demography, as populations are drawn to specific nodes within the borderlands (Nugent 2012). Borderlands are sometimes characterized by low population densities, but elsewhere asymmetrical borders suck in aspirant migrants, only to redistribute them in an uneven fashion across border spaces. The twin cities that have sprung up along the length of the US–Mexico border provide the classic instances. Here wealthier, but relatively small, American cities such as El Paso have become a focus for Mexican populations seeking a better life. Much larger "trampoline towns" like Ciudad Juarez have emerged on the Mexican side, replenished by fresh arrivals from across the country and even further afield. El Paso and Ciudad Juarez, or Laredo and Nuevo Laredo, are intimately connected despite the existence of a relatively hard border.[2]

Finally, a distinct politics of identity tends to play itself out in asymmetrical borderlands. For countries that seek to restrict immigration, it is often convenient to emphasize the "otherness" of those whom they seek to deny entry to. Hence at the southern borders of Europe, governments have asserted their right to restrict entry to migrants and refugees, whilst blurring the distinction between them—which is at least implicitly justified on the basis of religious and or/racial difference. At the same time, the phenomenon of the daily commute across the US–Mexico border demonstrates that governments can also create states of exception when it suits them. At the busiest crossing of all, between Tijuana and San Diego, some 90,000 people cross the border each day—many who live in the former and work in the latter. The flip side is that border populations may themselves claim a close bond with people on the other side of the line, subverting the state's claim to a monopoly of defining the terms of belonging. Hence the racialization of Mexicans has its counterpart in claims to affinity between Mexican Americans and their cousins from across the line. As Jiménez (2010) demonstrates, Mexican Americans in the border states generally empathize with the desire of their counterparts from Mexico to find a better life—which is ironically justified with reference to the American dream—but they are able to revive their own ethnic identity through regular contact with immigrants. This is despite some ambivalence about the illegality that pervades the process of gaining entry to the United States in the first place.

Symmetry and Affinity in African Border Regions

Uneven levels of state presence

When it comes to matters of state presence, there is clearly considerable variation across Africa. One of the ironies is that the states with the least institutional capacity have typically been tasked with maintaining the longest borders. This is especially true of those located in the Sahel and the Horn of Africa. Where forests or drylands have been deployed as a buffer, states have often maintained only a token presence at the physical border. The latter have provided ideal sites for the incubation of rebel insurgencies that have deployed the terrain to good effect. This has been true, for example, of the eastern Democratic Republic of Congo (DRC) and Sudan since the 1960s. Somalia is a singular case because the notional government does not control much territory outside of Mogadishu. But even states that might appear to have much greater capacity to control their borders have sometimes struggled to assert an effective presence when push has come to shove. The ease with which a combination of Tuareg secessionists fighting for the independence of Azawad, and Islamists affiliated with al-Qaeda, were able to cross borders and eventually overrun half of Mali in 2012 provides a pointed illustration of that reality. This is equally true of the manner in which Boko Haram established bases in the forest reserves of northeastern Nigeria and successfully beat back the Nigerian army over 2013/14. In this case, self-proclaimed jihadists claiming an adherence to Islamic State were able to exploit the lack of state presence in Nigeria as well as in the borderlands of Cameroon and Chad. In the process of defining a new moral community, and hence demarcating a social boundary, Boko Haram also identified Christians and most fellow Muslims as apostates who could justifiably be targeted for acts of violence. Uganda, Kenya, and Tanzania have found it convenient to locate large refugee camps in close proximity to international borders not merely to physically contain refugees, but also to establish a physical presence in marginal zones where state control has historically been tenuous. Whereas Uganda has established rather open settlements, Tanzania has sought to restrict movement beyond the confines of designated camps—thereby underlining the alterity of refugees and restricting their access to sources of income. The irony here is that the creation of a social boundary, in which refugees are pointedly placed outside the category of potential citizen, is what has enabled the state to stake out its physical borders.

It would be misleading to think of the border wilderness as anything like the norm because the margins in Africa are often rather densely populated (see below). They characteristically pulsate with economic activity, which in turn ensures that state institutions are very present on the ground. The African continent is currently undergoing a process of "re-spacing" through the combined effects of regional integration initiatives driven by various regional economic communities (RECs) and large-scale investments in infrastructure pursued by African governments, international financial institutions, China, the EU, and to a lesser extent by private corporations (Nugent 2018). Transport corridors, which are sometimes accorded the more grandiose label of development corridors, lie at the intersection of both of these sets of interventions. They typically have a seaport like Mombasa or Walvis Bay at one end and a capital city or a mining center at the other—with upgraded road and rail networks linking them together. There are, however, significant differences between the many corridors. Whereas investments in the Walvis Bay Corridors are heavily geared to the extraction of mineral resources (notably copper), the Northern and Central Corridors in East Africa are justified with reference to facilitating the flow of imported goods as well as non-mineral exports. The Abidjan–Lagos Corridor (home to some 35 million people) is different again, in that it is justified with reference to the vast sprawl stretching from Lagos along the coastline, which potentially creates synergies arising out of the agglomeration effects associated with urbanism.

The border towns that are dotted along the corridors have historically functioned as the choke points where customs, immigration, and police have conducted their formalities and regulated the passage of people and goods. The lengthy delays and corruption that are characteristic of border crossings have been widely cited as the reasons for the high cost of doing business in Africa. This has the greatest implications for the landlocked states of West and Central Africa, for whom transport costs amount to some 45 percent of the value of imports and 35 percent of the value of exports—as opposed to the global average of 5.4 percent and 8.8 percent respectively (Viljoen 2016). Much of the cost is directly related to the hours, and even days, wasted in crossing borders. Part of the reason is inadequate infrastructure, such as the lack of crossable bridges, but as important is the duplication of procedures. In the context of regional integration, the stated priority is to actively reduce barriers to the free movement of goods, but also to assist the mobility of citizens within a given REC. The Economic Community of West African States (ECOWAS) has been in the vanguard with respect to the freedom of movement of people since 1979, whereas the East African Community (EAC) has led the way in trade facilitation and infrastructural investment.[3]

Ironically, the emphasis on facilitating border flows has imparted a heightened significance to the state management of border crossings. The EU is seeking to export its own model of an integrated boundary management system that will enable state institutions at the border to share data between themselves. Other donors are involved in harmonizing record systems that will permit agencies, most notably customs, to create and access the same documents. At the same time, governments and donors are rolling out one-stop border posts where a range of state institutions from neighboring countries can work alongside each other, thereby halving the bureaucratic formalities. These reforms necessarily presume a mirroring of institutions at border crossings and require an active presence from both states. The construction of new border facilities and information systems frequently runs up against the realities of erratic electricity supplies and inadequate telecommunications infrastructure. Hence it has often been necessary to improve the connectivity of border towns. This upgrading has attracted ancillary businesses, most notably banks and logistics companies. Crucially for our purposes, it has also meant that a wider range of institutions and private actors has become invested in the dynamics of border towns.

However, significant tensions have emerged with respect to the management of mobility in particular. One arises out of the efforts of the EU to physically transplant its efforts to restrict the flow of would-be migrants. The European border force, Frontex, has enlisted African governments in a campaign to stem illegal migration at source by patrolling the West African coastline, but also by intercepting potential migrants at border crossings in the Sahel—long before the latter attempt the Sahara crossing (Andersson 2014: 100–36). Whereas freedom of movement is guaranteed to all ECOWAS citizens, people from coastal countries who enter the Sahel are often detained on a presumption of intent to reach Europe illegally—even though no actual crime has been committed. At the same time, African governments have sought to deal with the threat of terrorism by profiling border-crossers in ways that are in tension with the principle of freedom of movement. This is effected in part for reasons of national security and also in response to requests from external actors, most notably the United States and France. Given the ongoing campaign of al-Shabaab against Kenya and Uganda, for example, travellers who appear to be Somali are often singled out for special treatment in East Africa. Not surprisingly, the technologies of surveillance have become more sophisticated in recent years (Frowd 2018). While it is true that the implementation is often uneven, as well as inconsistent, the biometric border has traveled from airports to land borders, where finger prints are routinely taken. The concerns surrounding illegal immigration and terrorism together render border surveillance a genuine priority for African governments. Because this happens to coincide with the agenda of Western countries, it has been rather easy to secure external assistance to pay for the necessary equipment and training. While the integrated border management agenda is justified with reference to the benefits associated with more efficient data collection and sharing, it is clearly not devoid of political intent. It also complicates the regional integration agenda of RECs that have, for example, been seeking to dispense with passport requirements.

Networks of evasion

Networks of evasion are very extensive in most African border regions, relating more to the pursuit of trade than to migratory flows. Historically, there have been high levels of mobility within the continent, especially in West and Southern Africa. In the Senegambia region, for example, large numbers of migrants from Mali, Mauritania, Guinea, and Guinea-Bissau have resided in Senegal, while the Gambia has been home to substantial numbers of Senegalese. Crossing borders has been considered mundane, and governments have not considered it prudent or necessary to interfere too much—except during moments of inter-state crisis such as that which followed the border clash between Senegal and Mauritania and which set off tit-for-tat expulsions in the early 1990s. The southward extension of Frontex has brought some of the networks of evasion in North Africa to the Senegambia itself. But it does not (yet) appear that there are highly organized human-trafficking rings operating across most of sub-Saharan Africa. The issue of child trafficking between African countries is often said to be pervasive, and immigration officials are specifically trained to detect its incidence at border crossings. But evidence of pervasive trafficking networks is limited. Indeed, it is difficult to detect a strong economic driver even for domestic labor, given that a large pool of vulnerable children exists in most African countries anyway.

By contrast, the economic logic behind the trafficking in smuggled goods remains as powerful as ever. For the first three decades of independence, African countries pursued competitive economic strategies that created abundant opportunities for smuggling. In West Africa, for example, the more substantial countries like Nigeria, Senegal, and Ghana attempted to build national industries—which were typically state-owned—behind the protection of tariff walls. Neighboring countries—most notably Togo, Benin, and the Gambia—functioned as archetypal entrepôts, that is as microstates that had very little industry of their own but got by on the basis of tapping international trade. They actively encouraged the import of consumer goods through their ports, which were then taxed and dispatched across borders in the shape of contraband. This undercut fledgling industries, such as textiles or sugar production, in the neighboring countries. Under structural adjustment programs, much of the protection for state industries was removed, but a stimulus was provided to other forms of trade across borders (Walther 2014: 194–5). In the current era of regional integration, the harmonization of customs values and internal taxes has reduced many of the economic rents that formerly sustained smuggling. But the continued existence of different currencies, the retention of consumer subsidies (for example on petroleum products), and the remaining vestiges of industrial protectionism have all meant that smuggling remains a highly profitable business. Nigeria has, for example, delayed the implementation of a common external tariff and has insisted on upholding a list of prohibited imports and imposing high tariffs on "strategic" commodities, such as rice. The net effect has been to extend a renewed lease of life to the contraband trade centered on the port of Cotonou. Benin has embraced the logic of regional integration by promoting a rail link to Mali, but at the same time it has continued to function as a classic entrepôt state. Much of the smuggling across the continent is transacted in items of everyday consumption, such as wheat flour, Thai rice, and Chinese batteries. But there are also some items to which some value is attached and which require greater levels of organization within the supply chain. The attempt to sever the links between diamond mining and violent conflict through certification under the Kimberley Process has fueled smuggling across international borders—with the DRC being a major supplier of illicit diamonds to the rest of the world. Much of the trafficking in ivory for the Asian market, and skins used in Chinese medicine, takes place by road for the simple reason that these are easily concealed amongst other consignments and are difficult to detect without functioning scanners—which are a rare occurrence at most of Africa's land borders. The rerouting of the South American drugs trade, and in particular cocaine, through West Africa is a case of the internationalization of criminal networks (Klantschnig 2013)—with profound consequences for Guinea-Bissau, where it has become deeply entwined with the politics of the country. Although much of the narcotics trade has been routed through airports, improvements in the technologies of detection in countries like Ghana and Nigeria have meant that drugs have also entered Europe by boat and along land routes through the desert.

One of the distinctive patterns of cross-border trading in Africa is the role of ethnic and religious networks in cementing essential bonds of trust, both between partners of an equivalent size and between larger merchants and smaller traders. Long-distance trade has historically been associated with particular ethnic groups, such as the Dyula and Hausa of

West Africa, who remain deeply invested in cross-border trading to this day. But the emergence of lucrative seams of commerce since the 1970s has also facilitated the emergence of novel networks. A case in point would be the so-called Nana Benz of Togo, the market women who came to dominate the cloth trade from the Grand Marché in Lomé. After independence, Dutch and British wax prints were imported through the port by multinational trading firms and then distributed by the Nana Benz throughout the sub-region (Sylvanus 2016). Much of the cloth was sold into Ghana, whose own factories came close to collapse in the late 1970s and early 1980s. The lucrative textile trade was controlled by wealthy female traders, and in particular by Minas who originated from eastern Togo rather than from Lomé itself. They were, in turn, suppliers to a much larger group of middling and smaller traders. As the counterfeit cloth trade with China took off around the turn of the millennium, a much greater range of actors entered the field, and the Nana Benz forfeited their de facto monopoly. What stands out in this instance is the convergence between international commerce and cross-border flows on the one hand, and the demarcation of an entirely female domain that is spatially embodied within the urban landscape of Lomé on the other.

A rather different instance is that of the Mouride trading network of the Senegambia—which is Muslim, primarily Wolof in terms of its ethnic composition, and dominated by men. The Mourides are a Sufi religious order that was initially closely associated with the expansion of groundnut production in Senegal before its adherents turned their backs on farming and became heavily urbanized from the mid-1970s onward. The Mourides stand out from the other Muslim orders in the sub-region by virtue of an internal structure that is simultaneously hierarchical, being centered on the relationship between a religious *cheikh* and his *talibés* (followers), and yet flexible enough to facilitate its extension as a network. After independence, the Mouride capital of Touba was granted an exceptional status, likened by Senegalese to the Vatican, where state institutions like the police were absent from the scene. The Mourides became deeply implicated in the contraband trade with the Gambia in the 1970s, where they accessed Asian goods that sold more cheaply in Senegal than both the French equivalent and the products of local factories. In the 1980s and 1990s, the Mourides controlled much of the illicit trade across the greater Senegambia region and they remain prominently placed to this day—even if smuggling through the Gambia has lost much of its rationale as Chinese goods have entered directly through the port of Dakar. What was originally a village expanded rapidly, in large part by virtue of the commercial advantages that the unique status conferred, with the result that Touba grew to become Senegal's second city. The Mourides also moved in large numbers to Dakar, and subsequently became heavily invested in international migration, especially in the direction of France and Italy, where they became closely associated with street trading.

If we compare the Nana Benz and the Mourides, we can discern some of the complex ways in which border- and boundary-making have become intertwined. The Nana Benz carved out a distinct identity that was gendered and largely ethnic in character, and that depended on the reproduction of international borders and the economic rents associated with them. The space that they claimed as their own was physically concentrated at the commercial heart of the Togolese capital. At an earlier point in history, the Mourides created their own center that was deliberately located away from the colonial capital of Dakar. The religious network was built upon absolute allegiance to a *cheikh* who acted both as a religious interlocutor and a social protector. The Mouride order greatly expanded in numbers and influence when its adherents embraced the commercial advantages that came with cross-border trade and subsequently the opportunities for migration to Europe. The financial flows back to Senegal, which sustained both the religious leadership and extended families, have enabled the Mourides to adapt to changing circumstances. Today, there are multiple layers to the social identity of the Mourides. It is strongly associated with being Senegalese, and yet it actively embraces a worldliness that is threatened by stricter European immigration regimes. It is associated with Islam, but with innovations that make it distinct even from other Sufi orders in Senegal. And while the public perception of the Mourides emphasizes close solidarity between young men, they clearly have a substantial female following.

Under conditions where trade is characterized by high risk, whether by virtue of the nature of what is being traded or the insecure environment in which it is carried out, the networks tend to be more hierarchical and densely configured. While cigarette smuggling by boat between Libya and Egypt involves groups of young men who are connected through "tribal" ties, the trafficking in arms, people, and drugs between Libya and the Sahara is dominated by close-knit and heavily armed networks that do not hinge on kinship solidarities (Hüsken 2017: 907–9). The same is true of the "mafias" operating on the border between Mali and Algeria, which are based on personal ties rather than the established religiouscum-commercial networks, and are surrounded by a distinct aura of unsociability (Scheele 2012: 123). In regions where there is a high risk of banditry, militia attacks, or irregular seizures by state and quasi-state actors (it is not always so easy to tell them apart), merchants have to provide their own military security—or purchase it elsewhere. In the trade between the eastern DRC and its neighbors, where the risks are especially acute, a small number of players has come to dominate the most lucrative lines of trade. In the wake of the Rwandan genocide of 1994, and the flight of Hutu populations across the border, North and South Kivu became highly volatile regions of the DRC. Endemic insecurity did not sever trade, and indeed created its own war economy of sorts (Jackson 2006), but it did change the ways in which trust operated. Raeymaekers (2015) has explored the logics of a protection economy in which large merchants depended on the security afforded by military enforcers, but increasingly set the rules of the game themselves—thereby creating what he depicts as a hybridized system of governance. In a separate study of trade between the DRC and Uganda, Titeca (2012) similarly identifies the consolidation of economic power in the hands of a small group of well-connected "tycoons." In the Great Lakes region, the pervasive threat of spoliation is what enables the most lucrative commerce to remain concentrated in the hands of the few who possess the means to defend their interests. The effects are, therefore, broadly similar to the ways in which the high risks associated with trafficking across asymmetrical borders promotes hierarchical and highly concentrated networks.

Demography

As I have already indicated, border regions are frequently amongst the most densely populated, especially in West Africa, Central Africa and the Great Lakes region (Soi & Nugent 2017). Indeed, Africa has its own variants of the twinned towns and cities phenomenon. And much like on the US–Mexico border, the pattern is one of uneven growth between urban settlements. The cities of Kinshasa and Brazzaville provide the only instance in the world where two capital cities face each other across an international border defined by the Congo River.[4] In this case, Kinshasa is several times larger than Brazzaville. Together, they are home to some 13 million people, many of whom make a living in one way or another from trade across the dangerous river boundary. This is not likely to change, given that the prolific expansion of Kinshasa is predicted to continue unabated over the next three decades. Indeed, according to some projections Kinshasa will overtake Lagos and Cairo by 2025, with a projected population of 16.8 million people. In addition, a large number of Africa's capital cities are either located on an international border—typically along a navigable river—or within 50 kilometers of one. In several cases, capitals like Bangui and N'Djamena face smaller towns on the other side of the border which derive much of their vitality from the proximity between them. Finally, there are innumerable instances of border towns that have grown up in an intimate relationship with one another. In East Africa, there are several towns that share the same name: such as Busia, Uganda and Busia, Kenya, or Moyale, Kenya and Moyale, Ethiopia. In almost every case, the factors behind the consolidation of these urban clusters involve some combination between the selection of an administrative headquarters and the opportunities that derive from the existence of the border. A particularly fascinating example is Lomé and its Ghanaian neighbor, Aflao, whose border crossing literally opens into the downtown area of the Togolese capital. Aflao already existed in the seventeenth century, whereas Lomé was founded by smugglers seeking to escape British Customs duties after the declaration of the eastern border of the Gold Coast in 1879. After independence, Lomé expanded rapidly as the Togolese capital, but also as the epicenter of the contraband trade (see above). Aflao was an important partner in and beneficiary from this trade, which is reflected in the reality that its population grew significantly more quickly than other towns in Ghana. There is a close affinity between the populations of these settlements—given that specific quarters of the Togolese capital trace their origins to Aflao—but they have both drawn in populations from much further afield, including the Mina, who I have mentioned above.

Patterns of urban growth have also been shaped in significant ways by the security imbalances that have already been identified. Across Africa, high rates of urbanization are closely correlated with patterns of sustained violence—Angola being the classic case of a country that has experienced rural depopulation as a consequence of decades of civil war. Much of this urban growth is reflected at the geographical margins, where populations have a greater chance of seeking sanctuary across the border. Although the existence of large-scale refugee camps is well known, a pattern characteristic of relatively low-level insurgencies is one in which populations relocate to the more secure side of the border during times of trouble. Hence Gambian border towns have accommodated large numbers of people from the Casamance whenever the secessionist insurgency in Senegal has heated up, but then there has been a reverse flow when a semblance of normality has returned. These movements are based on established relationships, cemented by kinship and religious ties, between towns on the two sides of the border. Needless to say, these are towns where the livelihoods of much of the population revolves around the opportunities for cross-border trade.

Much as instability has been confined to the Casamance side of the Senegal–Gambia border, Uganda has experienced long periods of acute instability in a way that Kenya has not. Amidst the privation of the Amin years, when basic consumer goods ceased to be available in Uganda, a flourishing contraband trade with Kenya sprang up. This imparted a particular significance to the relationship between the two Busias. Smugglers from Busia, Uganda, often using bicycles, ran the gauntlet of military surveillance, but continued to take the risk because of attractive financial returns. However, because of the dangers associated with exhibiting wealth in Uganda at a time when the military was not bound by any rules, very little investment was evident. Most of the demographic growth and physical construction (especially well-stocked stores) was manifested in Busia, Kenya, a difference that was further magnified when the latter was elevated to an administrative center. When peace returned to the Ugandan side of the border, Busia, Uganda, assumed the role of a truck stop on the route from Mombasa. In recent years, however, Busia has acquired its own minor position within the Ugandan administrative hierarchy, and a range of businesses, including banks and filling stations, have grown up around the one-stop border post. There is a perception that property is more expensive in Kenya, while much of the electoral violence in recent years has played itself out in Busia, Kenya. This means that traders are much more likely to invest in Busia, Uganda, than before. The net consequence has been a narrowing of the gap between the towns with respect to both population and the quality of the built environment.

In the eastern DRC, a rather different pattern has taken shape based on the permanent displacement of rural populations toward the border. Goma has progressed from the status of a modest provincial town to a metropolis of more than 1 million people, while Bukavu is estimated to harbor a further 832,000. This is not a matter of the bright lights so much as a reflection of the reality that the city provides a relatively safe haven at a time when the rural hinterlands of North and South Kivu are rife with armed militias that routinely target civilian populations. The existence of the border provides a source of income for the many men and women who trade, transport goods, cook food, change money, and do all the other things that are associated with busy border crossings. What is striking is that the Rwandan towns of Gisenyi and Cyangugu, which face Goma and Bukavu across the border, have not expanded to anything like the same degree—despite the much greater level of physical security. The Rwandan administration clearly has no interest in encouraging Congolese settlement, with all the problems that this might entail. But it is equally true that displaced populations need to find a way of making a living, and this is easier in Goma than in Gisenyi, where economic activities are more closely regulated by the Rwandan state.[5] Despite the greater incidence of daily crime in Goma, border workers generally choose to reside there in preference to the more "orderly" Rwandan towns next door. The pattern that I have identified from the Uganda–Kenya border is therefore reversed in an interesting fashion.

The politics of identity

As has been widely noted, a discourse of autochthony has come into play across the continent over recent decades (Bøås & Dunn 2013; Geschiere 2009). In fact, there have been earlier iterations of something very similar, most notably with the expulsion of foreigners from Ghana in 1969 and from Nigeria in 1983, and the excision of the Ugandan Asians in 1972. In countries like Cameroon and Congo-Brazzaville, the struggle has really turned on claims to ownership of particular spaces, including specific urban *quartiers*, rather than arguments about national citizenship. But in Côte d'Ivoire and South Africa it has also been about defining the boundaries of national belonging, in which state categories and vernacular discourses of belonging have become closely intertwined. Inevitably, it has also involved some contestation over the ways in which national borders have been superimposed upon ethnic ones.

In the Ivoirien case, the political crisis turned on whether most northerners were actually Burkinabe. For southern activists seeking to advance the claims of putative autochthons, northerners were almost by definition suspect. The context was one in which a quarter of the population were immigrants by the 1990s, a large proportion of whom had been attracted to work on the cocoa farms of the forest belt. The complication in this case is that the borders of colonial Upper Volta changed several times over, enabling some supposed Burkinabe to make a historic claim to being Ivoirien at an earlier point in their history. Others laid claim to being Ivoirien on the basis of having been born in Côte d'Ivoire to parents who migrated decades before. And finally, most northerners insisted they had always been Ivoirien and had a right, as citizens, to reside, work, and acquire land in any part of the country. For the supporters of the former president Laurent Gbagbo, the invocation of a foreign threat was largely an exercise in seeking to reduce the number of northern voters, through exclusion from citizenship, rather than seeking to redraw the borders of Côte d'Ivoire.

In South Africa, the pressure to tackle illegal immigration has led the South African authorities to actively police urban spaces where foreigners reside in large numbers, and to resort to mass deportations—amounting to no fewer than 300,000 in 2007 alone (Landau 2010: 215). One of the cruel ironies of the recurring xenophobic attacks has been the targeting of South African Tsonga and Venda populations, who are collectively labeled as Shangaan. Because these groups straddle international borders, the assumption is that they are most likely foreigners who have crossed over from neighboring countries (Tafira 2011: 118). In this way, certain ethnicities are deemed to be unproblematically part of the nation while others are treated as alien or at least highly suspect—with language proficiency often providing the litmus test in any given, often charged, situation. The populations who are targeted, on the other hand, contend that their forebears were *in situ* before the borders were drawn.

The assumption that the contours of international borders neatly conform to ethnic boundaries is, of course, one that runs entirely counter to the view that populations were arbitrarily dissected by colonial borders. A.I. Asiwaju, who may fairly be regarded as the father of African border studies, edited a seminal volume in which he helpfully provided a checklist of partitioned ethnic groups (Asiwaju 1984: 252–9). The list is extensive, but even then it is incomplete. The Agotime who straddle the Ghana–Togo border, for example, are not included in the checklist, seemingly because they are bundled into the Ewe category. But such problems of classification also illustrate the difficulties of assuming clearly bounded ethnicities in the first place. Colonial borders helped to shape the way in which ethnic groups were classified, and the manner in which ethnicity was subsequently expressed. Hence the Agotime have tended to be assimilated to the Ewe category despite being an Adangbe splinter group with close links to the Ga of what is now coastal Ghana. On the Kenya–Uganda border, closely related populations do not deploy the same ethnonyms, although they are well aware of the affinities between them. The point nevertheless remains that closely related populations frequently live on two sides of a border, with the multiple ambiguities that this entails. The trap lies in conceiving of borderlanders as purely the victims—intended or otherwise—of a dispensation conjured up by external agents. Border populations have been equally adept at instrumentalizing borders and enlisting the support of states in the process. Elsewhere, I have examined the ways in which litigants involved in land disputes on the Ghana–Togo border deliberately conflated international borders with the borders between chiefdoms in order to stake contentious claims and to delegitimize those of their opponents (Nugent 2002). Similarly, Dereje (2011) has revealed how the Anywaa have sought to entrench the Ethiopia–Sudan border in a way that casts pastoralist Nuer populations, with whom they have been struggling over land, as foreigners. These instances demonstrate that borderlanders are as invested in the making of borders, and are often as adept at deploying the language of citizenship as the state and non-state actors are.

But there are also other ways in which populations relate to borders. As I have already indicated, border towns are often rather cosmopolitan places that suck in strangers from further afield. Hence, the visible presence of Igbo and Yoruba traders from southern Nigeria in towns on the northern Benin–Nigeria border (Walther 2014: 196), of Igbos trading in Gabonese border towns (Bennafla 2002: 137) and of Hausa traders operating in Agotime. The paramount chief of Aflao is distinctly proud of the fact that his town hosts migrants from across West Africa, and he speaks especially highly of the way in which the "Malians" (the largest group) have organized themselves.[6] However, it is also true that border populations may also lay claim to the border as a resource that belongs primarily to notional indigenes. As Flynn (1997) has demonstrated for the Benin–Nigeria border, locals may claim co-ownership of border spaces with the state by imposing their own controls and levies on what passes through. At the one-stop border posts on the Uganda–Kenya border it is striking that money changers insist on the right to operate inside the perimeter fence on the grounds that the facility is built on "their land." Such assertions of local ownership are, in practice, compatible with the presence of strangers who specialize in particular lines of commerce that indigenes have less of an interest in, or specialist knowledge of.

A rather different, but hardly contradictory, response is the assertion of a close affinity between people across the line. Borderlanders routinely intermarry, patronize rotating weekly markets, attend each other's schools and health clinics, and engage in joint religious observances. But it has not always been so easy to turn such daily interactions into an expression of a common identity. Governments tend to be acutely suspicious of efforts to discursively transcend the border because they regard it as a slippery slope to secessionism. Cross-border festivals afford a convenient way of making statements about the ties that bind, but in a manner that does not appear overtly threatening—especially when state actors can be drawn into the performance. The chief of Aflao is proud of the fact that his annual festival, *Godigbe*, attracts participants from Togo and as far afield as Benin. The festival therefore makes a statement about connectivity and affinity across two sets of borders. The Agotime have worked hard at promoting their own annual festival, *Agbamevoza*. During the three decades after independence when relations between the two sets of authorities were distinctly tense, it proved impossible to hold any public events in common, but the slow thaw from the mid-1990s provided an opportunity that Agotime leaders seized upon with alacrity. *Agbamevoza* is a week-long series of events that seeks to unify the Agotime around a shared sense of a place in history and their virtuosity in the production of the highest-quality *kente* cloth (Nugent 2019: 502–6). Whereas the events used to be held on the Ghana side of the border only, these days the festival shuttles back and forth across the line and involves the participation of state officials from both sides.

Ironically, however, because the border has been a hard one for so long, what it means to be Agotime in Ghana is not the same as what it means to be Agotime in Togo. As one informant explained, it is the "Ghanaians"—by which he also meant Ghanaian Agotime—who like to wear *kente* cloth on special occasions, whereas the Togolese prefer to don suits and wax prints. The Agotime seem to have succeeded in reminding the authorities that they are one people divided by an international border. The challenge now is to agree on what "Agotimeness" itself consists of. This conscious attempt to alter the meaning attached to the border is not to be confused with secessionist claims that have been on the rise across the continent. In subtle ways, festivals may even serve to reinscribe rather than challenge the legitimacy of the borders in question. But what they also do is to open up a space for negotiation about how the border is managed, much as they do in Laredo and Nuevo Laredo along the US–Mexico border.[7]

Conclusion

In this chapter I have deployed the asymmetrical border in other regions of the world as a foil for understanding the ways in which borders function and interact with social boundaries in Africa. I have avoided the temptation to draw overly sharp distinctions between Europe and the Americas on the one hand and Africa on the other, despite some very obvious differences. To be sure, along the familiar asymmetrical borders there are strict controls on migration, whereas the norm has been an acceptance of high levels of mobility across most of Africa, which is now formally sanctioned by regional integration agreements. Moreover, there are relatively few securitized borders in Africa—the heavily militarized Ethiopia–Eritrea border providing the obvious exception. Again, the development of hierarchical networks of evasion geared to the trafficking of people and narcotics has been a distinctive feature of asymmetrical borders. But as Europe has pushed its own border policing southward, and as much of the cocaine trade has shifted to Africa, some of the same dynamics are now present south of the Sahara. In addition, the phenomenon of twin cities and towns is widespread and underlines the transformative role of border flows and blockages. Whereas on the US–Mexico border peripheral urbanism is driven by the migration imperative, in Africa it is the economic opportunities that are encrusted around borders that draws people toward them. But even this has some parallels with the operations of the informal economy at the US–Mexico border.

I have gone on to argue that chronic insecurity creates effects that are similar to those we associate with evasion along asymmetrical borders. High risks to life and capital in the pursuit of cross-border commerce are conducive to the consolidation of hierarchical networks involving the primacy of political connections, fewer players, and tight-knit relationships based on something other than kinship. Insecurity is also closely bound up with demographic growth in border regions, although the patterns differ significantly by region. When it comes to affinities, one needs to be equally nuanced in thinking through the larger comparisons. Although it is common to conceive of the Mediterranean as marking a cultural boundary, it has historically functioned more as a crossroads between North Africa and southern Europe (Clancy-Smith 2011). And clearly, there are close affinities between Mexican Americans and their kinsmen across the southern border which have been revalorized in the context of the resurgence of white American nativism. Conversely, culturally similar populations in African border regions have not always made much of an effort to embrace their apparent similarities.

In unlocking the precise relationship between borders and boundaries, I have subjected four dimensions to closer investigation. When it comes to state presence, I have pointed to the challenges that some states have faced in controlling remote border regions that have provided a fertile breeding ground for insurgencies. I have also underlined some of the tensions between a regional integration agenda, which seeks to facilitate the freedom of movement of citizens of member states, and a security agenda which seeks to impose more effective regulation. The efforts of the EU to tie African states into measures designed to restrict migratory flows has added a further layer of complexity. The net effect has been to forge new strategies of surveillance and practices of selective exclusion.

Secondly, I have demonstrated that networks of evasion have proliferated in African border regions by virtue of the economic rents that conflicting economic policies have generated—and which migration controls are currently reinvigorating. Cross-border trade has often been associated with particular ethnic groups whose niche has been cemented over many years. But illicit trade has also spawned new networks as well as transforming older ones. I have compared the case of the Nana Benz of Lomé—whose location at the epicenter of a regional trade in contraband textiles helped to cement their dominance over the urban marketplace—with that of the Mouride brotherhood which began with deep roots in groundnut farming and subsequently mutated into a transnational network, with one foot in contraband and another in international migration. In both cases, the demarcation of a social boundary was closely bound up with participation in cross-border exchange.

This is closely related to the third point concerning the demography of borderlands. Border areas have often witnessed amongst the most sustained growth, by virtue of the livelihoods that grow up around trade but also because of the relative safety that urbanism provide in unstable regions. Border towns and cities are typically cosmopolitan, as they suck in populations of diverse national and ethnic origins.

In the final section on the politics of identity, I have pointed to the many ambiguities surrounding the ways in which international borders are exploited, challenged and internalized by local populations. While some actors have sought to exclude or target particular groups on the principle that their ethnic affiliation necessarily renders them foreign, borderlanders have not been above invoking state actors in defense of their own territorial claims. Even where groups such as the Agotime seek to transcend the border and rekindle a shared sense of community, they cannot escape the fact that the border has engendered a sense of difference over time. This is illustrative of the ways in which borders have served to inscribe social boundaries in a more general sense. In this, as in other respects, the African patterns are not so very different from those in other parts of the world. Or at least, there are enough commonalities to render the work of comparison potentially rewarding.

Notes

1. Some of the research for this article, especially the sections dealing with transport corridors and regional integration, was conducted as part of a European Research Council (ERC) Advanced Grant for a project entitled "African Governance and Space: Transport Corridors, Border Towns and Port Cities in Transition (AFRIGOS)" (ADG-2014-670851), for which I am the principal investigator. In East Africa, the research was conducted alongside Dr. Isabella Soi of the University of Cagliari, an affiliate of the project, whose insights I am grateful for.
2. Tijuana and San Diego are atypical in that the latter is slightly the larger city.
3. ECOWAS brings together the West African anglophone countries of Nigeria, Ghana, the Gambia, Sierra Leone, and Liberia, with the francophone countries of the West African Monetary Union (UEMOA), consisting of Senegal, Mali, Cote d'Ivoire, Burkina Faso, Togo, Niger, plus Guinea-Bissau. Guinea is a francophone member of ECOWAS, but is not part of UEMOA. In East Africa, the EAC is made up of Uganda, Kenya, Tanzania, Rwanda, Burundi, and South Sudan.
4. The Vatican is embedded in Rome, but this is clearly an exceptional case.
5. I am grateful to Hugh Lamarque for this insight.
6. Interview with Togbe Amenya Fiti V, Aflao, August 26, 2017.
7. I am grateful for having had the chance to read some of the drafts of a forthcoming book by Elaine Peña that deals with an annual festival in which a meeting on the bridge between the two Laredos is a highly symbolic moment.

References

Andersson, Ruben. 2014. *Illegality Inc.: Clandestine Migration and the Business of Bordering Europe.* Berkeley: University of California Press.
Asiwaju, A.I. (ed.). 1984. *Partitioned Africans: Ethnic Relations Across Africa's International Boundaries 1884–1984.* London: Hurst.
Bennafla, Karine. 2002. *Le commerce frontalier en Afrique centrale: acteurs, espaces, pratiques.* Paris: Karthala.
Bøås, Morten, and Kevin Dunn. 2013. *Politics of Origin in Africa: Autochthony, Citizenship and Conflict.* London: Zed Press.
Clancy-Smith, Julia. 2011. *Mediterraneans: North Africa and Europe in an Age of Migration c.1800–1900.* Berkeley: University of California Press.
Crush, Jonathan, Alan Jeeves, and David Yudelman. 1991. *South Africa's Labor Empire: A History of Black Migrancy to the Gold Mines.* Boulder, CO: Westview Press.

De Genova, Nicholas. 2012. "Border, Scene and Obscene." In Thomas Wilson and Hastings Donnan (eds), *A Companion to Border Studies*, 492–503. Chichester: Wiley-Blackwell.

Dereje, Feyissa. 2011. *Playing Different Games: The Paradox of Anywaa and Nuer Identification Strategies in the Gambella Region, Ethiopia*. Oxford: Berghahn.

Flynn, Donna K. 1997. "'We Are the Border': Identity, Exchange and the State along the Benin–Nigeria Border." *American Ethnologist* 24(2): 311–30.

Frowd, Philippe M. 2018. *Security at the Borders: Transnational Practices and Technologies in West Africa*. Cambridge: Cambridge University Press.

Geschiere, Peter. 2009. *The Perils of Belonging: Autochthony, Citizenship and Exclusion in Africa and Europe*. Chicago: University of Chicago Press.

Hüsken, Thomas. 2017. "The Practice and Culture of Smuggling in the Borderland of Egypt and Libya." *International Affairs* 93(4): 897–915.

Jackson, Stephen. 2006. "Borderlands and the Transformation of War Economies: Lessons from the DR Congo." *Conflict, Security and Development* 6(3): 425–47.

Jiménez, Tomas R. 2010. *Replenished Ethnicity: Mexican Americans, Immigration, and Identity*. Berkeley: University of California Press.

Klantschnig, Gernot. 2013. *Crime, Drugs and the State in Africa: The Nigerian Connection*. Leiden: Brill.

Landau, Loren B. 2010. "Loving the Alien? Citizenship, Law and the Future in South Africa's Demonic Society." *African Affairs* 109/435: 213–30.

Nugent, Paul. 2002. *Smugglers, Secessionists and Loyal Citizens on the Ghana–Togo Frontier: The Lie of the Borderlands since 1914*. Oxford/Athens: James Currey/Ohio University Press.

——— 2012. "Border Towns and Cities in Comparative Perspective." In Thomas Wilson and Hastings Donnan (eds), *A Companion to Border Studies*, 557–72. Chichester: Wiley-Blackwell.

——— 2018. "Africa's Re-Enchantment with Big Infrastructure: White Elephants Dancing in Virtuous Circles?" In Jon Schubert, Ulf Engel, and Elisio Macamo (eds), *Extractive Industries and Changing State Dynamics in Africa: Beyond the Resource Curse*, 22–39. Abingdon: Routledge.

——— 2019. *Boundaries, Communities and State-Making in West Africa: The Centrality of the Margins*. Cambridge: Cambridge University Press.

Payan, Tony. 2006. *The Three US–Mexico Border Wars: Drugs, Immigration, and Homeland Security*. Santa Barbara: Praeger.

Raeymaekers, Timothy. 2015. *Violent Capitalism and Hybrid Identity in the Eastern Congo: Power to the Margins*. Cambridge: Cambridge University Press.

Scheele, Judith. 2012. *Smugglers and Saints of the Sahara: Regional Connectivity in the Twentieth Century*. Cambridge: Cambridge University Press.

Soi, Isabella, and Paul Nugent. 2017. "Peripheral Urbanism in Africa: Border Towns and Twin Towns in Africa." *Journal of Borderlands Studies* 32(4): 535–56.

Sylvanus, Nina. 2016. *Patterns in Circulation: Cloth, Gender, and Materiality in West Africa*. Chicago: University of Chicago Press.

Tafira, Kenneth. 2011. "Is Xenophobia Racism?" *Anthropology Southern Africa* 34(3/4): 114–21.

Titeca, Kristof. 2012. "Tycoons and Contraband: Informal Cross-Border Trade in West Nile, North-Western Uganda." *Journal of Eastern African Studies* 6(1): 47–63.

Viljoen, Willemien. 2016. "Transport Costs and Efficiency in West and Central Africa." Unpublished report. Stellenbosch: Tralac.

Walther, Olivier. 2014. "Trade Networks in West Africa: A Social Network Approach." *Journal of Modern African Studies* 52(2): 179–204.

Notes on Contributors

Didier Fassin is James D. Wolfensohn Professor at the Institute for Advanced Study in Princeton, and Director of Studies at the École des Hautes Études en Sciences Sociales in Paris. Anthropologist, sociologist and physician, he has extensively written on moral and political issues in contemporary societies. His recent books include *The Will to Punish* (Oxford University Press) and *Life: A Critical User's Manual* (Polity).

Tugba Basaran is Deputy Director and Senior Researcher at the Centre for the Study of Global Human Movement, University of Cambridge. Her research provides reflections on violence, law and human rights in liberal societies. It draws upon political theory, socio-legal studies and international political sociology. Her publications include *Security, Law and Borders: At the Limits of Liberties* (Routledge).

Linda Bosniak is Distinguished Professor of Law at Rutgers University. She has written extensively and across the disciplines on questions of nationalism, borders, citizenship, equality, and the liberal legal subject. She has a forthcoming volume on territorial personhood as a legal category and is the author of *The Citizen and the Alien: Dilemmas of Contemporary Membership* (Princeton University Press).

Ilana Feldman is Professor of Anthropology, History and International Affairs at George Washington University. She works on the Palestinian experience, both inside and outside of Palestine. She recently authored *Police Encounters: Security and Surveillance in Gaza under Egyptian Rule* (Stanford University Press) and *Life Lived in Relief: Humanitarian Predicaments and Palestinian Refugee Politics* (University of California Press).

Mayanthi Fernando is Associate Professor of Anthropology at UC Santa Cruz. Her research interests include Islam, secularism, liberalism, and gender/sexuality. She is currently working on the secularity of post-humanism and on the regulation of Muslim intimacies in Europe. She published *The Republic Unsettled: Muslim French and the Contradictions of Secularism* (Duke University Press).

Michael Hanchard is Professor of African Studies at the University of Pennsylvania. His research combines a specialization in comparative politics with an interest in contemporary political theory, encompassing themes of nationalism, racism, xenophobia and citizenship. He recently authored *Party/Politics: Horizons in Black Political Thought* (Oxford University Press), and *The Spectre of Race: How Discrimination Haunts Western Democracy* (Princeton University Press).

Sherally Munshi is Associate Professor of Law at Georgetown University. Her work examines the ways in which colonial histories shape contemporary legal regimes. Her writings have appeared in various journals, including the *Yale Journal of Law & Humanities* and the *American Journal of Comparative Law*.

Mae Ngai is the Lung Family Professor of Asian American Studies and Professor of History at Columbia University. She dedicates her research to immigration, citizenship, and nationalism, focusing on Chinese migrants in the United States in the nineteenth and twentieth centuries. She is the author of *Impossible Subjects: Illegal Aliens and the Making of Modern America* (Princeton University Press), and of *The Lucky Ones: One Family and the Extraordinary Invention of Chinese America* (Houghton Mifflin Harcourt).

Paul Nugent is Professor of Comparative African History at the University of Edinburgh where he is divided between the Centre of African Studies and the School of History Classics and Archaeology. He straddles the disciplines of History and Political Studies. He has written extensively on African boundaries and is concluding a history of South African wine industry from phylloxera to the present. His most recent book is *Boundaries, Communities and State-Making in West Africa* (Cambridge University Press).

Ayşe Parla is Assistant Professor of Anthropology at Boston University. Her work on transnational migration, precarious labor, differentiated citizenship, and the governance of diversity is situated at the intersections of the politico-legal and the affective-moral realms in Turkey and its borderlands. She recently authored *Precarious Hope: Migration and the Limits of Belonging in Turkey* (Stanford University Press).

Rhacel Salazar Parreñas is Professor of Sociology and Gender and Sexuality Studies at the University of Southern California. She is an ethnographer who writes on labor migration from the Philippines. Her recent books include *Illicit Flirtations: Labor, Migration and Sex Trafficking in Tokyo* and *Servants of Globalization: Migration and Domestic Work* (both at Stanford University Press).

Kristin Surak is Associate Professor of Politics at SOAS, University of London. She has conducted research on international migration, nationalism, culture, and political sociology. She recently published *Making Tea, Making Japan: Cultural Nationalism in Practice* (Stanford University Press), and has a forthcoming book *Citizenship 4 Sale: Millionaires, Microstates, and Mobility* (Harvard University Press).

Index

Abidjan–Lagos Corridor, 238
abjected space, 216
Achick, Tong, 106
Adangbe population group, 248
Afghan immigrants, 13
Africa: asymmetrical borders/borderlands, 233–53; border distinctions, 8, 233–34; demography of, 244–47; evasion networks, 240–44; politics of identity, 247–50; racial inferiority rationales, 145; state presence levels, 236–40. *See also* specific African countries
African Americans: incarceration of, 13, 15n4; racial diversity in nation-states, 144; racial subordination of, 110; slavery in US, 158
Agbamevoza festival, 250
Agotime population, 248, 249, 250, 252
Alaoui, Myriam Hachimi, 88
Algeria, 4, 73, 90–91, 243
Alien and Sedition Acts (1798), 158
alien citizens, 108–11
al-Qaeda, 237
Amara, Fadela, 89–91
American Civil Liberties Union, 120
American Civil War, 104
American Convention on Human Rights, 175
American Friends Service Committee (AFSC), 214, 218–19
American imperialism, 136
American nation-states, 149
American nativism, 251
American Revolution, 145
Anderson, Benedict, 148
Angola, 233, 245
anti-Catholicism, 109
anti-Chinese movement, 106–7
anti-deportation stance, 202–4
anti-immigration measures, 173
antiracist movements, 128
anti-Semitism, 109
Anywaa population, 249
Arendt, Hannah, 1, 13–14, 172, 173

Armenia, 58–59, 68, 75n1
Armenian Genocide (1915), 9, 69–70, 72–74
Armistice Demarcation Line, 217
arranged marriages, 85
articles of commerce, 104–5
Aryan racial supremacy, 164
Asia, 8, 24
Asian Americans, 104, 111, 125, 145
Asiatic Barred Zone Act, 119–20, 126–27, 138. *See also* Immigration Act
Asiwaju, A.I., 248
Assing, Norman. *See* Yuan Sheng
asylum seekers, 103, 113
asymmetrical borders/borderlands, 233–36, 233–53
Austria, 7
authoritarianism, 22, 27, 29, 33, 114, 190

Balibar, Etienne, 4
Balkan Wars (1912/1913), 65, 70
banlieues (immigrant suburbs), 89
bare life, defined, 171
Barth, Fredrik, 4
Beit Hanoun, Gaza Strip: borderland and, 216–21; colonization and, 226–28; cycles of ruination and rebuilding, 224–26; introduction to, 11, 214–16
Benin, 240
Benin–Nigeria border, 249
Benjamin, Walter, 2
Bigler, John, 105–6
binational couples: family and government history/relations, 83–84; gender equality and, 87–88, 93; introduction to, 79–83; policing intimacy, 85–87; repression of women, 93–96
blood kinship of migrants: race as irrelevant category, 65–71; race codes, 58–60; racial kin/consanguines, 59–62, 71–73; restrictive definition of migrant, 62–65
Bolivar, Simon, 145, 149, 150–51
Bonilla-Silva, Eduardo, 128
border interiorization, 194

borders and boundaries: citizenship by investment, 27–29; as colonization, 226–28; cultural boundary, 251; differences and similarities between, 3–8; ethno-racial boundaries, 5–6, 9, 61–63, 72, 75, 88, 146, 248; exclusionary nature of, 23; introduction to, 1–3; legal bordering, 170, 175–82; political and moral economies of, 8–12; sovereign relationships and, 12–14
border ubiquitization, 193
Brazil, 10, 24, 64, 149–51
British Indian immigration, 120–23, 125
British parliamentary democracy, 151
Brown v. Board of Education (1954), 114, 138
Brubaker, Rogers, 147
brutalization forms, 13
Bulgaria, 5, 9, 60–61, 70–72, 74
Burundi, 25

Canada: abolishment of slavery, 149–50; migrant domestic workers in, 46–47, 55; visa-free access to, 30–31; white-settler dominions, 120–23
capitalism, 21, 23, 29, 148
cash-for-passport exchanges, 26
castas system in Latin America, 145
Catholic Church, 109, 145, 156–57
Central Africa, 238, 244
Central American asylum seekers, 113
Chad, 135, 233, 237
Chae Chan Ping, 107
Chamberlain, Joseph, 121
Cheney, Dick, 118
Chile, 149–50
China: African trade with, 242; anti-Chinese movement, 106–7; citizenship by investment, 32; European investors in, 115n6; foreign investment/ownership, 28; HNWIs in, 24; persecution of Tibetans in, 4; population concerns, 139; Qing government, 107; racial and ethno-national hierarchies in, 146; Scott Act and, 107; UNHWIs in, 27–28, 32; visa-free access, 24
Chinese Exclusion Act (1882), 10, 105, 114n5, 119
Chinese exclusion laws, 104–8, 113
Chinese migrants, 7, 10
Chirac, Jacques, 158
Christian apostates, 237

Christian refugees, 132
Christian Science Monitor, 223
Church, Denver S., 126
citizenship by investment (CBI): borders and boundaries, 27–29; global inequalities, 23–26, 24; implications of, 29–34; introduction to, 21–23; overview of, 26–27
Citizenship Clause of the Fourteenth Amendment, 111
citizenship laws, 68, 151
citizenship perimeter, 3–4
civil rights, 21, 128, 152
civil society, 111, 194
class distinctions, 21–22, 32, 181
Cleveland, Grover, 122
Clinton, Hillary, 131
Cold War, 5, 109, 164
Colombia, 149–51
colonial borders in Africa, 248
colonization, 226–28
color-blindness (race neutrality), 128–29
communalism *(communautarisme)*, Muslim, 88–93, 95
communism, 28–29, 62, 164
Communist Party, 28
Comprehensive Pre-Departure Education Program, 39–40
conservative liberalism, 148–51
contrat d'accueil et d'intégration (CAI), 87–88
Convention 189. *See* Domestic Workers Convention
Côte d'Ivoire, 247–48
creole elites, 149–51
criminal aliens, 196
criminalization of immigrant presence, 191, 197
criollo elites, 149
cross-border exchange/trading, 241–43, 246, 251–52
cross-border festivals, 250
cross-border mobility/movement, 25, 61
cubic air ordinance, 106–7
cultural boundary, 251
cultural sensitivity of migrant workers, 47–48
Customs and Border Protection (CBP), 198
Cyprus, 26, 27, 30, 216

Daily Alta, 106
Dakar, 242–43

Declaration of the Rights of Man and Citizen, 88
Deferred Action for Childhood Arrivals (DACA), 103, 196, 201, 209n27
Demafelis, Joanna, 50–51
democracy: British parliamentary democracy, 151; ethno-national chauvinism and, 148–49; exceptionalism and, 193; national identity and, 83, 164; nation-states and, 146, 148
Democratic Party, 59, 105, 107
democratic republicanism, 146, 149, 165
Democratic Republic of Congo (DRC), 237, 244, 246
denial of legal personality, 170–72
Denmark, 8, 45–46, 139, 156
deportation orders, 86
deportation rights, 10
detainee rights, 173–74, 181
discrimination: British Indian immigration, 125; disability discrimination, 6; ethnic discrimination, 4–5, 9–10, 138; gender discrimination, 6; legalized discrimination, 68; of migrants, 7; national origin and, 138; per-country limit discrimination, 138–39; racism, 9–10, 63, 127–29; religious discrimination, 4–5, 112, 132, 134; segregation forms, 13, 110, 113–14, 125, 172. *See also* inequality concerns
domestic violence, 85, 197
domestic workers. *See* migrant domestic workers
Domestic Workers Convention, 43–47
DREAM Act (2001), 11, 137, 201, 209n27
Dred Scott v. Sandford (1857), 162–63
drug cartels, 235
Dubois, Laurent, 154

East Africa, 238–39, 245
East African Community (EAC), 238
economic citizens, 30–32
Economic Community of West African States (ECOWAS), 238, 239, 253n3
economic free zones, 11
Egypt, 1, 26–27, 215–21, 226
El-Haj, Nadia Abu, 68
El Salvador, 139
employment conditions of migrant domestic workers, 52–54
endogamy, 88, 93, 95, 147
enforcement of immigration laws, 195–96

England, 7, 27, 145, 162
English law, medieval, 171
entrepreneurial wealth, 27–30, 32
Erder, Sema, 63–64
Ergin, Murat, 67
Escombe, Henry, 121–22
Ethiopia, 43, 47, 245, 251
Ethiopia–Sudan border, 249
ethnic discrimination, 4–5, 9–10, 138
ethnic marriages, 88
ethnic nationalism, 73
ethno-racial boundaries, 5–6, 9, 61–63, 72, 75, 88, 146, 248
Europe: asymmetrical borders and, 251; border distinctions, 8; HNWIs in, 24; immigration and, 12, 104; Islamophobia in, 13; refugee crisis in, 4–5
European colonialism, 136
European Convention on Human Rights, 80, 175
European Court of Human Rights, 175
European nation-states, 149
Europeanness of Turks, 68
European Union (EU), 5, 8, 12, 27, 233
evasion networks, 240–44
Ewe population group, 248
exceptionalism, 64, 65–66, 193, 236
exclusion/exclusionary forms: Chinese Exclusion Act, 10, 105, 114n5, 119; function of citizenship, 13, 22; Japanese internment during World War II, 110–11; Muslim ban, 1–3, 10, 103–4, 111, 114n1, 118–20, 131–36; political exclusion of slaves, 150; racial exclusion by design, 123–27; racism and rhetorical discipline, 127–29; rhetorical defiance and, 129–31; state policies for migrant domestic workers, 45–47; summary of, 136–40; wealth and power asymmetries, 233; white-settler dominions, 120–23
Executive Order 13767 (Trump), 195
Executive Order 13769 (Trump). *See* Muslim ban
expedited removal policy, 109

faith-based humanitarianism, 200
family-as-instrument paradigm, 96
family-sponsored migration, 103
Farris, Sarah, 82, 85
favoritism policies, 71
femonationalism, 82
Filipino undocumented migrants, 39–43

Fong Yue Ting v. US (1893), 108
foreign commerce, 104–5
foreigners, migrants defined as, 72
foreign investment/ownership, 28
Foucault, Michel, 83–84, 95
Fourteenth Amendment (US Constitution), 111
France: border distinctions, 3–4, 6, 8; gender equality and, 87–88, 97n9; Muslim communalism, 88–93, 95; nationalism of marriage, sex and romance, 82–83; *sans papier* movement, 60–61
freedom of movement, 44, 88–89, 204, 238–39, 252
Freeman, Edward Augustus, 145
free "people of color" *(gens de couleur)*, 154
French nationalism, 2, 82–83, 87, 95–96
French Revolution, 88, 152, 158
Freyre, Gilberto, 145

Gambia, 240, 242, 245–46
Gandhi, Mohandas, 122
Ga population group, 248
Garvis, Roy, 163
Gaza Strip. *See* Beit Hanoun, Gaza Strip
Gbagbo, Laurent, 248
gender discrimination, 6
gender equality, 9, 87–88, 93, 97n9
Georgia, 29, 159
German law, 169, 171
Germany, 1, 7, 64, 68, 76n12, 165
Ghana, 240, 241, 248, 250
Ghana-Togo border, 248–49
Giuliani, Rudolph, 133
global inequalities, 23–26, 24
global regulation of migrant domestic work, 43–45
Global South, 5, 12
Godigbe festival, 250
governmentality, 84, 95
Government of India Act (1858), 121
Gran Colombia, 150–51
Great Britain, 7–8
Great Depression, 110
green-card marriages *(mariages blancs)*, 83
Gregory, Roger, 137
gross domestic product (GDP), 30
Guantanamo Bay detention camp, 173–74
Guatemala, 13
Guinea, 240

Guinea-Bissau, 240–41
Gül, Abdullah, 74

Haaretz, 223
Hab Wa, 106
Haiti: per-country limit discrimination, 139; racial regimes of, 151–57; revolution in, 145, 150–51; termination of humanitarian protection programs, 196
Haitian Constitution (1805), 155
Haitian Revolution, 10, 151–59
Helg, Aline, 151
HereToStay slogan, 201–6
Herrenvolk ("master race") notions, 165
high net worth individuals (HNWIs), 23–25, 34n2
Hindu ban, 10, 119, 125
Hindu literacy test, 125–26
Hobbes, Thomas, 178
Hong Kong, 24, 28, 34n4, 55
human rights violations. *See* outlawing and human rights violations
Hungary, 5, 64

Igbo population, 249
illegal aliens, 110, 191
illegal immigrants/immigration, 2, 11, 109, 239, 248
illegalized presence. *See* territorial presence of illegalized migrants in US
illiberalization, 180, 195
immigrants/immigration: Afghan immigrants, 13; anti-immigration measures, 173; British Indian immigration, 120–23, 125; criminalization of immigrant presence, 191, 197; enforcement of immigration laws, 195–96; ethnic boundary and, 4; Executive Order 13769 and, 1–3; illegal immigrants/immigration, 2, 11, 109, 239, 248; irregular immigrants, 85, 189, 193–96, 199, 201–2; Jews, 1, 4; justice activism, 204; Latinos, 2; Mexico, 2, 191–92; nonimmigrant visa, 46; plenary power, 104–10, 138, plenary ; repatriate immigration, 64; surveillance and, 12; undocumented immigrants/migrants, 13, 39, 103, 118; Zimbabwean immigrants, 13. *See also* migrants/migration
immigrants/immigration policy in US: Chinese exclusion laws, 104–8; intro-

duction to, 103–4; racialized alienage, 108–11; Trump administration, 15n3, 103–4, 111–14, 195–99. *See also* territorial presence of illegalized migrants in US; Trump, Donald
Immigration Act (1917), 10, 126–27
Immigration Act (1924), 104
Immigration and Customs Enforcement (ICE), 12, 113, 118, 197–98
Immigration and Nationality Act (1952), 163–65
Immigration and Nationality Act (1965), 112, 134, 138–39
Immigration Bureau, 109
Immigration Restriction Act (1897), 121–22
incarceration of African Americans, 13, 15n4
indefinite detention, 173
India, 24, 43, 139
Indonesia, 43
inequality concerns: citizenship and, 21–23; gender equality, 9, 87–88, 93, 97n9; global inequalities, 23–26, 24; institutionalized inequality, 150; migrant domestic workers, 54–56; sovereign equality, 235. *See also* discrimination
International Covenant on Civil and Political Rights (1966), 174, 183n4
International Labour Organization (ILO), 43–44
International Monetary Fund (IMF), 28
international textile trade, 12
investment migration, 22, 26–27, 29, 31–32
Iran, 1, 131, 135
Iraq, 1, 70, 131, 133–34
irregular immigrants, 85, 189, 193–96, 199, 201–2
Islamic State, 237
Islamist militant organizations, 12
Islamophobia, 3, 13
Israel, 4–5, 7, 11. *See also* Beit Hanoun, Gaza Strip
Italy, 7, 15n6, 31, 46, 243

Jabalia refugee camp, 222
Jacobinism, 152–53
James, C.L.R., 152, 155
"Janus-faced nature" (El-Haj), 68
Japan, 24, 125–26, 146
Japanese immigrants, 24, 124, 164

Japanese internment during World War II, 104, 110–11, 136, 138
Jews/Judaism: anti-Semitism and, 73; discrimination against, 58, 68, 73; immigration and, 1, 4, 64; Nuremberg Laws, 183n2; Palestinian territories, 226
Jiang Zemin, 28
Jim Crow era, 138
John, Kevin R., 109
Johnson, Lyndon, 138
judicial jurisdiction limits, 177–78
Justice and Development Party, 74

kafala system, 52, 54
Kaftka, Franz, 169
Kazakhstan, 29
Kelly, John, 196
Kenya, 237, 245–46, 248
Kenya–Uganda border, 239, 247, 248–49
Kevorkian, Raymond, 70
Kimberley Process, 241, 242
Kuwait, 24, 50
Kyrgyzstan, 1

labor precarity. *See* migrant domestic workers
labor standards and migrant domestic workers, 54
Labor Standards Law, 46
language training of migrant workers, 48
Latin America: *castas* system, 145; immigration waves, 161; military state violence in Latin, 62; nation states, 144–45; Pan-Americanism in, 150; racial regimes in, 148–51; second passports in, 35n9; suffrage in, 148
Latino immigration bans, 2
law enforcement expansion, 198–99
Law of Absent Property, 226
Law on the Protection of Foreigners (Turkey), 63
Lebanon, 40, 224, 226
legal bordering, 170, 175–82
legalized discrimination, 68
legal personality, 170–72
Lei Rio Branco, 151
Le Play, Frédéric, 84
Les Amoureux au Ban Public (ABP) movement, 80, 96n2
Les Amoureux au ban public documentary, 79–83, 94

liberal-legalism, 190, 191–95, 205–6, 207n2
Libya, 1, 5, 7
literacy test, 121–22, 125–26

Macron, Emmanuel, 2, 3
male chauvinists, 90, 92
male oppression, 90
Mali, 237, 240–41, 243, 249
Malta, 22, 27, 30
Malta Today, 22
Manila, 40–41
mariage gris, 83, 94
Marshall, T.H., 21–23
Mauritania, 240
McCarran–Walter Act. *See* Immigration and Nationality Act
medieval English law, 171
Mediterranean as cultural boundary, 251
Méliane, Loubna, 91–92
Merriam, Charles, 166
Mexico: as American possession, 139; asylum seekers from, 113; exceptionalism and US border, 236; immigration ban against, 2, 7; Trump administration immigration policies against, 191–92; US–Mexico border, 15n5, 191, 235–36, 244, 250–51
Middle Eastern countries: diverse geographies of, 61; European Union interface with, 233; illegal immigrants and, 109; migrant domestic workers in, 8, 39–42, 46, 49–50; protection policies for migrant domestic work, 49–50; Turkish migrants from, 70; weapon expansion in, 13; women refugees from, 62. *See also* specific Middle Eastern countries
migrant domestic workers: employment conditions, 52–54; exclusionary state policies for, 45–47; global regulation of, 43–45; introduction to, 39–43; minimum wage for, 42, 44, 46, 51; protection policies in Philippines, 47–52; summary of, 54–56
migrants/migration: Chinese migrants, 7, 10; defined as foreigners, 72; family-sponsored migration, 103; Filipino undocumented migrants, 39–43; investment migration, 22, 26–27, 29, 31–32; language training of migrant workers, 48; from less-developed countries, 31; Mexican migrants, 7; nonimmigrant visa, 46; rape of undocumented migrants, 40–41, 66; restrictive definition of, 62–65; undocumented immigrants/migrants, 13, 39, 103, 118; West Indian migrants, 7. *See also* blood kinship of migrants; immigrants/immigration; territorial presence of illegalized migrants in US
minimum wage for domestic workers, 42, 44, 46, 51
Morocco, 5
Mourides of Senegal, 12, 242–43
mulatto oppression in Haiti, 154–55
Muslim ban, 1–3, 10, 103–4, 111, 114n1, 118–20, 131–36
Muslims: Alevi population in Turkey, 73; communalism, 88–93, 95; Executive Order 13769 in US, 1–3; gender equality and, 9; patriarchal Islamic norms, 83, 92–93, 96; regulation of marriage, 91; Sunni Muslims, 59, 73; targeting for violence, 237
Myanmar, 4

Nakba, 11, 215, 228
Nana Benz, 12, 243, 252
Natal Compromise, 122
Natal Law, 121–22
national jurisprudence on jurisdiction, 175
national wealth, 28
nation-state systems, 144–46
Native Americans, 104, 145
nativism, 136, 251
natural law-grounded humanitarianism, 200
Nauma, Pascal, 66–67
Navarro-Yashin, Yael, 216
Nazi Germany, 68, 76n12
Neveu Kringelbach, Hélène, 85–86
New Sanctuary Movement, 199
New York Times, 217, 221
Nicaragua, 196
Nigeria, 12, 233, 237, 240–41
Ni putes ni soumises (Amara), 89–91
Ni Putes Ni Soumises (NPNS, Neither Whores Nor Doormats) movement, 89–91
No Borders network, 23
No Go Zones in Gaza, 228
nonadmission to the law. *See* outlawing and human rights violations
nonimmigrant visa, 46

normalization, 64
Norris v. the City of Boston (1849), 161
North Africa, 12, 62, 87, 90, 235, 240, 251
North America, 8, 12, 226. *See also* Canada; Mexico; United States
North Korea, 135, 207n5
Nuer population, 249
Nuremberg Laws, 171, 183n2

Obama, Barack, 113, 131, 137, 192, 196, 198
Occupied Territories, 4, 11, 227
Organisation for Economic Co-operation and Development (OECD), 23
Ortiz, Fernando, 145
Oslo Accords (1993), 223, 227
Ottoman Empire, 64, 69–70
outlawing and human rights violations: core obstacles to rights access, 172–75; introduction to, 169–70; legal bordering, 176–78; legal personality, 170–72; outside the law, defined, 178–80; reflections of, 180–83
outside the law, defined, 178–80
Overseas Workers Welfare Administration (OWWA), 40, 47–49

Pakistan, 1
Palestine, 4, 11–12, 215–28
Pan-Americanism in Latin America, 150
Papua New Guinea, 173
participatory democracy, 149
"Passenger Cases" in US, 161–62
patriarchal Islamic norms, 83, 92–93, 96
Paylan, Garo, 59
Pennsylvania Society for Promoting the Abolition of Slavery, 160
people of color *(gens de couleur)*, 154
People's Democratic Party, 59
People's Republican Party, 73–74
per-country limit discrimination, 138–39
performative citizenship, 73
permanent residents (green cards), 103
Petion, Alexander, 151
petit blancs, 154–55
Philippine Overseas Employment Administration (POEA), 47, 48
Philippines, 39–43, 47–52, 139
plenary power, 104–8, 138, plenary
Plyer v. Doe (1982), 198
policing intimacy, 85–87
political-economic transformations, 27
political exclusion of slaves, 150
political instrumentalization, 71
politics of congruence, 174
politics of identity, 247–50
Pre-Departure Education Program for Household Service Workers, 49
Pre-Departure Orientation Seminar (PDOS), 39–40, 49–51
private international law, 174–75
privately held wealth, 28
privatization of state assets, 28
public wealth, 29

Qing government, 107

race as irrelevant category, 65–71
race codes, 58–60
racial discrimination, 9–10, 63, 127–29
racial exclusion by design, 123–27
racialized alienage, 108–11
racial kin/consanguines, 59–62, 71–73
racial orders, 146–48
racial regimes of the Americas: conservative liberalism, 148–51; Haiti, 151–57; Immigration and Nationality Act, 163–65; nation-state systems, 144–46; racial orders and, 146–48; summary of, 165–66; United States, 157–63
racial registry, 160
racism and rhetorical discipline, 127–29
racist exile law, 63
radical Islamic terrorism, 131
Raker, John, 125–26
rape of undocumented migrants, 40–41, 66
rebel insurgencies, 236–37
Reed, James, 127
refugee camps, 219, 222, 237
refugee crisis in Europe, 4–5
regional economic communities (RECs), 237
religiosity, 73
religious discrimination, 4–5, 112, 132, 134
repatriate immigration, 64
repression of women, 93–96
residence permits/visas, 5, 9, 31, 85, 87
right to be recognized before the law, 170–72
Roberts, John, 135–36
Rodriques, Nina, 145
Romania, 5, 64
Roman law, 169, 170–71

Roy, Sara, 221–22
rule of law, 22, 27, 146, 150, 177, 182, 195
Russia: fall of communism, 28; foreign investment/ownership, 28; foreign transfers, 32; HNWIs in, 8, 24, 27; public wealth, 29; repatriate immigration of Jews, 64; UNHWIs in, 29; US executive orders and, 1; visa-free access, 24
Rwanda, 244, 247

Saint-Domingue rebellion, 158–59
Saint Kitts, 26, 30–34
sanctuary cities, 111, 198
sanctuary policies, 199–207, 209n24
sanctuary practices, 11
sans papier movement, 60–61
Saudi Arabia, 1, 24, 41, 45
Sawt al-'Uruba, 218
Schengen Area, 2
Scott, Joan, 84
second-class citizenship, 34, 72
secret race codes, 58–60
securitization toward non-citizens, 169
segregation forms, 13, 110, 113–14, 125, 172
self-deportation, 191
Senegal, 240, 242–43, 245–46
Sephardic Jewish ancestry, 33
September 11, 2001 attacks, 158
servility requirements of domestic workers, 51–52
Sessions, Jeff, 197
Settlement Law (Turkey), 63
sex/sexuality, governance of, 84
sexual assault/harassment, 40
sexual nationalism, 82
Shangaan population group, 248
Sharon, Ariel, 221, 223
Silverstein, Paul, 73
simulated marriages, 85
Singapore, 8, 44–47, 53, 54
slavery: abolishment of, 149–50; of African Americans in US, 158; denial of legal personality, 171; Haitian Revolution and, 151–59; political exclusion of slaves, 150
Smith, Ron, 228
Smith v. Turner (1849), 161
social class, 6
social exclusion, 169
social rights, 21
Somalia, 1, 131, 135, 237

South Africa: asymmetries in, 233–34; British promise of protection, 122; politics of identity, 247–48; white rule in, 69, 120; Zimbabwean immigrants, 13
South American revolutions, 8, 145
South Korea, 24, 235
sovereign equality, 235
Soviet Union, 61, 64–65
Special Economic Zones, 28
Sri Lanka, 39, 43
state power and human rights, 174
state presence levels, 236–40
sub-Saharan Africa, 233–34
Sudan, 1, 249
suffrage in Latin America, 148
Sunni Muslims, 59, 73
Surkis, Judith, 86–87
surveillance and immigration, 12
Switzerland, 7
symbolic landscapes, 179–80
Syria, 1, 65–66, 69, 129, 131–35, 181, 226

Taiwan, 8, 28, 45–46, 55
Taney, Roger B., 162–63
Technical Education and Skills Department Authority (TESDA), 47, 48
Temporary Protected Status program, 103
territorial citizenship, 62
territorial presence of illegalized migrants in US: introduction to, 189–91; liberal-legalist territorialism, 190, 191–95; resistance and sanctuary policies, 199–207
territorial principle, 175
terrorists/terrorism: accusations of, 2–3, 110; immigration laws and, 191–92, 239; Thermidor reaction, 152–53; US executive orders against, 1, 114n1, 130–32
Thermidor reaction, 152–53
Tibet, 4
Tocqueville, Alexis de, 145
Togo, 240, 242, 248–49, 250
totalitarianism, 147, 200
trampoline towns, 236
transborder membership politics, 71
transnational social field, 55
Tribal Twenties, 104
Trump, Donald: criminalization of immigration violations, 197; enforcement of immigration laws, 195–96; Executive Order 13769 by, 1–3, 114n1,

131; Immigration and Nationality Act, 112, 138–39; immigration policy under, 15n3, 103–4, 111–14, 195–99; law enforcement expansion, 198–99; liberal-legalist territorialism, 191; Muslim ban, 1–3, 10, 103–4, 111, 114n1, 118–20, 131–36; rhetorical defiance of, 129–31
Tsonga population, 248
Turkey: authoritarianism in, 33; immigration control, 5, 9; race codes, 58–60; racial kin/consanguines, 59–62, 71–73; restrictive definition of migrant, 62–65

Uganda, 66, 248
Uganda-Kenya border, 239, 247, 248–49
Ugandan Asians, 247
Ukraine, 29
ultra-fraudulent marriages, 83
ultra-high net worth individuals (UNHWIs), 23–24, 27–29, 34n2
UN Conciliation Commission, 217
undocumented immigrants/migrants, 13, 39, 103, 118
UN Emergence Force (UNEF), 215, 220
United Arab Emirates (UAE), 1, 9, 43, 52–55
United Nations (UN), 11
United Nations General Assembly, 170
United States (US): African Americans slavery in, 158; American imperialism, 136; American nation-states, 149; American Revolution, 145; Citizenship Clause of the Fourteenth Amendment, 111; global regulation of migrant domestic work, 46; Japanese internment during World War II, 104, 110–11, 136, 138; Jim Crow era, 138; nativism of, 251; "Passenger Cases" in, 161–62; racial regimes of, 157–63; US-Mexico border, 15n5, 191, 235–36, 244, 250–51. *See also* immigrants/immigration policy in US; Muslim ban; territorial presence of illegalized migrants in US; Trump, Donald
Universal Declaration of Human Rights (UDHR), 10, 69, 170, 172

UN Relief and Works Agency for Palestine Refugees (UNRWA), 215–16, 219–20
UN Truce Supervision Organization, 215
urbanism/urbanization, 238, 242, 245, 251–52
US Constitution, 108–9
US Department of Homeland Security, 112–13
US-Mexico border, 15n5, 191, 235–36, 244, 250–51
US Supreme Court, 103–4, 107, 112, 135–36, 160–61, 198
US Treasury, 28

Vatican recognition of Haitian sovereignty, 156–57
Venda population, 248
Venezuela, 135, 207n5
vigilante border militias, 198
virtual fences, 12
visa-free access, 24, 24–25, 30–31, 34n5
Vivre libre (Living free) (Méliane), 91–92

Walvis Bay Corridors, 238
Walzer, Michael, 205–6
West Africa, 238, 240, 241–42, 244, 249
Western imperialism, 125, 152
West Indian migrants, 7
whiteness of Turks, 68
white-settler dominions, 120–23
Wilson, Woodrow, 145
Wolfe, Patrick, 226
Wolof, 12, 242
women and Muslim repression, 93–96
World Bank, 25, 28
World War I, 69, 104
World War II, 104, 110–11, 144, 164
Wynn, James, 136–37

xenophobia, 3, 13, 109, 164, 248, 257

Yemen, 1, 131, 135
Yiannopoulos, Milo, 198
Yuan Sheng (Norman Assing), 105–6

Zimbabwe, 13, 234
Zionism, 69